# Labour Law and Lifelong Learning

Jari Murto • Valentina Franca
Editors

# Labour Law and Lifelong Learning

Springer

*Editors*
Jari Murto
Faculty of Law
University of Helsinki
Helsinki, Finland

Valentina Franca
Faculty of Public Administration
University of Ljubljana
Ljubljana, Slovenia

ISBN 978-3-032-11034-3 ISBN 978-3-032-11035-0 (eBook)
https://doi.org/10.1007/978-3-032-11035-0



This Springer imprint is published by the registered company Springer Nature Switzerland AG
The registered company address is: Gewerbestrasse 11, 6330 Cham, Switzerland

# Contents

# Introduction

**Jari Murto and Valentina Franca**

The social significance of lifelong learning has grown considerably in recent years. Topics such as employee upskilling, reskilling, employability, job security and just transition procedures have become highly relevant in society. These aspects are all interconnected with lifelong learning within the context of labour law. The traditional paradigm of transitioning from school or vocational education to permanent, stable employment is no longer a reality, highlighting the increased importance of lifelong learning. Although lifelong learning is an interesting and socially relevant phenomenon, it is also difficult and multifaceted. As such, the definition of lifelong learning is not unambiguous. Lifelong learning can be defined in two different ways: (1) the humanistic approach and (2) the human–capital approach. The humanistic approach involves self-development whereas the human–capital approach is a more labour market-centred and thus economic approach. Indeed, lifelong learning is a value-based concept, in addition to which its content has varied over time. This is also reflected in the regulation of lifelong learning: the same concept can appear at different times with different contents.

The importance of the European Union is sometimes neglected when it comes to increasing the importance of lifelong learning, both politically and in the form of legal regulation. For instance, the first principle of the **European Pillar of Social Rights** emphasises education, training and lifelong learning:

> Everyone has the right to quality and inclusive education, training and life-long learning in order to maintain and acquire skills that enable them to participate fully in society and manage successfully transitions in the labour market.

J. Murto (✉)
Faculty of Law, University of Helsinki, Helsinki, Finland
e-mail: jari.murto@helsinki.fi

V. Franca
Faculty of Public Administration, University of Ljubljana, Ljubljana, Slovenia
e-mail: valentina.franca@fu.uni-lj.si



J. Murto, V. Franca (eds.), *Labour Law and Lifelong Learning*,
https://doi.org/10.1007/978-3-032-11035-0_1

The Action Plan of the European Pillar of Social Rights concretises these goals. According to the Action Plan, at least 60 % of all adults should participate in training every year.[1] In the Action Plan, emphasising the importance of lifelong learning is one way to achieve a strong Social Europe by 2030. Upskilling and reskilling are therefore means to promote the creation of quality jobs and reduce poverty.[2]

The year 2023 was designated as the European Year of Skills, emphasising lifelong learning, particularly in the context of green and digital transitions, and supporting the European Union's competitiveness.[3] In 2025, the **Union of Skills** was launched with the aim of ensuring that people have the opportunity to engage in lifelong learning, including reskilling and upskilling measures, in line with the European Pillar of Social Rights.[4] In addition, the Union of Skills was emphasised in the political guidelines for the European Commission 2024–2029.[5] It is therefore right to expect that the EU will continue to take the initiative as a promoter and regulator of lifelong learning. For instance, the development of micro credentials gives an illustrative picture of the EU's innovation capacity in this sector.

Similarly, the increasing relevance of **active labour market policy** leads to lifelong learning becoming a fundamental part of contemporary labour law in various forms. The aim is to avoid unemployment, to promote the smooth re-employment of workers by helping them to develop new skills and, as a result, to support the functioning of the labour market at the level of the national economy. In this context, lifelong learning is closely linked to employability and employment security; lifelong learning can be seen, especially in EU regulation, as a key means of promoting the functioning of the labour market and labour market transitions. Indeed, the more fragmented the labour market becomes, the more important the development of lifelong learning activities will be. Consequently, the reskilling and upskilling of the workforce may even be referred to in the European Semester country-specific recommendations.

Lifelong learning is particularly intertwined with the **twin transition policies** that address both environmental (green) and technological (digital and AI) dimensions. It can even be argued that with the greater discussion of the green and digital transitions, the role of lifelong learning has also developed greater importance. Although labour law, or broadly labour market law, has used the concept of transition as a labour market, to describe the fact that careers are no longer static and traditional progressions from school to permanent work, but instead include interruptions and transitions. As these transitions are at the same time risks in the labour market, the twin transition has further emphasised lifelong learning measures as a part of risk management in transitions. It may be expected that this development will continue and strengthen in the future.

---

[1] The European Pillar of Social Rights Action Plan (2021).

[2] The European Pillar of Social Rights Action Plan (2021), pp. 9–10.

[3] European Year of Skills (2023).

[4] European Commission (2025).

[5] von der Leyen (2024).

From the perspective of labour law, particularly in relation to lifelong learning, **just transition** measures represent a fascinating legal phenomenon. The twin transitions of the 2020s have brought about significant social changes, highlighting the need to address new types of risks in the labour market. The traditional view of the relationship between labour law, learning and education—where individuals move from school to a stable, long-term employment relationship, and then to retirement—no longer holds true. This idealised image of working life has been disrupted. Instead, uncertainty and various labour market transitions have increased. Consequently, the regulation of employees' reskilling, upskilling and other lifelong learning measures has expanded and become more comprehensive.

Recent regulatory developments at both the EU and national levels suggest that lifelong learning is becoming an integral part of labour law. Despite its growing importance, the regulation of lifelong learning within labour law remains relatively under-researched. This may be due to the traditionally conservative and narrow understanding of labour law in many countries, compared to the current multifaceted and multi-level regulation of working life. Rather than excluding lifelong learning from the scope of labour law, researchers and practitioners should embrace the challenge and analyse its implications within this context.

There is clearly a need for legal research, particularly from a labour law perspective. While lifelong learning has been studied extensively within social sciences, education and economics, it requires comprehensive analysis from the labour law viewpoint. Lifelong learning is a complex and challenging topic, especially as a labour law phenomenon. This provides a genuine opportunity to reflect on the relationship between increasingly regulated lifelong learning and labour law, as well as labour law institutions.

However, the task has not been easy as there has been little previous research on labour law and lifelong learning. Another reason is that lifelong learning is a very complex legal phenomenon. Lifelong learning can be linked with a variety of instruments, and its regulation is multi-level and multifaceted. Lifelong learning measures may involve employment-related actions, such as employee upskilling during employment, or actions aimed at promoting the employee's smooth re-employment. In addition, lifelong learning measures can be activating labour market measures for people who are not even employed, i.e., unemployed persons. Furthermore, when examining lifelong learning through the lens of labour law, it is essential to consider the broader institutional framework, particularly the influence of social partners and the significance of collective agreements. These actors play a crucial role in shaping access to training opportunities, defining rights and obligations related to continuous education and ensuring that lifelong learning initiatives align with both workers' needs and labour market demands.

While this volume acknowledges the growing relevance of lifelong learning in contemporary labour markets, it is equally important to perceive the structural inequalities that shape access to such opportunities. Namely, lifelong learning is not equally accessible to all individuals; rather, it is deeply influenced by socio-economic background, age, health status and employment conditions. For instance, individuals from lower socio-economic groups may face financial barriers, limited access to digital infrastructure, or precarious employment that restricts their ability to participate in training programs. Older workers may encounter age-related biases or lack tailored learning pathways, while those with health challenges may require adaptive learning environments that are not always available. Moreover, in practice, workers in non-standard or insecure employment often lack the institutional support—such as paid training leave or employer-sponsored programmes—that facilitate lifelong learning.[6] These thematises are addressed partially and implicitly, but in part due to the diversity and extent of the thematises, it is necessary to delineate its scope; this book specifically concentrates on labour law and lifelong learning, rather than providing a comprehensive analysis of all dimensions related to lifelong learning in general.

The central aim of this book is twofold. First, it seeks to explore the multifaceted relationship between lifelong learning and labour law by analysing how lifelong learning intersects with various dimensions of labour regulation. Second, it aims to identify and articulate the key features of lifelong learning as a legal and policy phenomenon. Given the complexity of the subject, the relationship between lifelong learning and labour law is approached from multiple perspectives, including European Union policies and regulations, national labour (market) laws and the conceptual framing of lifelong learning as a fundamental labour right. The diversity of these approaches reflects the inherently interdisciplinary nature of the topic. As the themes addressed in different chapters may overlap, cross-references are provided throughout the book to guide readers and facilitate a more integrated understanding. In doing so, this volume contributes to filling a significant gap in academic research by offering a comprehensive legal analysis of lifelong learning within the broader context of labour law.

Despite the growing significance of lifelong learning in contemporary labour markets, scholarly contributions from the labour law perspective remain relatively limited. One contributing factor is the conceptual complexity of lifelong learning, which resists a uniform definition across legal, cultural and institutional contexts. Lifelong learning encompasses both normative and temporal dimensions—it is simultaneously a societal value promoting continuous personal and professional development, and a time-related concept that spans the entirety of an individual's working life. For the purposes of this book, we have adopted a definition of lifelong learning based on the European Commission's 2001 definition:

> All learning activity undertaken throughout life, with the aim of improving knowledge, skills, and competences within a personal, civic, social, and/or employment-related perspective.[7]

This definition was adopted because it is sufficiently comprehensive and broad, allowing for the conceptualisation and analysis of various dimensions or approaches of lifelong learning within the context of labour law. Various approaches are explored in different chapters of the book, with varying emphases depending on the

---

[6] See. e.g. OECD (2025), pp. 39–68.

[7] European Commission (2001).

chapter. The book does not prioritise one approach over the other; rather, both are considered essential for understanding lifelong learning as an integral part of contemporary labour law.

The book's approach highlights that the regulation of lifelong learning spans all levels of labour law: from the International Labour Organization (ILO) and European Union regulations to national laws, collective agreements at various levels, employment contracts and employer policies and guidelines. Consequently, the concept of lifelong learning is multi-level and multi-faceted. Additionally, various national characteristics influence how lifelong learning is understood and structured within the context of labour law.

This multi-dimensional approach is reflected in the various chapters of the book. While the authors do not focus on country-specific analyses, each naturally views lifelong learning in the context of labour law through their own perspectives, shaped by national regulations, institutions and industrial relations.[8] Therefore, this must be taken into account when reading the different chapters of the book. In addition, it must be noted that although the authors are from different countries, this is not a comparative study. However, some examples from different countries or legal systems are used.

## 1 Structure of the Book

In this book, we implement a rather traditional structure. First, we analyse the phenomenon from the point of view of international and EU regulation, and thereafter we rely on the traditional division of individual and collective labour law.

The book consists of four parts and conclusions.

In the first **PART I**, the relationship between the lifelong learning and labour law is analysed in **Chapter "Lifelong Learning and Labour Law : Mapping the New Phenomenon in the Systematics of Labour Law" by *Jari Murto***. In this chapter, we seek to understand how lifelong learning can be systematised as part of the contemporary labour law systematics. Thus, the prevailing systematics of labour law is critically assessed, although the aim of the chapter is not to redefine labour law but to consider how new dimensions could be included in the systematics of labour law. The chapter examines how the external boundaries and internal systematics of the fields of law are usually determined. Thereafter, the possibility of expanding our understanding of labour law in such a way that it would also cover labour market law is considered. The actual analysis examines the different types of labour law regulation and assesses their relationship to the systematics of labour law and labour law institutions in 2020.

---

[8] In the book the relationship between labour law and lifelong learning is analysed mainly from the European perspective.

**PART II** of the book explores lifelong learning as part of employment policy. Thus, European Union regulation policies and initiatives play an important role in this chapter. However, this is useful, as lifelong learning is a difficult phenomenon to understand without a sufficient description of the EU background.

In **Chapter "Exploring the Future of Lifelong Learning through the Tapestry of European Policy History"**, ***Flore Claus*** describes and analyses the trajectory of the regulation of lifelong learning in the context of the European Union. The chapter outlines how lifelong learning policies and regulation have evolved as part of the EU's development. Lifelong learning has a long history as part of EU policies since the establishment of the European Economic Community in 1957, but the significance of lifelong learning was strengthened by the influence of European Employment policy and finally with the launch of European Pillar of Social Rights (2017). Therefore, Claus employs contextual analysis in her chapter to intertwine the development of lifelong learning with more general social and legal trajectories.

**In Chapter "Legal Foundations of Lifelong learning and Labour Law in Europe"**, ***Felicia Kain*** examines the regulation of lifelong learning in international norms and the regulation of the European Union. The analysis focuses, among other things, on the question of whether lifelong learning is protected and if the existing legal acts protect existing structures or instead call for the expansion of structures. The chapter provides a diverse picture of a very wide range of regulation that creates an international and European legal framework for lifelong learning, especially in the context of labour law and working life.

**In Chapter "EU Recommendations on Micro-credentials and Individual Learning Accounts: Soft (law) Steps Towards Common EU Employment Markets?", Matti Urpilainen** describes and analyses two new recent institutions based on the recommendations of the European Union Commission. These are micro-credentials and individual learning accounts. As employees' upskilling and reskilling has increased in importance, can the Commission's recommendations for micro-credentials and individual learning accounts, given in 2022, be seen as concrete steps in EU's employment policy? Since the Commission's recommendations are aimed at Member States, **Urpilainen** analyses how and why these non-binding soft law instruments can be interpreted as instruments for promoting lifelong learning across the EU. Although the recommendations are soft law instruments per se, the chapter addresses how and to what extent they could affect the coordination of lifelong learning in the EU, perhaps more strongly than their soft law nature would require.

**In Chapter "Apprenticeship in Europe: A Learning Hybrid Model Between Education and Work", Giorgio Impellizzieri** analyses apprenticeship, which constitutes an interesting and traditional legal institution at the intersection of learning and work life, and a certain type of transition from school to work. Although apprenticeship can easily be included in lifelong learning, it raises complex labour law issues, such as how the minimum content of training is determined in apprenticeship and to what extent the apprentice is covered by labour law protection. In this regard, the apprenticeship agreement is similar to various types of traineeships as a transition between education and work life. As the partial employment nature of the apprenticeship has also been noted on the European Union level, **Impellizzieri** analyses recent European regulatory initiatives, i.e. the 2018 European Council Recommendation on a European Framework for Quality and Effective Apprenticeships as well as the 2024 Proposal for a Directive on improving working conditions in traineeships.

**PART III** of the book explores the collective dimension of lifelong learning in labour law. Since collective agreements are an essential regulatory instrument for determining terms of employment in many countries, it is appropriate that the role of collective agreements is also studied when structuring lifelong learning in the context of labour law.

**Chapter "Social Dialogue and Lifelong Learning: The Difficult Interplay at EU Level and National Level"**, written by **Valentina Franca** and **Alexander De Becker**, analyses the development of the EU Social Dialogue and its historical roots in general, as well as the role of social dialogue in the context of lifelong learning. The scope of social dialogue has expanded and therefore the number of subjects of social dialogue has also increased. The main aim of this chapter is to examine to what extent lifelong learning fits into the current competences which are granted to the EU and to the social partners at EU level. Also, the contrary option, how the relationship between EU-level social dialogue and lifelong learning can be seen, is taken into account. Based on multilayered analysis, the chapter provides a viewpoint concerning the interplay between the EU Social Dialogue, the Social Dialogue in various EU Member States and lifelong learning.

After the European level analysis, the understanding of lifelong learning is deepened **in Chapter "Regulating Lifelong Learning Under Collective Agreements" by Caroline Johansson** through the analysis of collective agreements. Understanding the role and content of collective agreements in each country requires an understanding of industrial relations, on what level bargaining is conducted and how these affect the content of the collective agreements. In this chapter, **Johansson** illustrates the potential of collective agreements as a source of lifelong learning measures, especially in Sweden. Johansson outlines various thematic aspects of regulating lifelong learning under collective agreements as well as the question of the advantages and disadvantages of regulating lifelong learning in collective agreements, also taking into account the level— local, sectoral or cross-sectoral/confederate—at which the agreement is concluded. Thus, the chapter provides an interesting overview of the current state of lifelong learning in collective agreements and how collective agreements can be a regulatory instrument to define and regulate in particular profession- or sector-specific needs for employee reskilling and upskilling.

**In Chapter "Regulating Lifelong Learning Under Collective Agreements",** the focus is on works councils and their role as promoters of lifelong learning. **Jaqueline Stein** and **Katharina Ruhwedel** present the main features of work council institutions—especially in Germany—and analyse how work councils, as intermediaries between employers and employees on a company level, could be the institution where the needs of lifelong learning are mapped and applicable measures are developed. For this purpose, the distinction of preventive measures–reactive measures is employed. The chapter also highlights a fairly new legal innovation—still in its development phase—in lifelong learning in the context of labour law: company training mentors. While company training mentors can be considered a new type of personnel representative, the concept simultaneously illustrates how lifelong learning is gradually revealing various manifestations in the field of labour law.

**PART IV** examines the connection between lifelong learning and labour law from the individual perspective. Chapters in Part IV are also complemented with the future-oriented and critical approach.

**Agnieszka Zwolińska** addresses **in Chapter "Works Councils as Promoters of Lifelong Learning : Opportunities and Challenges"** the identification and analysis of legal institutions that may increase the freedom of the employees with regard to lifelong learning. The chapter examines—mainly on the basis of international agreements and EU regulation —how employees are informed about the possibilities of lifelong learning or how participation in lifelong learning measures is taken into account in recording an employee's working time. Special attention is paid to employee rights, especially how enforceable such rights are.

**Chapter "Lifelong Learning as a Contractual Issue: Is it an Employer's Obligation or an Empty Right?", written by Peter Sipka**, focuses on the role of employment contracts as an instrument for determining lifelong learning measures. This analysis is based on the starting points of individual labour law, which illustrates the fact that in different countries, the traditions of industrial relations and legal cultures and the weight and importance of different regulatory instruments vary. Since the reskilling and upskilling of employees naturally requires financial investment from the employer, the approach of this chapter is critical to a certain degree, especially when considering to what extent it is the employer's obligation to cover the costs of lifelong learning measures, especially if these measures may benefit another employer or even the functioning of the labour market on a wide scale.

**Beryl ter Haar** outlines in **Chapter "Lifelong Learning and Work in the Future"** the relationship between lifelong learning and labour law after the transitions (green and digital) have been made, as well as in the context of future work. One starting point in the chapter is how it would be possible to understand the relationship between lifelong learning and labour law if it is more than just the employee improving their employability. The chapter discusses, based on various theories, how lifelong learning can be understood in the context of future work, which also includes the question of how lifelong learning is not only important from an economic perspective, for the employee to remain employable, but also in improving employees' own talents.

## References

European Commission (2001) Communication from the commission, Making a European Area of Lifelong learning a reality. COM (2001) 678. https://eur-lex.europa.eu/LexUriServ/LexUriServ.do?uri=COM:2001:0678:FIN:EN:PDF

European Commission (2025) Communication from the Commission to the European Parliament, the European Council, the Council, the European Economic and Social Committee and the Committee of the Regions: The Union of Skills. COM (2025) 90 final. https://employment-social-affairs.ec.europa.eu/document/download/915b147d-c5af-44bb-9820-c252d872fd31_en?filename=Communication%20-%20Union%20of%20Skills.pdf

European Year of Skills (2023). https://commission.europa.eu/strategy-and-policy/priorities-2019-2024/europe-fit-digital-age/european-year-skills-2023_en

OECD (2025) Trends in Adult Learning: New Data from the 2023 Survey of Adult Skills, Getting Skills Right, OECD Publishing, Paris, https://doi.org/10.1787/ec0624a6-en.

The European Pillar of Social Rights Action Plan (2021). https://op.europa.eu/webpub/empl/european-pillar-of-social-rights/downloads/KE0921008ENN.pdf

von der Leyen U (2024) Europe's choice: political guidelines for the next European Commission 2024–2029. Strasbourg. https://commission.europa.eu/document/download/e6cd4328-673c-4e7a-8683-f63ffb2cf648_en?filename=Political%20Guidelines%202024-2029_EN.pdf

**Jari Murto** is associate professor of Labour and Social Law at the University of Helsinki, Finland. His main research interests are doctrines of labour law, determination of the terms of employment, regulation of labour market transitions, lifelong learning, industrial relations and labour market policy at the national and EU levels. Murto is a founder and co-leader of the international research group "Labour law and lifelong learning". Murto has extensive experience as a labour law expert on several multidisciplinary research projects combining legal and empirical research. Murto has acted as a national expert in several international networks.

**Valentina Franca, PhD,** works as an associate professor and researcher of labour law and social security law at the Faculty of Public Administration, University of Ljubljana, Slovenia. Her research includes numerous studies, books and articles in the field of collective labour relations, digitalisation in labour relations and new forms of work. She is a member of the editorial boards of scientific journals and participates as a national expert in international associations such as the Worker Participation Network at the ETUI Institute in Brussels and CEELEX at the International Labor Organization. She is also an active researcher in national and international projects for various organisations, such as Eurofound, EIGE, OECD, EC and the like, and lecturer at various professional and scientific conferences.

# The Role of Lifelong Learning in the Labour Law Frameworks

# Lifelong Learning and Labour Law: Mapping the New Phenomenon in the Systematics of Labour Law

**Jari Murto**

## 1 Introduction

The question of how we define labour law and what components labour law is composed of is relevant in several ways. Even at the beginning of their studies, students are presented with a legal system divided into branches of law, as this makes it easier to perceive and understand the legislation. Thus, the division into branches of law puts pedagogical function into practice.[1] During studies, the branches of law form a map of the legal system for lawyers, based on which the place of each legal phenomenon in the legal system is identified.[2] At the same time, the branches of law become a part of the self-understanding of lawyers and researchers as well as their legal mind.[3] Lawyers usually say they are specialised in a certain branch of law.[4]

Branches of law have arisen to describe the legal and social reality at a given time, although often on a national basis. This has affected the definition of the branch of law and how the boundaries of the branch of law as well as relations with other branches of law have been understood. The development, enlargement and diversity of legal norms entails the risk that the definition of the branch of law no longer captures all relevant legal norms that it should describe. The concept of a

[1] Tuori (2007), p. 109.

[2] Langille (2006), pp. 14–17.

[3] See the concept of legal mind e.g. Brożek (2019).

[4] Langille (2006), p. 17.

J. Murto (✉)
Faculty of Law, University of Helsinki, Helsinki, Finland
e-mail: jari.murto@helsinki.fi


J. Murto, V. Franca (eds.), *Labour Law and Lifelong Learning*,
https://doi.org/10.1007/978-3-032-11035-0_2

branch of law can then be considered 'mummified'.[5] Labour law is a good example of a branch of law in which the scope of relevant legal norms has expanded in recent years as a result of social and economic development, as new kinds of legal and social phenomena have entered the sphere of regulation. Therefore, there has been discussion about the concepts, functions and ideas of labour law.[6]

Lifelong learning is an illustrative example of a phenomenon created by social development and lifelong learning-related legal regulation. However, the relationship between lifelong learning and labour law is not unambiguous and little systematic attention has been paid to lifelong learning in labour law research. Lifelong learning is a broad concept that has several different meanings, and therefore it is not easy to fit it into the existing legal doctrines and frameworks of labour law.

The aim of this chapter is to analyse the relationship between lifelong learning and labour law. As a proviso, it must be mentioned that the purpose of this paragraph is not to redefine labour law but instead to outline and reflect on how a new type of phenomenon—lifelong learning—could be understood in the context of contemporary labour law and its systematics.

The research task is divided into the following research questions.

(1) How can the external and internal systematisation (subsystems) of labour law be perceived in general level?
(2) How could it be possible to extend our understanding of labour law, taking lifelong learning into account?
(3) What are the key dimensions of labour law in the context of lifelong learning?

These three questions will be answered next. To begin with, components that can define the boundaries of labour law are outlined and then different types of internal sub-systems of modern labour law are presented (Sect. 2). Next, we reflect on opportunities to extend understanding concerning labour law, particularly regarding lifelong learning as a legal phenomenon (Sect. 3). This is followed by an analysis of lifelong learning emphasising three key labour law perspectives (Sect. 4).

[5] Tuori (2007), pp. 145–146.

[6] See Hendrickx (2012), p. 108–109.

## 2 Systematics of Labour Law : External and Internal Systematic of Labour Law

The branch of law is an essential legal concept. However, it is not an unambiguous task to define it; it can be done in several different ways. Defining branches of law can be based on the main principle,[7] main concepts,[8] paradigm, [9] doctrines[10] or the social goal pursued by the regulation of that branch of law.[11] Often, the definition of a branch of law is influenced by a typical subject of regulation in that branch of law.[12]

The following is a brief description of the external and internal systematics of labour law, which are traditional tools for defining branches of law and their limits. An external perspective means the boundaries of the branch of law in relation to other branches of law, and an internal perspective means the internal systematics or subsystems within each branch of law.[13] The purpose of this chapter is to provide a background understanding for when the relationship of lifelong learning and labour law is outlined later in this chapter; thus, the aim is not to redefine labour law.

### *2.1 External Systemics of Labour Law : Considering the Boundaries of Labour Law?*

At the first stage of its development, labour law was conceived as part of contract law. However, since it was not a question of equal contracting parties, it soon became a characteristic feature and purpose of labour law norms to protect the weaker party— employee or worker—in this legal relationship. Thus, the principle of worker protection became the starting point and meta-principle of labour law. As a legal branch , labour law has evolved to cover those legal rules that aim to protect a person working in an employment relationship or in an employee position.

[7] Tuori (2007), p. 108.

[8] Bogg et al. (2015).

[9] Collins (2015), p. 48. – He uses expression "central case or paradigm".

[10] Bogg et al. (2015).

[11] Tuori (2007), p. 108.

[12] Tuori (2007), p. 118.

[13] See Collins (2015), pp. 46–50.

Performing work in an employment relationship is a key determinant of labour law. This has had an impact on the research of labour law, as the focus has been on the status and rights—mainly based on legislation and/or collective agreements—of an employee working in an employment relationship. On the other hand, less attention has been paid in the research to persons who are not working in the employment relationship. Can such persons be excluded from labour law research and the protection provided by labour legislation? Generally speaking, it is a question of what is understood as the central concept of labour law: namely, the fundamental concepts often determine our understanding of the branch of law and its limits.

The question of the central concept of labour law is not unambiguous. The central concept could be, for example, *work*. However, labour law is not defined on the basis of the concept of work. Taking into account the origins of this branch of law, it is understandable that the employee is one of the fundamental concepts of labour law; after all, labour law is intended to protect a person working in an employee position. Another central concept could be that of the *employment contract*. The position of the employment contract appears to be strong in labour law, especially for historical reasons, because labour law has developed as an independent branch of law from contract law. However, when it comes to determining terms of employment, the concept of an *employment relationship* becomes more essential.[14] It can also be considered whether the concept of the *employer* could be a fundamental concept of labour law. After all, the employer provides the work, and the employer is also the responsible party. Thus, it is no wonder that the position of the employer and the functional concept of the employer became a research interest a few years ago.[15]

From the perspective of lifelong learning, it is interesting to consider whether the *labour market* could be one of the fundamental concepts of labour law. This would broaden the perspective of labour law, as interest would be focused not only on the relationship between employees and employers, but instead more broadly on the activities of job seekers and employers in the labour market.[16] Such a starting point would be supported, for example, by the fact that, within the EU, labour law is—more strongly than national systems— related to the labour market and to promote the functioning of the labour market. The reason why labour market regulation is rarely structured as part of labour law is probably the nature of the regulation: labour market law falls mainly under the scope of public law.

Indeed, it can be argued that the structuring of labour law has a strong impact on understanding labour law as part of private law. Of course, there is a natural explanation for this. Labour law became 'independent' by disengaging itself from contract law when the regulation of paid labour work became a significant social phenomenon and thus subject to regulation. Therefore, understanding labour law as

[14] How the concept of an employment contract and employment relationship is understood in different countries varies.

[15] See e.g. Prassl (2015) and Selberg (2017).

[16] See e.g. Bruun (2023), pp. 31–32.

just one type of contract no longer corresponded to legal or social reality. However, there can be many opinions on how successfully labour law managed to disengage from the contract law by developing its own labour law doctrines. There are also country-specific differences.[17]

Labour law also has a traditional link with social security law and social law. Since employees' social security is often organised on the basis of paid employment, it has made sense to structure such regulation as part of labour law. At the same time, it should be noted that how the relationship of social security law and labour law is perceived must be seen in its temporal context.

It is important to note that labour law is a dynamic branch of law, and labour law regulation has expanded over time. Thus, labour law has either a stronger or weaker relationship with several other branches of law, and consequently labour law phenomena are intertwined with the doctrines and phenomena of other branches of law.[18] Thus, the need for dialogue between different branches of law has increased. However, at the same time, it should be noted that the branch of law is not a trivial matter; it defines and legitimises various actors—legal scholars and practitioners as well as other legal experts who can produce legal expertise such as new legal norms, institutions, reasoning[19] and, in general, the vocabulary and concepts by which we perceive labour law.

## 2.2 *The Internal Systematics of Labour Law : What Kind of Subsystems Are Included in Labour Law?*

By analysing labour law from an internal perspective, it is possible to obtain a more accurate picture of the content of labour law. The dichotomy between individual and collective labour law is a frequently used and traditional way of structuring labour law. In this case, the system of labour law is seen as being built on two types of contracts: an employment contract and a collective agreement. It is possible to obtain a more diverse picture of labour law when it is structured into different subsystems based on their functions. Thus, a system of employment contracts, collective agreements and employees' participation,[20] occupational safety and health legislation, social security and labour market law can be distinguished.[21] Moreover, from an internal perspective, labour law can be structured by paying attention to the subject matter of regulation or material terms of employment (working time, occupational safety, termination of an employment contract). Furthermore, labour law

[17] See Freedland (2015), p. 43.

[18] Collins (2015), pp. 47–48.

[19] Doorey (2017), pp. 209–210.

[20] Kairinen (2009), pp. 55–60.

[21] Tiitinen (2005), p. 1.

can often also be structured according to regulatory levels: legislation, collective agreements, company-specific norms[22] and employment contracts.

Clearly, the internal systematics of labour law can be structured in several different ways. This can easily be seen by browsing the table of contents of labour law textbooks[23] or reviews of the essential content of labour law.[24] Often, the general doctrines, main principles and concepts of labour law, as well as the development of industrial relations, are described. After the general part, the content of labour law is presented in a hybrid way by combining (1) the level of regulation (individual collective—labour law) and a more detailed description of the regulation of various types of (2) material working conditions (working time, occupational safety and health, termination of an employment contract, etc.).

Labour law has also been structured by dividing it into (1) employment contract law, (2) collective agreement and co-operation law, (3) occupational safety and health (working time, annual leave and occupational safety and health regulation), (4) social security legislation and (5) labour market law.[25] Despite the structuring, social security legislation and labour market law is excluded from traditional labour law. This is probably because these areas, which are mainly governed by public law, do not fit into the traditional understanding that labour law is part of private law. In this understanding, the division of private law–public law would de facto determine the boundaries of labour law at the same time: public law norm material, such as labour market law, would not be covered by labour law, and thus, as a rule, would be excluded from labour law. [26]

Due to political and social changes, labour law has become more diverse. New areas such as equal treatment of men and women, non-discrimination,[27] and the protection of employees' privacy[28] have developed. This can be seen, for instance, in the ILO agreements and recommendations, in which the division into individual and collective labour law is not so relevant due to the diversity of agreements and standards.[29] However, in this regard, it is also possible to rely on a more traditional

[22] Murto (2015), pp. 107–118.

[23] See e.g. Bruun (2022), Finland; Sigeman and Sjödin (2022), Sweden.

[24] ICLG (2025): (1) Terms and Conditions of Employment, (2) Employee Representation and Industrial Relations, (3) Discrimination, (4) Maternity and Family Leave Rights, (5) Business Sales, (6) Termination of Employment, (7) Protecting Business Interests Following Termination, (8) Data Protection and Employee Privacy and (9) The Future. See also Global Legal Insights (2024): (1) General labour market trends and latest/likely trends in employment litigation, (2) Redundancies, business transfers and reorganisations, (3) Business protection and restrictive covenants, (4) Discrimination protection, (5) Protection against dismissal, (6) Statutory employment protection rights (such as notice entitlements, whistleblowing, holiday, parental and maternity leave, etc.), (7) Worker consultation, trade unions and industrial action, (8) Employee privacy, (9) Other recent developments in the field of employment and labour law.

[25] Tiitinen (2005), p. 1.

[26] Tiitinen (2005), p. 1.

[27] See e.g. Fredman (2015), pp. 257–274.

[28] Eklund (2021), pp. 13–21.

[29] See as an example ILO Library, General Surveys: Reports by Theme.

systematic approach and structure to the content of international labour standards: Chapter 1. Freedom of Association and Social Dialogue, Chapter 2. Labour and Employment and Chapter 3. Social Security.[30] Similarly, the European Social Charter is thematically and diversely built on working life-related phenomena, without division into individual and collective labour law.[31]

In particular, the EU has played a significant role in the development of labour law and the emergence of new subsystems. The division between individual and collective labour law has long been weaker in EU labour law than in national systems; however, it is not completely absent in European labour law either.[32] That said, the European Pillar of Social Rights are not based on the dichotomy of individual-collective in labour law, but the three main chapters are titled as Chapter II: Equal opportunities and access to the labour market, Chapter II: Fair working conditions; Chapter III: Social protection and inclusion.[33]

As described above, there appears to be two types of self-understanding in labour law. On the one hand, labour law is traditionally understood on a national basis, emphasising labour law as part of private law as well as the dichotomy of individual and collective labour law. However, it is necessary to examine to what extent this corresponds to increasingly pluralistic regulation and contributes to the perception and structuring of new legal phenomena, especially in the context of EU regulation. Even though the scope of labour law has widened, and this has—at least to some extent—influenced labour law research and the ever-greater fragmentation of labour law, with the increase in the number of actors constantly challenging the self-understanding of labour law and labour law research.

Lifelong learning is one—but at the same time also illustrative—such social phenomenon that challenges the boundaries, internal systematics and self-understanding of labour law. However, it is not just a social phenomenon. As the regulation of lifelong learning is gradually expanding, lifelong learning needs to be taken into account more seriously when considering labour law as a branch of the discipline of law.

## 3 How Can Lifelong Learning Be Systematised as Part of Contemporary Labour Law?

When considering how it would be possible to systematise lifelong learning as part of the systematics of labour law, it is necessary to break away from the traditional approach. Instead, different types of EU regulation, which simultaneously determine the regulation of lifelong learning and the development of these institutions,

[30] Servais (2022), pp. 5–15.

[31] Council of Europe (1996).

[32] Bogg et al. (2016).

[33] The European Pillar of Social Rights.

should be taken into account. At the same time, it seems necessary to adopt a broader view of the scope of labour law, i.e. what kind of regulation and legal phenomena should be included within the scope of labour law in the 2020s.

When aiming to systematise lifelong learning to contemporary labour law, Bruun's four-field offers an interesting starting point. Although there are also traditional dimensions of individual and collective labour law, Bruun has outlined two new dimensions to the internal systematics of labour law: (1) “Fundamental rights” and (2) “Access justice.[34] In fact, it can be stated that Bruun’s four-field already offers, on a general level, a fresh view of the systematics of contemporary labour law. Especially when the goal is to try to structure lifelong learning in the context of labour law, “access justice” or, more precisely, “access to the labour market” is a useful and interesting starting point.

With the dimension of access justice, Bruun describes a legal standard that aims to promote access to work or the labour market for the individuals. This is an important addition to the traditional framework of labour law in order not to exclude relevant norms and legal phenomena from labour law. When the labour law norms are structured taking “access justice” into account, one can read the kind of regulation that aims to help the employee reach—but also to stay in—the labour market. In particular, EU labour law and labour market regulation explains why it has been necessary to add “access justice” as a new dimension of labour law.[35] However, examples can also be found in national regulation.[36]

The dimension of access justice can also be connected to the model of the transitional labour market, developed by Schmid in 1998.[37] The idea of the transitional labour market model is to distinguish between different transitions during employees’ careers, and thus transitions characteristic of modern working life. One transition is from education to working life, but the model identifies different types of models to meet the needs of employees’ upskilling and reskilling. Indeed, the role of lifelong learning as a risk management tool has been identified as a model of transitional labour market.[38]

Access justice dimension can be connected to the concept of employability. EU regulation has shifted from traditional labour law towards employment and labour supply issues in the 2000s. Employability embodies the idea that the employee and job seeker would have the ability to find employment and thus manage labour market transitions. Although employability stresses individual responsibility, it also

[34] Bruun (2017), pp. 26–29.

[35] Bruun (2017), pp. 27–28.

[36] Employment Contract Act 55/2001 Chap. 1 § 3a (2001). Concluding a fixed-term employment contract with a long-term unemployed person.

[37] Schmid (1998).

[38] Schmid (2015), pp. 88–89.

emphasises the provision of services that facilitate labour market transitions.[39] The EU often relies on the idea of promoting employability in its arguments.[40]

Access justice or access to labour market dimension is a broad concept, but at the same time, it embodies in a meaningful way the relationship between traditional labour law and labour market law. Thus, the dimension of access justice articulates the prevailing division between insiders and outsiders in the labour market, and the fact that these groups can be seen differently for the purpose of legislation should have a stronger influence on understanding labour law and research on it.[41]

In this way, labour law is also more broadly included in the scope of labour market institutions.[42] Such an extension to the understanding of labour law, without paying too much attention to the private law–public law dichotomy, will update labour law to reflect current regulation. At the same time as labour law is extended beyond the employee–employer relationship, consideration should be given to how labour law research should take phenomena outside of traditional labour law into account.

Based on the above, it is possible—and necessary—to consider whether lifelong learning and its regulation is a phenomenon outside labour law, or to what extent labour law can already include elements that can be considered as an indication of lifelong learning. This will be considered in the next subchapter.

## 4 Different Dimensions of Lifelong Learning from the Perspective of Labour Law

Lifelong learning is a broad and multifaceted phenomenon in the context of labour law and the labour market. The following outlines the main labour law components of lifelong learning from three different perspectives: (1) during an employment relationship, (2) the role of social partners and (3) labour market measures. The analysis is based primarily on Finnish legislation, which serves as an example in this subchapter.

### *4.1 Lifelong Learning and Employment Relationship*

An employee performs duties in accordance with his or her employment contract in an employment relationship. In other words, the employee sells his/ her skills and working hours for the employer to use. In the past—in the traditional model—the

[39] Zekic (2016), pp. 554–560 and pp. 574–575.

[40] See e.g. Council of the European Union (2022).

[41] See Bruun (2017), pp. 27–29.

[42] Finkin (2019), pp. 1115–1116.

employee moved directly from school to work. However, for this transition, various legal arrangements have been developed, aimed at ensuring that the employee's skills meet the employer's needs as well as possible.

Apprenticeship training has been a traditional way of learning the skills needed for a particular employer. It combines working and competence development when an apprentice performs his or her work.[43] A somewhat similar concept has been developed in Finland, called the Education Agreement. This is not about work in an employment relationship, but specifically about learning. The training agreement is therefore agreed between the training provider and the workplace providing the training.[44]

Today, there are several different types of trainee or internship positions that can be considered to include elements of lifelong learning, as they are work-based or work-related learning schemes.[45] On the one hand, an internship may be included in regular studies, but, on the other hand, it may be a work of an employment nature, for example a seasonal/summer job or other type of fixed-term work.[46] Traineeship is based on the fact that both private and public sector employers now have increasingly customised trainee or graduate programmes. Traineeships, on the one hand, provide the student with a way to get to know the work tasks in their field and gain work experience; on the other hand, trainee programmes also provide an opportunity to get to know future employees.

The competence development of employees or personnel has been a part of the management of the employer for a long time. This is evident, for example, in the diversified HRM/HRD-related[47] competence development guidelines and policies, which are based on the employer's unilateral decision-making. The company-specific competence development policies and guidelines mentioned above also guide the procedures for an individual employee.[48]

In addition to the training at the discretion of the employer described above, the employer has a statutory or collective agreement obligation in certain cases. This has also been taken into account in Directive (EU) 2019/1152 on transparent and predictable working conditions in the European Union, Article 13 ‘Mandatory

[43] See in this volume Impellizzieri G, Apprenticeship in Europe: A Learning Hybrid Model Between Education and Work –The Integration of Training and Employment Between Regulation, Opportunities, and Risks.

[44] Act on Vocational Education and Training (517/2017), Sect. 71. See also Murto (2018), pp. 97–103.

[45] Rosin (2017), p. 11.

[46] Rosin (2017), p. 11. She has distinguished four different types of traineeships: (1) traineeships organised as part of vocational and higher education; (2) traineeships forming part of active labour market services; (3) traineeships for new graduates (open-market traineeships) and (4) cross-border traineeships.

[47] Human resource management /human resource development.

[48] See legal status of employer’s unilaterally decided policies and guidelines for instance Murto (2015), pp. 249–255.

training'. It requires member states to ensure that the training that a worker needs to complete work must be free of charge and take place during working hours.[49]

Since reskilling and upskilling of employees and personnel has become increasingly important, it is not only within the scope of the employer's unilateral decision-making but also part of the co-operation procedure, i.e. employees' participation. This can be seen as an expression of the fact that the up-to-date competence of employees is in the best interest of the employer and the personnel. In regular dialogue, employer and employee shall cover the competence requirements of personnel and the development of competence.[50] In addition, when the workplace community development plan is drawn up, the following two lifelong learning issues shall be included: First, the current state and foreseeable trends that may have an impact on personnel competence requirements; and second, objectives and measures for developing and maintaining the competence of personnel.[51] This makes it possible to take company-specific special needs into account and coordinate them with the non-legal HR procedures of the company.[52]

Employee upskilling and reskilling plays a key role when it is a question of collective redundancy. The legal phenomenon can be determined as transition security, and its idea is to promote employees' smooth re-employment through cooperation between employees, employers, and employment authorities in the event of collective redundancy. From the perspective of lifelong learning, the most important point is that employees enjoy the right to participate in a month-long employee-funded training programme that furthers their prospects of finding employment, but only if the employee employs more than 30 people and the employee has been employed for over five years. The value of the coaching or training must correspond to the employee's pay for at least one month. If that employee's pay is less than the average monthly earnings of personnel at the same workplace, the value of training should correspond to at least the average wage of the employees given notice.[53] The content of the training or coaching is not specified in the legislation, only that it promotes the employee's re-employment. The content of coaching or training can be agreed in a collective agreement,[54] and thus it can be defined in more detail than it is in the legislation. Furthermore, employees are encouraged to take part in training or coaching because the value of the training is not the taxable income of the employee.

Employers are, in addition, obligated to compose a transition security action plan as a part of cooperation negotiations and to investigate, together with employment authorities, how to support dismissed employees. One key element of the action

---

[49] See implementation of this directive in selected countries; See in this volume Sipka P, Lifelong Learning: An Obligation for the Employer or an Empty Right?, Section 4.2.

[50] Co-operation Act (1333/2021) Chap. 2, Sect. 8.

[51] Co-operation Act (1333/2021) Chap. 2, Sect. 9.

[52] See also Government proposal 159/2021, pp. 76–83.

[53] Employment Contract Act 55/2001 Chap. 7 § 13 (2001).

[54] Employment Contract Act 55/2001 Chap. 13 § 7 (2001). It is thus semi-dispositive legislation.

plan is to define the principles of how to help employees to find new employment or training.[55]

As noted above, labour law has a fairly long history of measures that fall within the scope of lifelong learning, particularly apprenticeship. However, this legal phenomenon has also become more diverse with the development of various types of traineeships. The latest development is transition security in the context of collective redundancy. This embodies the goal of a smooth re-employment, in which up-to-date skills play a key role.

## 4.2 *Lifelong Learning and the Role of Social Partners and Collective Agreements*

Collective agreements and social partners are key labour law institutions. However, the role of collective agreements cannot be understood without taking each country's industrial relations into account. This also affects the role and importance of collective agreements and social partners when considering lifelong learning and employee reskilling and upskilling regulation. From the perspective of the systematics of collective agreements but also of labour law as a whole, two essential questions arise: (1) whether lifelong learning has been agreed in collective agreements and (2) if so, what is contained in the provisions agreed under those collective agreements.

The role of social partners is acknowledged in several international norms directly[56] or indirectly related to the regulation of lifelong learning, e.g. according to the European Pillar of Social Rights, Principle 8, "social partners shall be consulted on the design and implementation of economic, employment and social policies according to national practice".[57] Although the EU seems to want to strengthen the participation of social partners in the context of lifelong learning,[58] this leaves open the question of how and at what level, in different national traditions, lifelong learning issues may be agreed upon.

In addition to traditional sectoral collective agreements, labour market-related lifelong learning can also be agreed upon between labour market confederations. Examples include the new Main Agreements (Den nya huvudavtal 2022)[59] agreed in Sweden and the Tripartite Agreement on Adult and Continuing Education

[55] Act 1333/2021 on Co-operation within Undertakings Ch. 3 § 21 (2021).

[56] Art. 5 Human Resources Development Convention.

[57] European Pillar of Social Rights, Principle 8.

[58] "Calls upon Member States, in close cooperation with the social partners, to strengthen skills and labour market policies that promote lifelong learning, including adult upskilling and reskilling, as well as labour market participation, notably of underrepresented groups." See Council of the European Union (2025), p. 8.

[59] See in this volume Johansson C, Regulating lifelong learning in collective agreements, Sect. 3.4.1 and Huvudavtal om trygghet, omställning och anställningsskydd.

(Trepartsaftale om langsigtede investeringer i voksen-, efter- og videreuddannelse 2023)[60] agreed in Denmark. The implementation of employee competence development through labour market agreements has also been considered in Norway.[61] In addition, Finland, especially, Akava, the union for highly skilled workers, has highlighted the need to consider how to create operating models for the development of employee competence between central confederations,[62] by sector in collective agreements or recommendations, or by defining company-specific procedures.[63]

Some openings for employee reskilling and upskilling may already have been agreed in collective agreements. They may, however, be of an aspirational or recommendational nature.[64] However, the fact that provisions in collective agreements appear in the first stage of an effort can be seen as part of the process of juridification:[65] first, the issues of lifelong learning are agreed upon as conditions of a kind, but they can also be established over time as conditions that create enforceable rights for individual employees. The two examples below give an idea of how the regulations for lifelong learning in collective agreements are evolving.

> The unions recommend that the employer and senior staff member aged 55 or over hold an annual discussion on the measures that support the competence and retention of an older employee.[66]

> **Exchange of holiday allowance for the development of skills**
>
> The employee has the right to exchange the holiday bonus pay or part of the holiday bonus pay for the corresponding paid leave. The leave will be used according to current Study Leave Act, or other corresponding right to study leave, self-motivated training to develop the employee's competence, if the change of holiday allowance would not cause significant inconvenience to the company.
>
> The employee should make the request as early as possible. The employer has the right, upon request, to obtain a reasoned explanation of what the employee is using his holiday pay leave for.[67]

The question is whether lifelong learning has been agreed upon in collective agreements and, if so, to what extent it varies between countries. It is interesting to note that as early as 10 years ago, in 2015, when Eurofund analysed merging topics addressed by collective bargaining since 2000 (economic themes, employment themes and work-related themes), several themes linked to lifelong learning were observed: (1) Mobility and career pathways, employment and redeployment, (2)

---

[60] Trepartsaftale om langsigtede investeringer i voksen-, efter- og videreuddannelse.

[61] NOU 2025:1 Felles ansvar, felles gevinst, Partssamarbeid for kompetanseutvikling i arbeidslivet; See also Norwegian International Labour Office (2019), pp. 23–24.

[62] Ahtela (2024), p. 7.

[63] Ahtela (2024), p. 36.

[64] See in this volume Johansson C, Regulating lifelong learning in collective agreements, Sect. 2.3.

[65] Blichner and Molander (2005).

[66] Collective agreement for senior salaried employees in technology industries between Technology Industry Employers of Finland and Federation of Professional and Managerial Staff (YTN), Sect. 4.4.

[67] Commerce sector collective agreement, amendments (2025) 23 §.

Employability and training (vocational training and lifelong learning), (3) Prevention of skills shortages and (4) Apprenticeship.[68] Thus, it can be assumed that the procedures and content of lifelong learning will also be increasingly agreed upon in collective agreements in the future. This makes it possible to combine sector-specific knowledge about needs for upskilling and reskilling in each sector. In this case, the provisions in collective agreements concerning lifelong learning measures would possibly evolve from general aspirations towards more tailored training plans specific to the sector, or even company. This would make it possible to meet the needs of both employees and employers in acquiring up-to-date skills and competences.

An illustrative and interesting example of the potential of collective agreements to be tools for the development of a lifelong learning framework in the context of labour law is provided by company training mentors in Germany.[69] Company training mentors exemplify fresh thinking on how to develop new labour law institutions—in work councils or collective agreements—and thus respond to new challenges in working life.

However, the fact that lifelong learning could be developed as part of collective agreements would above all require the trade unions to prioritise lifelong learning in the negotiations of collective agreements. Although lifelong learning is not a traditional collective agreement issue, its importance is growing, and it is important to employees and employers alike. Furthermore, in addition to sectoral collective agreements, confederation level and cross-sectoral agreements could be used when agreeing on broader, cross-sectoral issues, such as funding. Depending on the national model, this may also be a pathway to legislation.

## *4.3 Lifelong Learning and Activating Labour Market Measures*

Traditionally, when an employee becomes unemployed, he or she is paid unemployment benefit. This compensates the employee for the loss of income. While the status of active labour market policies has strengthened, a variety of active labour market measures have developed alongside monetary unemployment benefits. These emphasise the promotion of re-employment and the development of the skills of the unemployed person to meet the needs of the labour market.

As a rule, a full-time student is not entitled to unemployment benefit because they are not available to the labour market.[70] However, in Finland, certain derogations have arisen when an unemployed person may study even if he or she receives unemployment benefits. First, it is possible to study part-time and receive unem-

[68] Eurofound (2015), pp. 35–36.

[69] See in this volume Ruhdwedel K and Stein J, Works councils as promoters of lifelong learning – opportunities and challenges, Sect. 3.3.

[70] Unemployment Security Act (1209/2002) Chap. 2, Sect. 10.

ployment benefits as long as studying does not prevent the acceptance of full-time work.[71] Second, it is possible to accomplish short-term study supported by unemployment benefit, if person is over the age of 25, the studies do not last longer than six months and the studies provide transferable professional skills.[72]

The third derogation is that it is possible to study independently and voluntarily. Prerequisites are that the person is over 25 years old, employment authorities consider that independent studying is the most appropriate way to improve the person's professional skills and that the person has agreed independent studies with the employment authorities in their job-seeking plan.[73] It is worth noting that independent studying is defined in the legislation as a service which aims to promote (re) employment,[74] so it can be seen as a voluntary development of the person's employment. Self-motivated studies while receiving unemployment benefits were made possible in 2010.[75] The rationale for the change is, among other things, to improve adults' skills and their opportunities to obtain or maintain a job as well as to increase the availability of skilled labour.[76]

In the context of labour market measures, it is a customary practice for public authorities, i.e. employment authorities, to also be involved in organising or funding these measures. Moreover, it should be noted that employers can also participate in the organisation of training or labour market measures. The question is not only the employee's reskilling and/or upskilling but also that the employer has a significant interest that employees and hired employees have appropriate and up-to-date skills and knowledge.[77] The aim of joint purchase training in Finland is to foster labour market orientation, in addition to which training will be tailored to the needs of the employer and the trainees. Joint purchase training covers three kinds of training:

*Targeted Training*: When changes in the company require an upskilling of its employees. The aim is to avoid lay-offs or dismissals that threaten employees through education. Thus, these preventive measures could preserve jobs and extend working careers. The employer pays about 30–50% of the total cost of the training, depending on the size of the employer.[78]

*Recruitment Training*: If employees cannot find competent employees or skilled personnel will not be graduating soon in the field. The trainees who complete the training successfully will be employed by the company. The Centres for

[71] Unemployment Security Act (1209/2002) Chap. 2, Sect. 10.

[72] Unemployment Security Act (1209/2002) Chap. 2, Sect. 10 b.

[73] Unemployment Security Act (1209/2002) Chap. 2, Sect. 10 b.

[74] Unemployment Security Act (1209/2002) Chap. 2, Sect. 10 b.

[75] Government's proposal to Parliament (178/2009), amending the Public Employment Service Act, p. 8.

[76] Larja and Räisänen (2020), pp. 9–10.

[77] Act on the Organisation of Employment Services (380/2023) Chap. 7 Sect. 62.

[78] Murto (2018), pp. 67–68.

Economic Development, Transport and the Environment (ELY Centres) will pay 70% of the training costs and the employer 30%[79]

*Change Training*: The aim of Change Training is to help redundant workers to find a new occupation as a result of collective redundancies. The aim of training is to prevent and reduce unemployment among redundant employees, to promote fluent re-employment and/or improve their professional skills.[80]

It seems clear that reskilling and upskilling is a growing trend in the context of labour market measures. It has also been described as "from job security towards employment security". [81] This phenomenon is related to the fact that an employee should develop his/her own employment security or labour market security so that they can retain their jobs with the current employee or, in case of a lay-off, to become re-employed smoothly.[82] Ultimately, it is about employability,[83] and therefore such labour market measures that promote employees' re/upskilling constitute an increasingly essential toolbox to support various transitions in the labour market.

This European-wide transition to a supply-based approach in labour market policies has also been examined from a partly critical perspective. It would not be a question of protecting the worker against changes in the market, but rather of European employment policy contributing a tool for the workforce to survive in the constantly changing labour markets by means of upskilling, reskilling and training, and thus strive to develop employability.[84]

Activating labour market measures demonstrate that regulation of lifelong learning can already be interpreted as a key element of labour law. It is true that, to accept this interpretation, labour law must be understood more broadly than the traditional definition, i.e. labour market law. At the same time, activating labour market measures highlights the fact that the regulation of lifelong learning is characterised to some extent by a tripartite framework in which, in addition to the employee and the employer, there is a third party—a financier, an education provider, etc.

## 5 Conclusions

The aim of this chapter was to reflect on and analyse how lifelong learning could be understood in the context of labour law. One starting point was that labour law can be understood in a rather traditional and conservative way: labour law is a part of private law, and systematisation is based on the dichotomy of individual vs. collective labour law. Nevertheless, how labour law is understood affects what kind of

[79] Murto (2018), pp. 68–69.

[80] Murto (2018), pp. 69–70.

[81] Zekic (2016), p. 549.

[82] Barnard (2021), pp. 1207–1208.

[83] Zekic (2016), pp. 554–560 and 574–575.

[84] Ashiagbor (2005), p. 38.

regulation as well as social and legal phenomena are either excluded or included in labour law.

Although the assumption of a traditional understanding of labour law was the starting point, it should be noted that interesting openings have also been made in labour law. Specifically, "access justice", developed by Bruun, is a concept that describes labour law regulation which promotes the transition to the labour market, re-employment and retaining jobs with the current employer. The relationship between labour law and lifelong learning measures has become increasingly significant in all these transitions.

The chapter outlined three key dimensions of labour law in the context of lifelong learning. The analysis was based mainly on Finnish labour law, which served as an example. It was interesting to note that labour law contains quite a lot of different types of lifelong learning measures: Transition to work and apprenticeships or different type of traineeships, development of employee competences as a part of regular co-operation procedure as well as transition security in the context of collective redundancies to promote smooth re-employment.

The role of collective agreements in regulating lifelong learning appears to be limited, albeit evolving. However, it is worth noting that there are country-specific differences. However, lifelong learning measures are quite traditional terms of employment, which could be bargained in collective agreements, and this has also been identified. In addition, cross-sectoral agreements concerning lifelong learning measures in the labour market have been concluded between labour market confederations in Sweden and Denmark.

Lifelong learning measures are often related to activating labour market measures. This is understandable when upskilling and reskilling aims to promote a person's employability in the transitional labour market. Therefore, in the context of labour market law, lifelong learning appears to be a natural part of labour law.

Finally, it is justified to state that lifelong learning measures can be systematised as a part of modern labour law and its systematics. Even today, labour law covers many lifelong learning measures, even though they are not called by that name. Lifelong learning measures have evolved within the sphere of labour law while maintaining their own terminology. Lifelong learning could be challenged from the perspective of the traditional understanding of labour law, but at the same time, it must be stated that lifelong learning is such an important legal and societal phenomenon that there is a need for further labour law research.

## References

Ahtela J (2024) Sopiminen, osallistuminen ja luottamus: Mitä voimme oppia Ruotsin ja Saksan työmarkkinajärjestelmistä? Akava Works raportti 1/2024 https://akavaworks.fi/wp-content/uploads/sites/2/2024/01/Akava-Works-1-2024-Sopiminen-osallistuminen-ja-luottamus.pdf

Ashiagbor D (2005) The European employment strategy: labour market regulation and new governance. Oxford Monographs on Labour Law, Oxford

Barnard C (2021) EU ‘Social’ policy from employment law to labour market reform. In: Craig P, de Búrca G (eds) The evolution of EU law. OUP, Oxford

Blichner L, Molander A (2005) What is juridification? Working Paper No. 14, Arena, Centre for European Studies, University of Oslo https://www.sv.uio.no/arena/english/research/publications/arena-working-papers/2001-2010/2005/wp05_14.pdf

Bogg A, Costello C, Davies ACL, Prassl J (2015) Introduction, exploring the autonomy. In: Bogg A et. al (eds) The autonomy of labour law, 1st edn Hart Publishing, Oxford, pp 1–28

Bogg A, Costello C, Davies ACL (eds) (2016) Research handbook on EU labour law. Edward Elgar Publishing, Cheltenham. https://doi.org/10.4337/9781783471126

Brożek B (2019) The legal mind: a new introduction to legal epistemology. CUP, Cambridge

Bruun N (2017) The old and new foundations of labour law. In: Ahlberg K, Bruun N (eds) The new foundations of labour law. Peter Lang, Frankfurt am Main, pp 17–35

Bruun N (2022) Työoikeuden perusteet. Alma Talent, Helsinki

Bruun N (2023) Nordic labour law research – past, present and future. Nordic J Lab Law. https://www.karnovgroup.no/publikasjoner/tidsskrifter/nordic-journal-of-labour-law

Collective agreement for senior salaried employees in technology industries between Technology Industry Employers of Finland and Federation of Professional and Managerial Staff (YTN)

Collins H (2015) Contractual autonomy. In: Bogg A et al (eds) The autonomy of labour law, 1st edn. Hart Publishing, Oxford, pp 45–72

Commerce sector collective agreement, amendments (2025). https://www.pam.fi/wp-content/uploads/2025/03/LIITE-1-Sovitut-tekstimuutokset-Kaupan-tyoehtosopimukseen.pdf

Council of Europe (1996) European Social Charter (Revised). European Treaty Series No. 163, Strasbourg

Council of the European Union (2022) Council Decision on guidelines for the employment policies of the Member States and The Council Recommendation on a European approach to micro-credentials for lifelong learning and employability. 2022/C 242/03

Council of the European Union (2025) Draft Council Conclusions on the 2025 Joint Employment Report. 6460/25 https://data.consilium.europa.eu/doc/document/ST-6460-2025-INIT/en/pdf

Doorey DJ (2017) Just transitions law: putting labour law to work on climate change. J Environ Law Pract 30(2):201–239. https://ssrn.com/abstract=2938590

Eklund M (2021) Integritet och övervakning i arbetslivet: Juridiska perspektiv på arbetsgivarens rätt att övervaka arbetstagare. Helsingfors universitet, juridiska fakulteten, Helsinki

Eurofound (2015) Collective bargaining in Europe in the 21st century. Publications Office of the European Union, Luxembourg. https://www.eurofound.europa.eu/en/publications/2015/collective-bargaining-europe-21st-century

Finkin MW (2019) Comparative labour law. In: Reimann M, Zimmermann R (eds) The Oxford handbook of comparative law, 2nd edn. Oxford Handbooks, pp 1110–1136

Fredman S (2015) Equality law: labour law or an autonomous field? In: Bogg A et al (eds) The autonomy of labour law, 1st edn. Hart Publishing, Oxford, pp 257–276

Global Legal Insights (2024) Employment & Labour Laws and Regulations 2024. https://www.globallegalinsights.com/practice-areas/employment-and-labour-laws-and-regulations/

Hendrickx F (2012) Foundations and Functions of Contemporary Labour Law. Eur. Lab Law J. 3(2):108–129. https://doi.org/10.1177/201395251200300202

Huvudavtal om trygghet, omställning och anställningsskydd concluded by Svenskt Näringsliv and LO. https://www.livsmedelsforetagen.se/app/uploads/2023/03/huvudavtal-lo94.pdf

ICLG (2025) Employment & Labour Law in 30 jurisdictions https://iclg.com/practice-areas/employment-and-labour-laws-and-regulations

ILO Library, General Surveys: Reports by Theme https://libguides.ilo.org/general_surveys/theme

International Labour Office (2019) Getting and staying together: 100 years of social dialogue and tripartism in Norway. ILO, Geneva. https://www.ilo.org/sites/default/files/wcmsp5/groups/public/@ed_dialogue/@dialogue/documents/publication/wcms_709868.pdf

Kairinen M (2009) Työoikeus perusteineen. Työelämän tietopalvelu OY, Raisio

Langille B (2006) Labour law's back pages. In: Davidov G, Langille B (eds) Boundaries and frontiers of labour law: goals and means in the regulation of work, 1st edn. Bloomsbury Publishing, London, pp 13–36. https://doi.org/10.5040/9781472563804
Larja L, Räisänen H (2020) Omaehtoinen opiskelu työttömyysetuudella. TEM-analyyseja 99/2020, Työ- ja elinkeinoministeriö
Murto J (2015) Ryhmänormit yrityksessä: tutkimus työntekijäryhmiä koskevien normien asemasta. Suomalainen Lakimiesyhdistys
Murto J (2018) Työnhakijan ja työntekijän osaamisen kehittäminen työvoimapolitiikan osana. Helsingin yliopiston oikeustieteellinen tiedekunta, Helsinki
Prassl J (2015) The concept of the employer. OUP, Oxford
Rosin A (2017) Labour law protection of trainees. Turun yliopisto
Schmid G (1998) Transitional labour markets: a new European employment strategy. WZB Discussion Paper, No. SP I 1998-206, WZB Social Science Center, Berlin. https://nbn-resolving.org/urn:nbn:de:0168-ssoar-128858
Schmid G (2015) Sharing risks of labour market transitions. Br J Ind Relat 53(1):70–93. https://doi.org/10.1111/bjir.12041
Selberg N (2017) Arbetsgivarbegreppet och arbetsrättsligt ansvar i komplexa arbetsorganisationer, Lunds universitet, Juridiska fakulteten
Servais J-M (2022) International labour law. Wolters Kluwer Law International, Alphen aan den Rijn
Sigeman T, Sjödin E (2022) Arbetsrätten: en översikt. Norstedts Juridik
The European Pillar of Social Rights. https://employment-social-affairs.ec.europa.eu/european-pillar-social-rights-20-principles_en
Tiitinen K-P (2005) Työoikeuden pääasiat. Helsingin yliopisto, Helsinki
Trepartsaftale om langsigtede investeringer i voksen-, efter- og videreuddannelse (2023). https://www.uvm.dk/-/media/filer/uvm/aktuelt/pdf23/sep/230912-trepartsaftale-om-langsigtede-investeringer-i-voksen%2D%2D-efter%2D%2Dog-videreuddannelse.pdf
Tuori K (2007) Oikeuden ratio ja voluntas. WSOYpro, Helsinki
Zekic N (2016) Job security or employment security: what's in a name? Eur Lab Law J. 7(4):548–575

**Jari Murto** is associate professor of Labour and Social Law at the University of Helsinki, Finland. His main research interests are doctrines of labour law, determination of the terms of employment, regulation of labour market transitions, lifelong learning, industrial relations and labour market policy at the national and EU levels. Murto is a founder and co-leader of the international research group "Labour law and lifelong learning". Murto has extensive experience as a labour law expert on several multidisciplinary research projects combining legal and empirical research. Murto has acted as a national expert in several international networks.

# Lifelong Learning as Employment Policy

# Exploring the Future of Lifelong Learning Through the Tapestry of European Policy History

**Flore Claus**

## 1 Lifelong Learning at EU level: A Tale in Four Chapters

Lifelong learning as an EU policy matter is more relevant than ever. However, the 'right' to lifelong learning—as stated in the first principle of the European Pillar of Social Rights—is not arbitrary.[1] This 'right' stems from a long and complex policy history, with roots in the establishment of the European Economic Community in 1957 and subsequent developments leading to the European Union as we know it today. Any discussion of the EU and labour law today would be incomplete without an examination of its policymaking history, characterised by numerous milestones and policy decisions. This chapter seeks to address the central question: "1) How has the EU lifelong learning policy developed since 1957, 2) how has the EU's role in shaping this policy transformed, and 3) what might this indicate about the future?". Two elements are critical to understanding this question: context and timing.

In terms of *context*, lifelong learning has been embraced as a policy theme not only within the European Union but also by key international organisations such as UNESCO, the International Labour Organization (ILO), and the Organisation for Economic Co-operation and Development (OECD). These organisations contribute

[1]The right to lifelong learning, as established in the European Pillar of Social Rights, is further examined in this volume Kain F, Legal Foundations of Lifelong Learning and labour law in Europe, Sect. 2.2.

F. Claus (✉)
Research Foundation Flanders (FWO) – Faculty of Law and Criminology - Department of Criminology, Criminal Law and Social Law, Ghent University, Ghent, Belgium
e-mail: flore.claus@ugent.be



J. Murto, V. Franca (eds.), *Labour Law and Lifelong Learning*,
https://doi.org/10.1007/978-3-032-11035-0_3

to global approaches to lifelong learning. Analysing the evolution of EU policies on lifelong learning, particularly in relation to the employment relationship, requires an understanding of the European Union's distinct characteristics compared to other international organisations. Broadly, lifelong learning can be viewed through two perspectives: the humanistic approach, which emphasises self-development, and the human-capital approach, which focuses on addressing labour market challenges.[2] Limiting the analysis to the EU's historical trajectory without considering simultaneous international developments would risk presenting an incomplete account. To address this, the first part of this chapter explores global and supranational perspectives on lifelong learning.

Following this global perspective, the European Union can be examined in detail. Since context and timing are both crucial to the history of EU lifelong learning policy, it is framed as 'a tale in four chapters'. In the early days of the European Union, then known as the European Economic Community, only sporadic initiatives promoted lifelong learning. Thus, the first chapter encompasses forty years of policy history: 'Primary notions of lifelong learning in European policy history'. Around 2000, however, a momentum emerged, marked by significant EU-level milestones which forms the second chapter: 'Focusing on open method of coordination with found legitimacy'. Nevertheless, progress was not straightforward. A period of economic and financial recession eventually led to various new initiatives and a third chapter: 'From a period of crisis to new policy opportunities'. This ultimately resulted in the inclusion of a right to lifelong learning in a key EU instrument, the European Pillar of Social Rights, which forms the last chapter of this tale: '*The European Pillar of Social Rights as start of a new era*'.

The common thread in policy history is the various European strategies from which new initiatives and concrete actions have emerged. This chapter charts the evolution of policy and therefore emphasises soft law provisions related to lifelong learning rather than its legal definition. It provides a deeper understanding of the path the EU has already taken and how past policy choices influence current and future decisions. To grasp how lifelong learning will evolve, it is essential to understand the past while also considering developments beyond the EU's borders. The analysis first examines global and supranational perspectives.

## 2 Shaping Lifelong Learning Policies: Global and Supranational Perspectives

Although the research interest in lifelong learning from a labour law perspective arose only recently, it is not a new phenomenon. Lifelong learning has a deep-rooted historical and cultural tradition. The integration of lifelong education into

[2] Elfert and Rubenson (2023), p. 1219.

policy frameworks began in the 1960s.[3] Since the European Union's role became significant in the 1990s, the preceding three decades other international organisations were relevant for the development of lifelong learning as a policy theme. As mentioned in the introduction, both context and timing are crucial in shaping a policy framework for lifelong learning. This is the case not only for the EU but also for other organisations such as UNESCO and the OECD. However, each starts from its own perspective and follows a unique trajectory. This can be described as 'institutional entrenchment': due to the specific characteristics, it is challenging to deviate from the path shaped by earlier decisions.[4]

An example of this is the contrast between the humanistic perspective, which views lifelong learning as a means of self-development, and the human-capital perspective, which frames lifelong learning as a transformative factor for a sustainable labour market. The evolution of these differing approaches is also influenced by timing.[5] Twice, a major historical moment led to the creation of lifelong learning policy proposals: the Second World War for the first generation of lifelong learning proposals, as discussed in the late 1960s context, and the fall of the Berlin Wall for the wave of new proposals in the 1990s.[6]

## 2.1 *First Lifelong Learning Policies in the Late 1960s*

The idea of lifelong learning (then known as 'lifelong education') first appeared in United Nations policy documents in 1965.[7] Two key UNESCO reports, the Faure report (1972) and the Delors report (1996), are central to the development of the concept. The Faure report, developed after the Second World War, was produced by the International Commission on the Development of Education, chaired by Edgar Faure. It framed 'lifelong education' as essential for human self-development, emphasising the continuous need for learning to survive and evolve.[8] While an important milestone, the report is more abstract and philosophical in nature.[9]

In addition to the United Nations, the OECD also took the initiative to reflect on how they envisioned lifelong education.[10] Unlike UNESCO, the OECD laid the foundations for the human-capitalist perspective, linked with the labour market,

---

[3] Lee (2022), p. 694.

[4] Pierson (2000), p. 252.

[5] Rubenson describes these as different 'generations' of lifelong learning. The second generation, emerging in the 1980s, marked a shift towards neoliberalism, with less emphasis on the state and more on private actors, making it less significant than the first and third generations; see Elfert and Rubenson (2023), pp. 1219–1221.

[6] Ibid.

[7] UNESCO (1966), para 34. It was referred to as 'continuing education'.

[8] Faure et al. (1972), p. 158.

[9] Elfert (2015), p. 89.

[10] Field (2001), p. 6.

which later influenced EU policies.[11] The OECD did not adopt UNESCO's utopian approach, but aligned more with what Field described as "human capital thinking, albeit laced with a few dashes of social democracy".[12] The OECD views 'recurrent education' as a means of maintaining agility within a career. It serves to preserve the flexibility of the workforce and provides alternative opportunities in the event of unemployment.[13] It also focused on practical implementation, emphasising support for the labour market, such as paid educational leave which allows workers time off for further training.[14] The OECD's approach also aligns with actions taken by the International Labour Organization (ILO), which established two significant conventions at ILO level connecting education and the labour market: ILO Convention No. 140 on Paid Educational Leave in 1972 and ILO Convention No. 142 on Human Resources Development in 1974.[15]

The first generation of lifelong learning policies lacked traction, focusing mainly on government responsibility with little involvement from private actors.[16] Additionally, there were no favourable conditions to develop a global lifelong learning culture. The economic crisis and political tensions sidelined lifelong learning.[17] The fall of the Berlin Wall marked the end of the Cold War, two decades later, catalysed a new stage in the lifelong learning policies.[18]

## 2.2 *Lifelong Learning Policies in the 1990s*

The 1990s were shaped by globalisation and technological change.[19] Several organisations, including UNESCO, the OECD and the EU, refocused on lifelong learning as a policy theme.[20] Each international organisation responded differently to these developments. UNESCO led the way with the Delors report in 1996; making a return to a humanistic approach despite societal challenges and prevailing neoliberalism.[21] This demonstrates 'institutional entrenchment': once the humanistic approach was chosen, other perspectives, such as the human-capitalist view, seemed

---

[11] See in this volume, Kain F, Legal Foundations of Lifelong Learning and labour law in Europe and Franca V and De Becker A, Social Dialogue and Lifelong learning: the difficult interplay at EU-level and national level.

[12] Field (2001), p. 6.

[13] Kallen and Bengtsson (1973), pp. 42–43.

[14] See Elfert and Rubenson (2023), pp. 1221–1222 and Field (2001), p. 7.

[15] International Labour Organization (1974), Convention concerning Paid Educational Leave (No. 140).

[16] Elfert and Rubenson (2023), p. 1226.

[17] Field (2001), pp. 7–8.

[18] Ibid.

[19] Borg and Mayo (2005), pp. 208–209.

[20] Hake (1999), p. 54 and Elfert (2015), pp. 90–91.

[21] Delors (1996), pp. 20–22 and p. 37; see also Elfert (2015), p. 91.

less relevant.[22] The key shift, despite different viewpoints on lifelong learning, was the terminology. Initially, terms such as 'lifelong education' and 'recurrent education' were commonly used. Terms like 'lifelong education' and 'recurrent education' became outdated with the introduction of 'lifelong learning' in the 1990s, particularly in the Delors Report. This change reflects a broader view on education, recognising learning as a lifelong continuum, not confined to specific times or places.[23]

The reasoning of 'institutional entrenchment' can also be applied to other organisations, such as the ILO and OECD. Unlike UNESCO's Delors report, the OECD's vision of lifelong learning was shaped by neoliberal tendencies.[24] The divergence in perspectives, evident in the first generation of lifelong learning policies in the late 1960s, became more pronounced in the 1990s. According to the OECD, lifelong learning enhances economic growth by developing a more efficient workforce capable of boosting productivity.[25] The 'human capital' concept emerged to capture the value of workers' skills, instrumental in driving labour productivity.[26] This perspective was shared by the ILO which in its Recommendation No. 195 on Human Resources Development (2004) connects lifelong learning and employability. Employability, which will also resurface in European discourse, refers to transferable skills and qualifications that help individuals access, maintain and progress in decent work while adapting to evolving labour markets and technology.[27]

This introduction focuses on the context and timing of key developments in lifelong learning policies. It can be argued that each institution follows their own path: once a path is taken, whether shaped by a human-capital approach or a humanistic vision, it tends to persist. This narrative now shifts its focus to a key player: the European Union. The EU, like the ILO and OECD, follows a similar path but with own distinct features. A unique aspect of the EU is its regional character, enabling closer alignment with its member states and the utilisation of various legal instruments (whether directly enforceable or not).[28] The EU's evolving approach to lifelong learning, shaped by the Maastricht Treaty in 1993, is explored in the following section on European policy history.

---

[22] Pierson (2000), p. 252.

[23] One reason for the conceptual shift is the individualisation of the concept; see Biesta (2006), pp. 175–176 and Delors (1996), p. 100.

[24] OECD (1989) and OECD (1996).

[25] OECD (2006), p. 156.

[26] OECD (2006), p. 154.

[27] Art. 2 a), d) ILO Human Resources Development Recommendation No. 195 (2004).

[28] This distinctive nature of the EU is further discussed in Clapman and Bourke Martignoni (2006), pp. 236–239.

# 3 Primary Notions of Lifelong Learning in the European Union Policy History

The first part of our narrative spans a broad period of time, reflecting the complexities surrounding the European Union's competence (then: the European Economic Community) to adopt lifelong learning policies. A significant turning point was the Maastricht Treaty in 1993, marking the beginning of the European Union's efforts to shape the concept of lifelong learning.

## *3.1 The Issue of Competence*

In the early years of the European Economic Community, there was a lack of attention to lifelong learning. The focus was on establishing an internal market, a common market, among the various member states.[29] Additionally, the European Economic Community did not have jurisdiction, although Article 128 of the Treaty of Rome in 1957 did provide for the possibility of adopting initiatives regarding training: "The Council shall, on a proposal of the Commission and after the Economic and Social Committee has been consulted, establish general principles for the implementation of a common policy of occupational training capable of contributing to the harmonious development both of national economies and of the Common Market".[30]

Education, including training and lifelong learning,[31] was perceived by member states as a national competence. In the early 1990s, the rising influence of globalisation and economic trends sparked policy interest in lifelong learning.[32] The Maastricht Treaty established a legal basis for EU initiatives, specifically article 126 and 127.[33] Article 126 outlines the EU's role in supporting and cooperation on education, while article 127 focused on vocational training. Both articles uphold the principle of subsidiarity.[34]

Even though the Maastricht Treaty was a significant first step, however, uncertainties remained regarding the EU's role. The Maastricht Treaty distinguishes

---

[29] Field (1998), p. 26.

[30] EEC Treaty or Treaty of Rome: Treaty Establishing the European Economic Community, 25 March 1957, 298 U.N.T.S. 3, 4 Eur. Y.B. 412.

[31] A strict distinction between 'education,' 'training,' and '(lifelong) learning' is difficult at this early stage, as these terms evolved over time and were complicated by linguistic differences between the French 'éducation' and the English 'learning'; see Elfert (2015), p. 187.

[32] This timing also UNESCO and the OECD to renew their focus on lifelong learning as a policy theme; see Hake (1999), p. 54 and Elfert (2015), 90–91.

[33] Art. 126-127 Treaty on the European Union (TEU) C 191/1, Pb.L. 29 July 1992, 112. 235 of the treaty Establishing the European Economic Community.

[34] Art. 5(3) TEU.

education from vocational training, but the distinction is not yet fully defined.[35] The question also arises regarding how the European Union will exercise this competence after the Maastricht Treaty. The issue remains where the competence under Articles 126 and 127 of the Treaty on European Union ends and where member states draw the line based on their exclusive competence over education.[36] Two EU policy documents try to clear the air.

### 3.2 Shaping the Concept of Lifelong Learning

The EU, while aligning more with the OECD's human-capitalist approach than UNESCO's humanistic vision, has introduced unique elements in defining lifelong learning.[37] These white papers represent the early stages of lifelong learning in the EU. After the Treaty of Maastricht, the White Paper *Growth, Competitiveness, Employment* in 1994 outlined several European objectives, though lacking legal value, it revealed the EU's policy vision.[38] It stresses the need for a right to ongoing training, advocating for cooperation between the public and private sectors and its importance in social dialogue.[39] Learning is seen as a mean to address youth unemployment and the challenges of a changing society, where globalisation intensifies competition.[40] Lifelong learning serves as a tool to tackle labour market challenges, described in the paper as "training, the catalyst of a changing society".[41]

In 1995, the White Paper *Teaching and Learning: Towards the Learning Society* further clarified the EU's position on lifelong learning, announcing the European Year of Lifelong Learning in 1996.[42] It introduces the concept of 'the learning society' as essential for moving beyond traditional career paths in light of the 1990's developments.[43] Education and training are viewed as critical for fostering self-awareness, belonging, growth and personal fulfilment. Learning is not confined to formal settings but extends to workplace environments and informal contexts. These diverse forms of learning strengthen individuals to shape their future and foster personal growth.[44]

---

[35] Lenaerts (1994), pp. 24–31.

[36] For article 126, the Treaty refers to the procedure of co-decision (article 189b TEU); for article 127, the Treaty refers to the procedure of cooperation (article 189c TEU). See Hake (1999), p. 58.

[37] See Sect. 2.2 Shaping lifelong learning: global and supranational perspectives.

[38] Lee (2008), p. 453.

[39] European Commission (1994), p. 17.

[40] Nordin (2011), p. 11.

[41] European Commission (1994), pp. 133–137.

[42] European Commission (1995), p. 66; European Parliament and of the Council, Decision No 2493/95/EC establishing 1996 as the 'European year of lifelong learning', 23 October 1995, Pub.L. 256/45; Lee (2008), p. 453.

[43] European Commission (1995), p. 2.

[44] Ibid.

This attempt to provide direction to European policy faced criticism for being too conservative and lacking innovation, focusing heavily on existing educational structures and linking learning primarily to the labour market. Additionally, member states reiterated their sovereignty and the principle of subsidiarity.[45]

In light of this human-capitalist perspective on lifelong learning and the responses to the two White Papers, the European Commission reassessed its role. Instead of taking a leading position, it adopted a supportive and inspiring role aligning with the principle of subsidiarity.[46] The Council of the EU echoed this perspective following the European Year of Lifelong Learning in 1996.[47] Despite the shift in approach of the EU, lifelong learning remains a significant policy theme, affirmed by the acceptance of lifelong learning as a policy priority in the Treaty of Amsterdam in 1997.[48] The remaining concerns about the EU competence were addressed with the Lisbon Strategy, a milestone marking the beginning of a new chapter.

## 4 Focusing on Open Method of Coordination with Found Legitimacy

The turn of the millennium marked a shift in EU lifelong learning policy. Context and timing remained crucial in shaping its direction. Following the 1990s, a period characterised by exploration and uncertainty, a change in the European Commission takes place. After the Santer Commission's early resignation, Romano Prodi's Commission introduced key policy documents, including the Lisbon Strategy and the EU Memorandum on Lifelong Learning.[49] However, its ambitious goals soon faced challenges.

### *4.1 The Lisbon Strategy: Paving the Way for Lifelong Learning Policy*

The onset of the new century immediately marked a pivotal moment in shaping the EU's lifelong learning policy. Three significant milestones from the year 2000 are worth nothing: (1) the *Lisbon Strategy*, (2) the *Memorandum on Lifelong Learning*,

---

[45] Field (1998), pp. 76–78; see also Hake (1999), pp. 15–17.

[46] Lee (2008), p. 452.

[47] Council of the European Union, Council Conclusion of 20 December 1996 on a strategy for lifelong learning, *Pb.L.* 97/C 7/02.

[48] Art. 126 and 127 of the Treaty of Maastricht were replaced by article 149 and 15 of the Treaty of Amsterdam. For the policy implications, see also art.109N *j*° art. 118C Treaty of Amsterdam Amending the Treaty on European Union, The Treaties Establishing the European Communities and Related Acts, 10 November 1997,*Pb.L.* 97/C 340/01.

[49] For the context on the change of Commissions, see Holford and Milana (2023), pp. 509–510.

and (3) *the Charter of Fundamental Rights of the European Union*. Article 14(1) of the Charter states: "Everyone has the right to education and to have access to vocational and continuing training".[50] The latter provision is undoubtedly crucial for situating the 'right to lifelong learning' within the EU's framework, though not a primary focus of this analysis. This contribution prioritises the in-depth analysis of the Lisbon Strategy and the EU Memorandum on Lifelong Learning, policy initiatives stemming from Article 14 of the Charter, rather than examining the legal significance of Article 14 itself.[51]

In March 2000, the Lisbon European Council held an extraordinary meeting where the—then 15[52]—member states gathered to strategise with the aim of enhancing economic conditions, social cohesion and employment. The Lisbon Strategy specifically focuses on the importance of lifelong learning and cooperation at EU level: "a European framework should define the new basic skills to be provided through lifelong learning".[53] The Council and Commission further highlighted lifelong learning as one of four key policy areas, stressing the role of social dialogue in fostering innovation.[54]

A crucial development was the introduction of the *open method of coordination* (OMC).[55] This approach encouraged policy alignment while respecting the member states' exclusive competence. With an open method of coordination, the emphasis is placed on disseminating best practices at the EU level to pursue greater convergence in policy among the various member states and thus achieve EU objectives.[56] Through mutual learning, the incorporation of best practices into EU policy was enabled. This helped alleviate concerns about the legitimacy of EU lifelong learning policies, establishing a democratic approach to functioning at a supranational level in cooperation with diverse member states.[57]

Shortly after, the Feira Council reinforced the lifelong learning's broader societal role, emphasising that its value extends beyond just an economic perspective, highlighting its role in fostering employment, social cohesion and citizenship.[58] The Feira Council highlights the shared responsibility of the Council, the Commission, and Member States to implement lifelong learning policies within their respective

---

[50] However, this Charter got only legally binding since the Treaty of Lisbon in 2009. Charter of Fundamental Rights of the European Union C 364/1, Pb.L. 18 December 2000.

[51] Therefore, see in this volume Kain F, Legal foundations of lifelong learning and labour law in Europe.

[52] Those countries were Germany, France, Italy, Netherlands, Belgium, Luxembourg (starting point in 1958); Denmark, Ireland and the UK (entered in 1973); Greece (entered in 1981); Spain and Portugal (entered in 1986); Austria, Finland and Sweden (entered in 1995).

[53] European Council (2000a), paras 25–28.

[54] Ibid., para 29.

[55] Ibid., paras 37–40.

[56] Ibid., para 37.

[57] Lee (2008), p. 456.

[58] European Council (2000b).

areas of competence and to collaborate with social partners.[59] Building on these developments, the *EU Memorandum on Lifelong Learning* marked a major step forward in advancing lifelong learning within the EU.

## 4.2 Defining Lifelong Learning: More than a Labour Market Remedy

The *EU Memorandum on Lifelong Learning* starts with a retrospective view, reflecting on key lessons from the 1996 European Year of Lifelong Learning and includes a broad consultation round with all the member states.[60] The Memorandum is an attempt to correct the EU policy direction as it identifies both employability and citizenship as two "equally important aims".[61] The pursuit of balance continued in the effort to define the concept of lifelong learning. The initial definition of lifelong learning in the Memorandum as "all purposeful learning activity undertaken on an ongoing basis with the aim of improving knowledge, skills, and competences" was refined after criticism for its narrow focus on employability[62] and neglecting implications of cultural or intellectual development. A broader perspective was later adopted in the Commission's follow-up communication, *Making a European Area of Lifelong Learning a Reality*, defining lifelong as "all learning activity undertaken throughout life, with the aim of improving knowledge, skills, and competences within a personal, civil, social, and/or employment-related perspective".[63]

In the years following, the policy progress was limited. The *Education and Training 2010 framework* highlighted the urgency of reforms for the Lisbon Strategy's success. The Council and Commission warned of persistent challenges, such as the low number of women in scientific and technological professions, the lack of adult participation in lifelong learning and nearly a fifth of young people failing to acquire competences.[64] These concerns resurfaced in the Lisbon Strategy's mid-term review.

---

[59] Ibid., para. 33.

[60] European Commission (2000).

[61] European Commission (2000), p. 5.

[62] In the conclusions of the Commission after the consultation round in 'Making a European Area of Lifelong Learning a Reality, employability is defined as "the capacity for people to be employed: it relates not only to the adequacy of their knowledge and competences but also to the incentives and opportunities offered to individuals to seek employment". European Commission (2001), p. 32.

[63] European Commission (2001), p. 32.

[64] Council (2004), p. 7.

### 4.3 A Failed Lisbon Strategy?

A couple of years after the milestone year of 2000, the Lisbon Strategy underwent evaluation. A 2004 mid-term review, led by Wim Kok at the request of the Commission, highlighted critical shortcomings.[65] Kok identified several reasons hindering the Strategy's implementation: lack of political action, an overly ambitious agenda and poor coordination among member states.[66] The Strategy's economic focus was also questioned, especially as Europe's productivity growth lagged behind other regions such as Asia and North America and demographic challenges mounted due to an aging population and declining birth rates.[67]

The open method of coordination proved inadequate in achieving the Strategy's goals.[68] To address this crisis, the Lisbon Strategy was relaunched in 2005 with a new policy, *Working together for growth and jobs: A new start for the Lisbon Strategy*, where new objectives were adopted within the European Commission to revitalise the Lisbon Strategy.[69] This included introducing a new lifelong learning programme and empowering member states to adopt their own lifelong learning strategies.[70]

An important initiative from the relaunch was the 2006 Key Competences for Lifelong Learning report, which outlined eight key competences to clarify lifelong learning. These competences compassed not only economic skills but also skills related to social inclusion and personal fulfilment.[71] Finally, the *European Parliament Resolution on adult learning: It is never too late to learn* reiterated the importance of lifelong learning and urged member states to promote a learning culture, particularly for vulnerable groups such as those with low educational qualifications or migrant backgrounds.[72] At the end of the decade, timing created a new turning point: the EU economic and financial crisis.[73]

[65] Nordin (2011), p. 13.

[66] Kok (2004), pp. 6–7.

[67] Holford (2023), p. 6.

[68] Nordin (2011), p. 13.

[69] European Commission (2005).

[70] Ibid., p. 27.

[71] For more information about the key competences see European Parliament and Council (2006), pp. 13–18.

[72] European Commission (2006), paras 2–3 and 21–25. See also Holford and Milana (2023), p. 514.

[73] Holford described it as "Lisbon laced with Kok" in Holford (2023), p. 7.

# 5 From a Period of Crisis to New Policy Opportunities

In the late 2000s, the EU faced crises, including economic instability and youth unemployment.[74] During this period of instability, new policy initiatives were launched. The 2009 Treaty of Lisbon introduced no significant legal changes, with education remaining a member-state competence, and the EU continuing to apply subsidiarity through the open method of coordination, as stated in Articles 165 and 166.[75] However, Article 9 of the Treaty on the Functioning of the EU strengthened the EU's mandate to promote lifelong learning: "In defining and implementing its policies and activities, the Union shall take into account requirements linked to the promotion of a high level of employment, the guarantee of adequate social protection, the fight against social exclusion, and a high level of education, training and protection of human health".[76]

While this contribution cannot be exhaustive, it highlights several significant policy initiatives implemented during this period to promote lifelong learning in Sec. 5.1. *A wave of new policy initiatives*. Those policy initiatives are utilised to their fullest extent, with a focus on monitoring objectives. This is further discussed in Sect. 5.2. *The European Semester as a control mechanism.*

## *5.1 A Wave of New Policy Initiatives*

Besides the economic and financial challenges in the late 2000s, the EU also faced concerns about demographic trends: an aging population, declining birth rates and a shrinking workforce. These trends led to a 'skills gap', where existing skills were insufficient for current needs.[77] Amidst this, and with the EU Commission now led by a more centre-right ideology, lifelong learning was framed as a human capital issue.[78] Focus shifted to creating learning opportunities aligned with the labour market needs, with lifelong learning treated as labour-market policy.

In response, the *European cooperation in education and training* (ET 2020) replaced the Lisbon Strategy.[79] Four objectives are outlined for the period 2010–2020, including encouraging lifelong learning in the member states. The first objective is "*Making lifelong learning and mobility a reality*", emphasising the need for a qualification structure and flexible learning pathways. To achieve this objective, bench-

[74] Holford and Milana (2023), pp. 514–515.

[75] Art. 6 TFEU; Art. 165–166 Treaty of Lisbon.

[76] Art. 9 TFEU.

[77] Volles (2014), p. 17.

[78] After Prodi (until 2004), two Commissions led by Barroso, one under Juncker, and the current Commissioner von der Leyen, also from the European People's Party, as noted by Holford and Milana (2023), p. 516.

[79] Council (2009), p. 2.

marks are provided such as the goal that at least 15% should take part in lifelong learning by 2020.[80] This goal is aligned with EU initiatives like the Europe 2020 Strategy and the European Semester.

Another significant initiative was the *European Qualifications Framework* (EQF) which stands out as one of the key policy initiatives at the EU level. The EQF does not feature an overarching recognition structure but provides a 'common reference framework', facilitating the translation of competencies within a member-state and enabling comparison with the reference framework of another member-state. It serves as a meta-framework, facilitating the mobility of students and workers across borders.[81] The EQF acknowledges all learning forms (informal, formal and non-formal)[82] and was reaffirmed by the Council Recommendation of 2012.[83] Later, in 2017, the European Qualifications Framework underwent a revision to improve qualification comparability.[84]

Focusing on vulnerable groups with low participation in lifelong learning, *the Council Recommendation on Upskilling Pathways*, targets adults with limited skills, knowledge and competences.[85] The recommendation highlights the issue that lifelong learning participation is four times lower among low-skilled individuals compared to those with tertiary qualifications. It presents lifelong learning not only from an economic perspective but also as a means of self-development, though the emphasis remains on linking it to the labour market, particularly job vacancies and skills.[86] A three-step approach is proposed, focusing on skills assessment, suitable learning offers and the validation of acquired skills.[87] To further enhance skills within the EU, the Commission launched the *Skills Agenda* in 2016, with actions to stimulate lifelong learning and improve young workers' employability. The approach is labour-market oriented, facilitating young workers' transition into the labour market following their studies.[88] Member states remain responsible for implementing these initiatives, but the European Semester provides a follow-up mechanism, reducing the voluntary nature of these soft law instruments.[89]

---

[80] This includes the population aged 25–64 that followed a training in the four weeks prior to the Labour Force Survey. Council (2009), p. 7.

[81] Méhaut and Winch (2012), p. 372.

[82] European Parliament and Council (2008).

[83] Council (2012).

[84] Council (2017).

[85] Council (2016).

[86] Council (2016), paras 1–2.

[87] Ibid., Art 3. Of course, this is "in accordance with national legislation, circumstances and available resources, and in close cooperation with social partners and education and training providers".

[88] European Commission (2016), p. 4.

[89] Ibid., p. 16.

### 5.2 *The European Semester as a Control Mechanism*

Although the principle of subsidiarity tends towards the adoption of *soft law* provisions, the EU lifelong learning policies are not an inefficacious endeavour. Since 2011, the European Semester has coordinated economic and financial policies, incorporating education and labour market evaluations which include lifelong learning, thus examining lifelong learning policies in various member states.[90] Based on the Europe 2020 Strategy, several benchmarks are evaluated, linking them with those formulated in the strategic plan Education and Training 2020. The European Semester functions as a form of *soft power*, issuing country-specific recommendations following policy reviews.[91]

Given the EU's diverse socio-economic landscape, each country emphasises its own priorities. Country-specific recommendations seek to balance overarching EU objectives with national contexts.[92] Moreover, the EU's influence extends beyond its borders through the open method of coordination. The European Qualifications Framework (EQF) exemplifies this by encouraging the development of national qualification frameworks (NQFs). Many member states and non-EU countries have adopted NQFs, demonstrating the broader impact of EU policy.[93]

In summary, these developments highlight how the economic crisis catalysed policy initiatives. By setting benchmarks in the *ET 2020* and the *Europe 2020 Strategy* and monitoring them through the European Semester, EU policies on lifelong learning do not remain a paper tiger.[94] The interest in lifelong learning as a labour market policy is further underscored by the following landmark: the right to lifelong learning as included in the European Pillar of Social Rights in 2017.

## 6 The European Pillar of Social Rights as Start of a New Era

As the final chapter in this tale of four, the European Pillar of Social Rights (EPSR) marks a significant milestone. In an attempt to put fundamental social rights higher on the EU agenda, the EPSR was promulgated in Gothenburg in 2017. The Pillar comprises 20 principles, with the first principle defining a right to lifelong learning: "Everyone has the right to high-quality and inclusive education, training and lifelong learning provision to acquire and maintain the skills needed to participate fully in society and successfully manage labour market transitions".[95] This 'right to lifelong learning' is not legally enforceable, but its implementation is pursued through

[90] Eeva (2024), pp. 193–194.

[91] Ibid., p. 186.

[92] Ibid., p. 192.

[93] Kleibrink (2011), p. 78.

[94] Holford and Milana (2023), p. 516.

[95] European Parliament, Council and Commission (2017).

alternative means.[96] This contribution does not delve into the (lack of) legal value but rather focuses on the context in which the European Union adopted the Pillar and the introduction of new EU monitoring instruments.[97]

### 6.1 *Juggling the Economic and Social Interpretation of Lifelong Learning*

After the economic crisis, lifelong learning was primarily seen as a labour market tool.[98] However, the context has changed. With Brexit, for the first time, a country has exited the EU after decades of expansion.[99] In this post-economic crisis and post-Brexit period, there is a renewed search for the social face of the EU. The European Pillar of Social Rights, however, largely reaffirms existing principles rather than creating new social rights.[100] Nevertheless, no recent EU policy document has been as explicit on lifelong learning: it is the first principle among the twenty in the Pillar. The first principle reflects ongoing tensions between economic, human-capitalist and social dimensions, affirming that "everyone has the right to lifelong learning" while linking it to the labour market.[101] Its legal value remains limited as it is largely a political instrument with no binding force.[102]

Despite its limited legal status, the Pillar's proclamation has had notable consequences.[103] The European Commission introduced the *European Pillar of Social Rights Action Plan*, translating its principles into concrete initiatives. One key objective is ensuring that "at least 60 % of all adults participate in training every year".[104] Achieving this objective depends on the member states, and it has already driven new national initiatives.[105] EU mechanisms have also been updated to monitor the progress towards this goal in the different member states.

[96] Rogowski (2019), pp. 283–304; Rambla and Kovacheva (2021), pp. 45–54.

[97] See in this volume Kain F, Legal foundations of lifelong learning and labour law in Europe Sect. 2.1.

[98] See 5.1. *A wave of new policies.*

[99] Garben (2019), p. 102.

[100] Ibid., p. 107.

[101] Art. 1 European Pillar of Social Rights.

[102] Ibid., p. 104.

[103] Holford and Milana (2023), p. 516.

[104] European Commission (2021), p. 11.

[105] See in this volume Kain F, Legal foundations of lifelong learning and labour law in Europe; Impellizieri G, Lifelong learning in national recovery and resilience plans and Urpilainen M, Promoting lifelong learning in the EU's employment policy – have financial incentives and economic coordination a role to play?.

## 6.2 *Monitoring After the European Pillar of Social Rights*

As part of the European Semester, a new monitoring instrument has been established: the European Social Scoreboard, which tracks member states' initiatives following the European Pillar of Social Rights. It features various indicators, including adult participation in learning over a four-week period and serves as an input in relation to the European Semester.[106] However, the Scoreboard has faced criticism for limited stakeholder involvement and a lack of context-specific indicators, reducing its effectiveness in tracking governmental action on the EPSR.[107] Additionally, there are the annual Employment Guidelines, shaping the development of a lifelong learning culture.[108] One of the 2024 guidelines, Guideline 6, highlights "enhancing labour supply and improving access to employment, lifelong acquisition of skills and competences" reinforcing the Commission's focus on lifelong learning.[109]

The European Semester generates country-specific recommendations, considering the Employment Guidelines and the Social Scoreboard indicators.[110] These country-specific recommendations of the Commission not only target the economic development of member states but also include an analysis of their actions concerning the implementation of lifelong learning policies. Some of these recommendations are more general such as "Step up policy efforts aimed at the provision and acquisition of skills and competences needed for the green transition".[111] Other are country-related, like Sweden's recommendation: "Develop the skills of disadvantaged groups, particularly people with migrant backgrounds, by adapting resources and methods to their needs, with a view to helping them integrate into the labour market".[112] This monitoring mechanism underscores the EU's influence on lifelong learning policy. However, its role remains supportive, in line with the principle of subsidiarity. With these final reflections on the EU's monitoring system, the uncovering of the EU lifelong learning policy as a tale of four chapters comes to a close.

---

106 Eurostat (2024) Social Scoreboard. https://ec.europa.eu/eurostat/cache/dashboard/social-scoreboard/. Accessed 15th October 2024.

107 Sabato and Corti (2018), pp. 57–58.

108 Art. 148 TFEU. European Commission (2018), p. 12.

109 European Commission (2024a), p. 1.

110 Eeva (2024), p. 192.

111 Such as Austria, France, Ireland... European Commission (2024b).

112 Ibid.

## 7 The Road Ahead for EU Lifelong Learning Policy: Final Reflections

This chapter discusses the development of lifelong learning within the EU framework, offering an overview and critically examining how context and timing have shaped the EU's path. *Contextual factors*, such as geopolitical, economic or institutional shifts, have catalysed EU policy changes. The change of EU Commissions around the turn of the millennium led to the Lisbon Strategy and the introduction of the Open Method of Coordination. Political and economic events, such as the 2008 financial crisis and the UK's departure from the EU, also drove new policy directions.

*Timing* has also been a crucial factor in European policymaking. Over time, interest in lifelong learning grew gradually, spurred by contextual factors. Reflecting on the past shows that significant steps were taken over three decades to shape EU lifelong learning policy. The relationship between the EU and its member states has evolved, as evidenced by developments in this area. Before the Maastricht Treaty, disagreements existed over the EU's role in lifelong learning policies. However, The Lisbon Strategy's open method of coordination introduced a framework respecting subsidiarity, with the European Commission monitoring policy implementation through indicators, benchmarks and country-specific recommendations. This 'soft governance' approach ensured that lifelong learning policies were translated into practice within member states.

In conclusion, while EU lifelong learning policy has evolved with changing circumstances, the human-capital perspective has remained central. Terms such as 'employability' and 'labour market' have consistently driven new initiatives. However, it would be simplistic to suggest that lifelong learning is solely viewed through an economic lens. The revised Memorandum on Lifelong Learning and the European Pillar of Social Rights highlight the search to find a difficult balance between both societal participation and labour market challenges. Nevertheless, the human-capital perspective continues to dominate, contrasting with other organisations like UNESCO, which prioritises a humanistic vision based on the right to self-fulfilment.

This enduring focus can be explained by the concept of *path dependence*. Although not universally defined, path dependence can be described as how earlier decisions shape future developments and limit the incentive to deviate from past choices.[113] While the literature on lifelong learning and path dependence is rather limited, it merits greater attention.[114] Path dependence not only explains why the EU remains committed to its past, current and future trajectory but also sheds light on the differences in interpretation among international organisations. These differences make a uniform definition of lifelong learning—whether as a right or a policy

---

[113] Pierson (2000), pp. 251–252; Husa (2018), p. 130.

[114] As quoted by Holford and Milana "path dependency made it inevitable, or at least overwhelmingly probable that the EU lifelong learning would adopt the discourse of competitiveness"; Holford and Milana (2023), p. 506.

theme—difficult to achieve. Once a path is taken, the costs of changing course often outweigh the convenience of continuing along the established route.[115] Therefore, it is valuable to understand the EU's policy history on lifelong learning, as it offers critical insights not only into past developments but also into future trajectories.

## References

Biesta G (2006) What's the point of lifelong learning if lifelong learning has no point? On the democratic deficit of policies for lifelong learning. Eur Educ Res J 5(3–4):169–180

Borg C, Mayo P (2005) The EU Memorandum on lifelong learning. Old wine in new bottles? Global Soc Educ 3(2):203–225

Clapman A, Bourke Martignoni J (2006) 'Are We There Yet?' In search of a coherent EU strategy on labour rights and external trade. In: Leary VA, Daniel W (eds) Social issues, globalisation and international institutions. Labour rights and the EU, ILO, OECD and WTO. Martinus Nijhoff Publishers, Leiden, pp 233–309

Council of the European Union (2004) Education & Training 2010. The success of the Lisbon Strategy hinges on urgent reforms; Joint interim report of the council and the commission on the implementation for the detailed work programme on the follow-up of the objectives of education and training systems in Europe. Official Journal C 104/1

Council of the European Union (2009) Council conclusions of 12 May 2009 on a strategic framework for European cooperation in education and training ('ET 2020'). Official Journal C-119/2

Council of the European Union (2012) Recommendation on the validation of non-formal and informal learning. Official Journal C-398/1

Council of the European Union (2016) Recommendation on Upskilling Pathways: New Opportunities for Adults. Official Journal C-484/01

Council of the European Union (2017) Recommendation on the European Qualifications Framework for lifelong learning and repealing the recommendation of the European Parliament and of the Council of 23 April 2008 on the establishment of the European Qualifications Framework for lifelong learning. Official Journal C-189/03

Delors J (1996) Learning: the treasure within. Report to UNECO of the International Commission on Education for the twenty-first century. UNESCO, Paris. https://unesdoc.unesco.org/ark:/48223/pf0000109590. Accessed 2 May 2024

Eeva K (2024) Governing through consensus? The European Semester, soft power and education governance in the EU. Eur Educ Res J 23(2):178–197. https://doi.org/10.1177/14749041211055601

Elfert M (2015) UNESCO, the Faure report, the Delors Report, and the political Utopia of lifelong learning. Eur J Educ 50(1):88–100

Elfert M, Rubenson K (2023) Lifelong learning: researching a contested concept in the twenty-first century. In: Evans K et al (eds) Third international handbook of lifelong learning. Springer International Handbooks of Education. Springer, Cham, pp 1220–1236

European Commission (1994) Growth, competitiveness, employment. The challenges and ways forward into the 21st century. White Paper, Office for Official Publications of the European Communities, Luxembourg

European Commission (1995) Teaching and Learning. Towards the Learning Society. White paper, Office for Official Publications of the European Communities, Luxembourg

European Commission (2000) Commission Staff Working Paper A Memorandum on Lifelong Learning. SEC(2000) 1832

---

[115] Pierson (2000), pp. 252–253.

European Commission (2001) Communication from the Commission. Making a European area of lifelong learning a reality. COM(2001) 678 final
European Commission (2005) Communication to the spring European Council. Working together for growth and jobs. A new start for the Lisbon Strategy. COM(2005) 24 final
European Commission (2006) Adult learning: It is never too late to learn. COM(2006) 614 final. https://eur-lex.europa.eu/legal-content/EN/TXT/?uri=celex%3A52006DC0614
European Commission (2016) Communication from the Commission to the European Parliament, the Council, the European Economic and Social Committee and the Committee of the Regions. A new Skills Agenda for Europe. Working together to strengthen human capital, employability and competitiveness. COM(2016) 381 final
European Commission (2018) The Implementation of the Circular Economy Package: Options To Address the Interface Between Chemical, Product and Waste Legislation. COM(2018) 32 final
European Commission (2021) The European Pillar of Social Rights Action Plan. COM(2021) 102 final
European Commission (2024a). Proposal for a Council Decision on Guidelines for the Employment Policies of the Member States. COM(2024) 599 final
European Commission (2024b). Country Specific recommendations database, https://ec.europa.eu/economy_finance/country-specific-recommendations-database/. Accessed 21 January 2025
European Council (2000a) Lisbon European Council 23 and 24 March 2000. Presidency Conclusions. https://www.europarl.europa.eu/summits/lis1_en.htm. Accessed 2 May 2024
European Council (2000b) Santa Maria da Feira European Council 19 and 20 June 2000. Presidency Conclusions. https://www.europarl.europa.eu/summits/fei1_en.htm. Accessed 2 May 2024
European Parliament and Council (2006) Recommendation on key competences for lifelong learning. Official Journal 926/EC
European Parliament and Council (2008) Recommendation on the establishment of the European Qualifications Framework for lifelong learning. Official Journal C-111/01
European Parliament, Council and Commission (2017) Interinstitutional Proclamation on the European Pillar of Social Rights. Official Journal C-428/10
Eurostat (2024) Social Scoreboard. https://ec.europa.eu/eurostat/cache/dashboard/social-scoreboard/. Accessed 15th October 2024
Faure E et al (1972) Learning to be: the world of education today and tomorrow. UNESCO, Paris. https://unesdoc.unesco.org/ark:/48223/pf0000001801/PDF/001801eng.pdf.multi. Accessed 2 May 2024
Field J (1998) European Dimensions. Education, Training and the European Union. Higher Education Policy Series (39). J. Kingsley Publishers, London, Bristol, PA
Field J (2001) Lifelong education. Int J Educ 20(1–2):3–15
Garben S (2019) The European pillar of social rights: an assessment of its meaning and significance. Camb Yearb Eur Leg Stud 21:101–127. https://doi.org/10.1017/cel.2019.3
Hake BJ (1999) Lifelong learning policies in the European Union: development and issues. Compare 29(1):53–69
Holford J (2023) Lifelong learning, the European Union, and the social inclusion of young adults: rethinking policy. In: Holford J et al. (eds) Lifelong learning, young adults and the challenges of disadvantage in Europe. Palgrave Studies in Adult Education and Lifelong Learning. Palgrave, Basingstoke. https://doi.org/10.1007/978-3-031-14109-6_1
Holford J, Milana M (2023) The European Union and lifelong learning policy. In: Evans K et al (eds) Third international handbook of lifelong learning. Springer International Handbooks of Education. Springer, Cham. https://doi.org/10.1007/978-3-031-19592-1_27
Husa J (2018) Developing legal system, legal transplants and path dependence: reflections on the rule of law. CJCL 6(2):129–150
Kallen D, Bengtsson J (1973) Recurrent Education: a strategy for lifelong learning. OECD, Washington
Kleibrink A (2011) The EU as a norm entrepreneur: the case of lifelong learning. Eur J Educ 46(1):70–84

Kok W (2004) Facing the challenge. The Lisbon strategy for growth and employment. Report from the High Level Group chaired by Wim Kok. Office for Official Publications of the European Communities, Luxembourg

Lee M (2022) Revisiting the Faure Report: contemporary legacy and challenged legitimacy. Int Rev Educ 68:691–707

Lee M, Thayer T, Madyun N (2008) The evolution of the European Union's lifelong learning policies: an institutional learning perspective. Comp Educ 44(4):445–463

Lenaerts K (1994) Education in European community law after Maastricht. Common Mark Law Rev 31(1):7–41

Méhaut P, Winch C (2012) The European qualification framework: skills, competences or knowledge? Eur Educ Res J 11(3):369–381

Nordin A (2011) Making the Lisbon Strategy happen: a new phase of lifelong learning discourse in European policy? Eur J Educ 10(1):11–20

OECD (1989) Education and the economy in a changing society. OECD Publishing, Paris

OECD (1996) Lifelong Learning for All. Meeting of the Education Committee at Ministerial Level 16-17 January 1996. OECD Publishing, Paris

OECD (2006) The returns to education: links between education, economic growth and social outcomes. In: OECD Education at a Glance 2006: OECD Indicators. OECD Publishing, Paris, pp 152–159

Pierson P (2000) Increasing returns, path dependence and the study of politics. Am Polit Sci Rev 94(2):251–267

Rambla X, Kovacheva S (2021) Constructing meaningful transitions in a vulnerable situation – the role of lifelong learning policies in European regions. Int J Soc Welf 32(1):45–54

Rogowski R (2019) The European Employment Strategy, the European Social Pillar and their Impact on Labour Law Reform in the European Union. Int J Comp L.L.I.R. 35(3):283–304

Sabato S, Corti F (2018) 'The times they are a-changin'?' The European pillar of social rights from debates to reality check. In: Vanhercke B, Ghailani D, Sabato S (eds) Social policy in the European Union: state of play 2018. Nineteenth annual report. European Trade Union Institute (ETUI) and European Social Observatory (OSE), Brussels, pp 51-68

United Nations Educational, Scientific and Cultural Organization, International Committee for the Advancement of Adult Education (1966). International Committee for the Advancement of Adult Education. Report of the third session. UNESCO/ED/219

Volles N (2014) Lifelong learning in the EU: changing conceptualisations, actors, and policies. Stud Higher Educ 41(2):343–363. https://doi.org/10.1080/03075079.2014.927852

**Flore Claus** is a PhD researcher at Ghent University's Department of Crim0inology, Criminal Law and Social Law. Supported by the Research Foundation–Flanders (FWO), her doctoral research explores the right to lifelong learning within the employment relationship. Through a mixed-method approach that bridges international and national perspectives, she investigates how lifelong learning can foster sustainable careers.

# Legal Foundations of Lifelong Learning and Labour Law in Europe

**Felicia Kain**

## 1 Introduction and Research Questions

Lifelong learning is not just a political agenda, but already part of the various legal systems in Europe (national law, international law and European law). It has developed into a pan-European field that exceeds purely national endeavours.[1] Before exploring the legal foundations of lifelong learning in more depth, it is necessary to specify how this term is understood. In accordance with the European Commission's understanding, it is defined as "All learning activity undertaken throughout life, with the aim of improving knowledge, skills, and competences within a personal, civic, social, and/or employment-related perspective."[2] It is therefore a holistic concept based on two main parameters: all kinds of education, on the one hand, and the learning duration throughout life, on the other.

How can the respective legal acts that are part of the lifelong learning concept within Europe be identified? It is clear that those legal bases that refer explicitly to lifelong learning are significant. The list of such documents is limited. However, there are important acts of law that do not refer explicitly to lifelong learning but do so thematically. At this point, reference must be made to the definition just mentioned. First, laws regarding vocational training are relevant because they concern—among other things—learning activity with regard to the employment-related perspective. Second, since the definition also targets other areas of life, such as

[1] For further reading see Léonard and Perin (2009), p. 285 sseq.

[2] European Commission (2001).

F. Kain (✉)
University of Vienna, Institute for Labour and Social Security Law, Vienna, Austria
e-mail: felicia.kain@univie.ac.at



J. Murto, V. Franca (eds.), *Labour Law and Lifelong Learning*,
https://doi.org/10.1007/978-3-032-11035-0_4

personal, civic or social perspectives, laws referring to education in general are important. This view is supported by the European Pillar of Social Rights Action Plan, as it determines that education and training systems play a key role in laying the foundations for lifelong learning.[3] The following explanations are therefore based on education and vocational training as a starting point for lawmaking activities in the area of lifelong learning. In order to reflect the lifelong aspect, the focus is on education and vocational training that goes beyond school education or initial training.

Within this chapter, the following research questions will be answered. First, which positive effects of the promotion of lifelong learning can be expected will be shown, and thus why it is so important. Next, the legal framework on an international and European level will be investigated to determine if lifelong learning is protected and if the existing legal acts protect existing structures or instead call for the expansion of structures. Lastly, whether lifelong learning could be seen as a fundamental and human right will be discussed.

## 2 Lifelong Learning Within Labour Law: Why Should We Promote Lifelong Learning?

One question that is worth answering at the beginning is why it is worth promoting lifelong learning at all. In other words, why is lifelong learning needed? In particular, the European Commission, the Council of the European Union and the ILO have been exploring the reasons. All of these institutions have issued legal acts that specify the objectives to be pursued in lifelong learning.

### *2.1 European Commission: Lifelong Learning as a Means of Tackling Upcoming Challenges*

One legal act that is relevant for the topic at hand is the **European Pillar of Social Rights (EPSR)**, an initiative launched by the European Commission. It must be understood as a recommendation or a joint declaration. It is therefore not binding in accordance with Article 288 TFEU. However, it has a practical significance that should not be neglected. First, it is to be used as a source of interpretation for European Union law. Second, it can be the basis or a source for new initiatives. Thus, it is of high de facto relevance.[4] The implementation of the EPSR is supported by the Commission's Action Plan on the EPSR, which concretises the objectives

[3] European Commission (2021) The European Pillar of Social Rights Action Plan, COM (2021) 102.

[4] Brameshuber (2022), p. 308 sseq; Deinert (2022), p. 283 sseq.

stated therein. According to the Action Plan, 60% of adults should participate in learning every year until the year 2030.

The first principle of the EPSR relates not only to education and training but also refers explicitly to lifelong learning.[5] It states that "Everyone has the right to quality and inclusive education, training and life-long learning in order to maintain and acquire skills that enable them to participate fully in society and manage successfully transitions in the labour market".[6] A look at the Action Plan shows that lifelong learning is largely used as a means of tackling other emerging challenges. It explicitly states the aim of preparing the workforce for the digital and green transition in the best possible way. Lifelong training also increases the resilience of the workforce, enabling it to recover more quickly when difficulties arise. Ultimately, an appealing further education and training programme should also attract new talent, which in turn should counteract the ageing and shrinking of the European workforce. Realising these goals requires continuous investment in education and training systems. The success of these developments will have a direct impact on Europe's competitiveness.[7]

## *2.2 Council of the European Union: Lifelong Learning Within and Beyond the Profession to Adapt to Changing Circumstances*

The Council of the European Union is pursuing similar objectives. This can be deduced from the following five **council recommendations** and **decisions** based on Art 165 and Art 166 TFEU. First, **key competence recommendation,**[8] which refers directly to the EPSR in Recital 1, shows that the council supports and is in line with the European Commission's initiative in the present field. It is interesting to note that this recommendation is not focused on pursuing social, economic or political objectives, as is usual in European Union law. It instead names personal fulfilment, health, employability and social inclusion as goals (Recital 2). Seeking these will help ensure Europe's resilience in times of rapid and profound change.

Second, **micro-credential recommendation**[9] also deals with the adaptation of employees to changing circumstances and takes into account emerging challenges

[5] For further reading regarding the historical perspective see Claus F, Exploring the Future of Lifelong learning through the Tapestry of European Policy History, section 6.

[6] Principle 1 of the European Pillar of Social Rights.

[7] European Commission (2021) The European Pillar of Social Rights Action Plan, COM (2021) 102.

[8] Council recommendation of 22 May 2018 on key competences for lifelong learning, 2018/C 189/01.

[9] Council recommendation of 16 June 2022 on a European approach to micro-credentials for lifelong learning and employability, 2022/C 243/02.

regarding the green and digital transition. The recommendation explicitly states that micro-credentials can be used to enhance—among other things—lifelong learning.[10]

Third, the **adult learning resolution**[11] falls along the same lines. According to this resolution, as in the other legal acts mentioned above, adult learning as an important part of lifelong learning should be used as a tool to meet challenges, going hand in hand with complex and frequent transitions as well as current and future difficulties. It is emphasised that "Adult learning needs a holistic approach including inter-sectoral and multi-stakeholder collaboration, and effective coordination at European, national, regional and local levels, respecting the diverse models of adult learning in the European Union and fully respecting the specific competences of the different policy levels".[12]

Fourth, the **VET recommendation**[13] explains why the expansion of vocational education and training is so important in our society. It contributes to adapting to labour market changes. Flexibility and opportunities for progression lie at the core of vocational education and training. Also, these areas are drivers for innovation and growth. They prepare the workforce for digital and green transitions and train people for occupations in high demand. Additionally, expansion of education promotes the equality of opportunities and underpins a culture of quality assurance. To sum up, the focus of this recommendation is on vocational education and training as a decisive factor in adapting to changing circumstances. These reasons in favour of expanding vocational education and training are therefore also reasons for expanding lifelong learning.

Fifth, the **common vocational training policy decision**[14] from 1963 must be highlighted. Of course, certain aspects of this legal act are no longer up to date. Nevertheless, it must be mentioned here because it shows how far back in time the endeavours concerning lifelong learning at European level go.[15] This council decision includes ten principles for pursuing a common vocational training policy and targets young persons as well as adults who are already employed. Even back then, vocational training and retraining were considered useful instruments for dealing with structural changes.

[10] For further reading regarding micro-credentials see in this volume Urpilainen M, EU recommendations on micro-credentials and individual learning accounts: soft (law) steps towards common EU employment markets?.

[11] Council of the European Union (2021).

[12] Council of the European Union (2021), para 23.

[13] Council of the European Union (2020).

[14] Council of the European Union (1963).

[15] For further reading regarding the historical perspective see in this volume Claus F, Exploring the Future of Lifelong learning through the Tapestry of European Policy History.

## 2.3 *ILO: Promotion of Lifelong Learning Instruments to Face Changing Framework Conditions*

The third body that has been involved in lifelong learning for a very long time and has highlighted why its promotion is so important is the ILO. A look at the respective annual figures shows that it had already issued a convention touching the present field in 1974.[16] It has adopted several relevant legal acts that shed light on the topic of lifelong learning from various angles.[17] It was already stated in the **ILO Constitution**[18] of 1919 that the improvement of the organisation of vocational education was urgently required.[19] The **ILO Philadelphia Declaration**[20] declares the goal of promoting programmes which target "the assurance of equality of educational and vocational opportunity".[21]

A concretisation of the overarching objectives of lifelong learning can be found in the **Human Resources Development Convention** from 1975[22] and in the **Human Resources Development Recommendation** from 2004,[23] which concretises the Convention. If ratified, ILO conventions are binding international treaties, while recommendations are non-binding instruments to provide guidance for national policy, legislation and practice.[24] The preamble of the Human Resources Development Recommendation accurately points out that "education, training and lifelong learning contribute significantly to promoting the interests of individuals, enterprises, the economy and society as a whole [...]"[25] because they tackle challenges such as high employment rates, the fight against poverty, social inclusion and sustainable economic growth in the global economy. Lifelong learning as a factor for personal development, access to culture and active citizenship also plays a role in pursuing one of the primary objectives of the ILO, which is the realisation of decent work for workers everywhere.

With the **Paid Educational Leave Convention**[26] as well as the **Paid Educational Leave Recommendation,**[27] there are more documents from the ILO that concern the overriding objectives of lifelong learning. Both were issued in 1974. According

---

[16] Paid Educational Leave Convention, 1974 (Nr C140).

[17] For further reading regarding the historical perspective see in this volume Claus F, Exploring the Future of Lifelong learning through the Tapestry of European Policy History, section 2.

[18] ILO Constitution, 1919 (hereinafter ILO Constitution).

[19] Preamble, ILO Constitution.

[20] ILO Declaration concerning the aims and purposes of the International Labour Organisation 1944 (hereinafter ILO Philadelphia Declaration).

[21] Art. III lit j Philadelphia Declaration.

[22] Human Resources Development Convention, 1975 (Nr V142).

[23] Human Resources Development Recommendation, 2004 (Nr R195).

[24] ILO, Conventions, Protocols and Recommendations.

[25] Preamble Human Resources Development Recommendation, 2004 (Nr R195).

[26] Paid Educational Leave Convention, 1974 (Nr C140).

[27] Paid Educational Leave Recommendation, June 5th, 1974 (Nr R148).

to these documents, the aim of the concept of educational leave is to address scientific and technological developments as well as the changing pattern of economic and social relations. Although the situation has changed, the aim of lifelong learning remains the same to this day. That aim is to prepare the workforce for changing framework conditions.[28]

Also, the **Quality Apprenticeships Recommendation** from 2023[29] refers explicitly to the term lifelong learning. It names quality apprenticeships as a means of providing lifelong learning opportunities, which consequently enhance resilience, transitions and employability. The recommendation includes specifications on how the respective states should incorporate their apprenticeship systems, how apprentices should be protected and measures to create an enabling environment.[30]

## *2.4 Analysis: Benefits for Individuals, Companies, the Economy and Society as a Whole*

The analysis of the legal acts shows that the Commission, the Council and the ILO essentially state the same objectives as to why lifelong learning should be supported. They focus on creating added value for individuals who make use of education throughout life, for the companies that these individuals work for, for the economy and for society as a whole.

Lifelong learning can have an impact on all these levels because they are intertwined. If a person continues their education, it leads to higher skills which makes them more valuable on the labour market in addition to their personal fulfilment. If employees or the self-employed who work for companies are better trained, the competitiveness of these companies improves. These two factors in combination mean that the labour market can adapt more easily to changing circumstances and thus become more resilient. This in turn is beneficial both for the economy and for society as a whole. If the economy and society as a whole are doing well, this leads to a higher standard of living for the population, regardless of whether they are still in work or not. The most important challenges to come are the green transition as well as the digital transition.[31] The green transformation in particular is already the subject of a number of legal acts under European and international law.[32] Lifelong

[28] Preamble, Paid Educational Leave Convention, 1974 (Nr C140).

[29] Quality Apprenticeships Recommendation, June 16th, 2023 (Nr R208).

[30] For further reading regarding apprenticeship within Europe, see in this volume Impellizzieri G, Apprenticeship in Europe: A Learning Hybrid Model Between Education and Work, section 4.

[31] On the digital and green transformation, see European Commission, The European Green Deal; Council of the European Union (2025).

[32] The green transformation is already emphasized by a series of legal acts under European and international law. See for example: United Nations (1987); United Nations (2015); European Commission (2019).

learning will be a crucial factor in ensuring Europe's position in the world during these upcoming challenges.

Because the development and enhancement of a transnational lifelong learning concept is so important, it needs not only political activism but also legal protection. As has already been shown, numerous relevant legal acts have been passed so far. However, these endeavours are not homogeneous. The various legal acts have different levels of legal force or only concern parts of the lifelong learning concept. A comprehensive analysis is therefore required of the extent to which lifelong learning is protected *de lege lata* and what the core contents of these legal acts are.

# 3 The Lifelong Learning Concept Within the European and International Legal Framework

## *3.1 Whole Lifelong Learning Concept Covered by Legislation*

A brief survey shows that the entire concept of lifelong learning is covered by legislation. As only a few acts cover the whole concept, most of them relate to partial areas. The analysis refers to the two defining parameters of lifelong learning, namely the scope of education, on the one hand, and its extension over a lifetime, on the other.

### 3.1.1 Relevant Legislation within International Law

The ILO issued several documents that cover the lifelong learning concept decades ago. Both, the **Human Resources Development Convention** and the **Human Resources Development Recommendation** refer explicitly to lifelong learning. Accordingly, the respective states have to adopt and develop policies and programmes for vocational guidance and training.[33] The development should take place with the assistance of social partners.[34] It is explicitly mentioned that programmes and information should be accessible to children, young persons and adults.[35] Educational systems should "meet the needs for vocational training throughout life".[36] Within the Human Resources Development Recommendation, lifelong learning is not only explicitly mentioned throughout the recommendation, but even defined. Art 2 states that "the term lifelong learning encompasses all learning activities undertaken throughout life for the development of competencies and

[33] Art. 1 Human Resources Development Convention.

[34] Art. 5 Human Resources Development Convention.

[35] Art. 3 Human Resources Development Convention.

[36] Art. 4 Human Resources Development Convention.

qualifications".[37] Consequently, its understanding is limited to vocational guidance and training. Although the wording refers to life as a whole, it can be inferred from the content that only working life is meant. The scope of the **Paid Educational Leave Convention** and the **Paid Educational Leave Recommendation** are also limited to working life. However, they are not limited to vocational training but also concern general, social, civic and trade union education. The **quality apprenticeships recommendation** is limited to vocational training as well as to working life.

**Art 2 Protocol 1 ECHR** contains an individual right to education and is binding for the contracting states. States cannot deny education within institutions they have chosen to set up. The key element of the right to education is therefore a prohibition of discrimination in access to educational institutions. Although the wording is negative, the law goes beyond this, and certain positive obligations can be derived. However, it is not possible to deduce a right to the establishment of new educational facilities.[38] According to the ECtHR, the right to education generally includes any person who wishes to make use of it.[39] The right to education is not absolute since constraints are possible. For example, states can restrict access to educational institutions where lifelong learning activities could be offered under certain conditions.[40] One example are entrance examinations.[41] The relevance of the right to education within the meaning of Art 2 Protocol 1 ECHR must be emphasised, because its scope covers large parts of the lifelong learning concept. This provision refers to higher education institutions and protects all people who want to access education institutions. Consequently, it protects the very aspect of 'lifelong' and is additionally not limited to vocational training.

**Art 10 ESC (revised)** contains a right to vocational training. The ESC (revised) is an act of international law and thus binding for the contracting states. However, it must be noted that the system of the ESC (revised) provides that the contracting states only have to "opt in" to a certain number of articles. The rights to which the respective states are bound therefore differ.[42] The term vocational training refers to all kinds of higher education.[43] The provision at hand covers various aspects of vocational training. According to this provision, vocational training should gener-

[37] Art. 2 lit a Human Resources Development Recommendation.

[38] Belgian linguistic case (1968), ECtHR, 1474/62.

[39] Velyo Velev v Bulgaria (2014), ECtHR, 16032/07.

[40] Belgian linguistic case (1968), ECtHR, 1474/62.

[41] Tarantino and others v Italy (2013), ECtHR, 25851/09, 29284/09 and 64090/09; for further reading see ECtHR, Guide on Article 2 of Protocol No. 1 to the European Convention on Human Rights (Version 20.02.2024), 8/24 sseq.

[42] Art. 10 in its entirety or certain paragraphs were selected by Austria, Andorra, Belgium, Bulgaria, Cyprus, Denmark, Estonia, Finland, France, Georgia, Germany, Greece, Hungary, Ireland, Italy, Latvia, Lithuania, Luxembourg, Malta, Montenegro, Netherlands, Norway, Poland, Portugal, Serbia, Slovak Republic, Slovenia, Spain, Sweden, Türkiye, Ukraine and the United Kingdom. It should also be noted that not all states in this list have ratified the ESC (revised) and that therefore for some of the states mentioned Art. 10 of the "original" ESC applies. The rights stated in the respective paragraphs are guaranteed for all nationals of these countries.

[43] Regarding the definition of the term see European Committee of Social Rights (2003).

ally be promoted and access to such training should be ensured, and social partners should be involved in the process. In particular, the inclusion of certain groups of people, such as disabled people, both genders, long-term unemployed and young people is emphasised.[44] It is essential that people of disadvantaged groups enter, remain and develop within the labour market to foster economic development and social cohesion. Art 10 ESC (revised) thus also supports, among other things, the existing endeavours of European social partners to pursue inclusion via training and skill development.[45]

It has to be highlighted that Art 10 ESC (revised) only protects that part of the lifelong learning concept that refers to vocational training. Therefore, it is mainly concerned with the employment-related perspective. It must also be emphasised that it refers to vocational training throughout working life. This is shown by several aspects within the provision at hand. First, Art 10 para 3 lit a ESC (revised) determines that the parties should provide or promote—among other things—adequate and readily available training facilities for adult workers as well as special facilities for the retraining of adult workers needed as a result of technological development or new trends in employment. Furthermore, Art 10 para 4 ESC (revised) contains a call to the contracting states to promote the reintegration of the long-term unemployed. Those contracting states that have ratified the relevant paragraphs are therefore obliged to meet these standards.

### 3.1.2 Relevant Legislation Within European Union Law

The European Union's Competence Regarding Lifelong Learning

Before discussing the specific legal acts of the European Union that protect the concept of lifelong learning, it is necessary to discuss competences. Is the European Union allowed to pass laws regarding lifelong learning? Art 14 CFR, which includes a right to education, does not provide a suitable basis for harmonisation actions. This is because the CFR does not establish any new competences.[46]

The European Union has a **competence** to support, coordinate and supplement, among other things, in the fields of education and vocational training on the basis of

[44] Lukas (2021), Art. 10 ESC Nr 10.13, 10.18, 10.21, 10.26, 10.29; European Committee of Social Rights (2003); European Committee of Social Rights (2007).

[45] Examples of such endeavours are the framework agreement on inclusive labour markets from 2010 as well as the subsequent report on the implementation of the European framework agreement on inclusive labour markets from 2014, see https://ec.europa.eu/employment_social/2010againstpoverty/export/sites/default/downloads/Events/event_123_Framework_agreement_ILM_25.03.10.pdf and https://www.businesseurope.eu/wp-content/uploads/2025/02/2015-00260-E-07f-1.pdf. Accessed on 06 May 2025.

[46] Art. 6 para 1 TEU.

Art 6 TFEU. This coordination competence[47] includes the incentive to cooperate with third countries as well as International Organisations. On this basis, the European Union can be a party in international agreements. The areas of education and vocational training are also dealt with in Art 165 and 166 TFEU.[48] The prevailing doctrine assumes that Art 165 TFEU is a *lex generalis* for the entire education sector and Art 166 TFEU is a *lex specialis* for vocational education and training. The concept of education within these provisions must be viewed comprehensively: it refers to state and private as well as institutionalised and non-institutionalised knowledge transfer.[49] As can be derived from the objectives, the focus is on social and employment policy. Both provisions have the same structure and distribute the competences between the respective member states and the European Union. What is taught and how education structures are organised is a matter for the member states, while the European Union should introduce a vocational training policy to support their actions.[50] Thus, the European Union shall promote the cooperation between the respective member states. This is both an authorisation and a limit to its competence. Excessive cuts in national legislative competences should be avoided.[51]

This division of competences is an expression of the principle of subsidiarity.[52] In simple terms, the European Unions' competences are quite limited, education and vocational training are primarily the responsibility of the member -states, and the European Union is barred from taking concrete harmonisation measures on this foundation.[53] Nonetheless, Arts 165 and 166 TFEU play an important role as a basis for the adoption of secondary legislation. To achieve the goals set out in these provisions, the Council can take measures together with the European Parliament and issue recommendations on the basis of a proposal from the Commission. These rights have also been exercised and relevant secondary legislation has been adopted.

The absence of an explicit harmonisation competence of the European Union does not mean that it is impossible to ensure appropriate standards. The ability to intervene could also be drawn from other, more general provisions.[54] Education is often an aspect of other competences, such as fundamental freedoms or the prohibition of discrimination.[55] The case law of the CJEU shows that the boundaries of jurisdiction within education and training are not set in stone. In *Casagrande*, the CJEU stated that "although educational and training policy is not as such included in the spheres which the Treaty has entrusted to the Community institutions, it does

[47] The term "coordination competence" for the competence to support, coordinate and supplement is generally used in contrast to the European Union's harmonisation competences.

[48] For further reading see Klamert (2019), Art. 6 TFEU Nr 1 sseq.

[49] Budischowsky (2023), Art. 165, 166 TFEU, Nr 34.

[50] Anderson (2015), p. 134 sseq; Blanke (2024) Art. 166 AEUV, Nr 18 sseq.

[51] Garben (2019), Art. 165 TFEU Nr 2 sseq; Budischowsky (2023) Art. 165, 166 AEUV, Nr 34.

[52] For further information see Granat (2018), p. 1 sseq.

[53] For further reading regarding education governance within the European Union see Volante (2016), p. 988 sseq.

[54] Kalteis (2019), Art. 14 GRC Nr 3.

[55] Ruffert (2022), Art. 165 TFEU Nr 2, 6 sseq.

not follow that the exercise of powers transferred to the Community is in some way limited if it is of such a nature as to affect the measures taken in the execution of a policy such as that of education and training".[56]

Even if the European Union has no harmonisation competence in the present field, requirements may arise from primary law which have a de facto harmonising effect. In other words, a "harmonization through the back door", as *Garben* aptly describes this phenomenon, is possible.[57] On the basis of fundamental freedoms, European Union law could thus also intervene in these areas. One example is the coordination of social security law, within which the European Union has exerted a strong influence on national social security systems.[58] The provisions on the coordination of benefits in kind in the event of illness result, for example, from the application of the free movement of goods and the freedom to provide services.[59] The fundamental freedoms in connection with Art 165 and Art 166 TFEU could therefore be a good basis for further legislative action by the European Union.[60]

## Acts of European Union law that Cover Lifelong Learning

First of all**, Art 14 CFR** must be mentioned. Art 14 para 1 CFR contains a comprehensive right to education, consisting of the right to education in it's core, the right to access to vocational training and the right to free compulsory education.[61] Since the CFR has the status of primary law, it is directly binding. The term education does not refer to all kinds of education, but rather to school education.[62] Vocational training within Art 14 CFR is any form of training that prepares the trainee for access to an occupation within the meaning of Art 15 CFR by imparting occupation-specific skills. In the literature, this also includes higher education at universities or comparable institutions.[63] The provision at hand hence protects general education, but only in schools and further vocational training. The duration of protection is therefore not lifelong but focused on primary education and limited to working life.

The **EPSR** is one of the few legal bases that covers the whole lifelong learning concept. This is because the understanding within this book is based on the European Commission's definition and the EPSR is an initiative of the European Commission. As already described in subchapter 2, it is a soft law instrument that focuses on the development of lifelong learning structures and has a high de facto relevance as

[56] Casagrande (1974), CJEU, C-9/74, ECLI:EU:C:1974:74.

[57] Garben (2019), Art. 165 TFEU Nr 4.

[58] It should be noted at this point that the coordination competences in the areas of social security and education are not identical.

[59] For further reading see Obermaier (2008), p. 15 sseq.

[60] It would be interesting to explore these possibilities further in future research.

[61] Sigg (2024), Art. 14 CFR Nr 1.

[62] Kingreen (2022), Art. 14 CFR Nr 3.

[63] Kempen (2016), Art. 14 CFR, Nr 9; Thiele (2023) Art. 14 CFR Nr 10.

source of interpretation. **Principle 1** is especially relevant to the topic at hand since it refers to both education in general as well as vocational training throughout life. But Principle 4 (active support to employment), Principle 5 (secure and adaptable employment), Principle 7 (information about employment conditions and protection in case of dismissals) and Principle 8 (social dialogue and involvement of workers) can also be associated with lifelong learning. How exactly these Principles will be intertwined with Principle 1, and lifelong learning in general, remains to be seen in the future.

As already mentioned, the European Union's competences regarding general education and vocational training are determined in Art 165 and Art 166 TFEU.[64] These competences have already been utilised and the council has issued several documents relating to lifelong learning. In fact, existing documents are regularly based on both Art 165 and Art 166 TFEU.[65] The **key competence recommendation**, the **micro-credential recommendation**, the **adult learning resolution** as well as the **VET recommendation** explicitly use the term lifelong learning and refer to the EPSR directly.[66] Since the EPSR was proclaimed— among others—by the European Commission and thus the Commission's understanding of the term is reflected in it, these recommendations capture the whole concept of lifelong learning. As already mentioned, the **common vocational training policy decision** was one of the earliest documents concerning the present topic. In terms of content, it is limited to vocational training but extends to the entire professional life. The decision points out that people should be able to receive basic, advanced and retraining in different stages of their working life.

## 3.2 *Protection-focused Acts and Action-focused Acts*

All the legal bases mentioned have in common that they protect and promote lifelong learning. An analysis of the respective legal acts shows that the content can be divided roughly on the basis of how they pursue these goals. Some acts focus on (1) the protection of existing education structures and some aim for an (2) expansion of structures. It should be noted that these objectives are regularly intertwined and a clear separation is not always possible. This should therefore be understood as a rough classification to illustrate the phenomenon.

[64] For further reading regarding the historical perspective see in this volume Claus F, Exploring the Future of Lifelong learning through the Tapestry of European Policy History, section 5.

[65] See for example Council of the European Union (2018) and Council of the European Union (2020).

[66] Recital 1 council recommendation on key competences for lifelong learning; Recital 7 council recommendation on a European approach to micro-credentials for lifelong learning and employability; Art. 1, 4 and 5 council resolution on a new European agenda for adult learning 2021-2030; Recital 2 council recommendation on vocational education and training (VET) for sustainable competitiveness, social fairness and resilience.

### 3.2.1 Protection of Existing Structures

Basically, all relevant legal acts protect structures that already exist. Those legal acts that only or mainly protect existing structures and do not contain a further call for expansion are predominantly binding legal acts. In concrete terms, these are the ECHR and the CFR. **Art 2 Protocol 1 ECHR** prohibits discrimination in access to educational institutions. However, it must be noted that no concrete right or order to expand educational facilities can be derived.

**Art 14 para 1 CFR** determines the right to obtain access to educational institutions in order to acquire the mentioned types of education. However, it does not include a positive obligation to establish such institutions.[67] This provision binds both the institutions of the European Union and the member states insofar as they fall within the scope of Union law. They are therefore not allowed to pass laws or take actions that restrict the right to education. Interference with the right to vocational training occurs when access to an institution is excluded or made more difficult by a regulation or by de facto behaviour. Such an impairment also arises in the event of unequal treatment on access. Regarding impairments of the right to vocational training, justification is possible on the basis of Art 52 para 1 CFR.[68] Accordingly, any interference must have a legal basis and respect the essence of the right to vocational training.[69] Furthermore, the principle of proportionality must be respected. As far as can be seen, the CJEU has not yet dealt with the right to education in detail. Problems in this area have so far been solved on the basis of the prohibition of discrimination and the free movement of labour.[70]

### 3.2.2 Call for Expansion of Lifelong Learning Structures

Art **10 ESC (revised)** includes a comprehensive call to strengthen and expand existing structures. The states are consistently encouraged to provide or promote certain policies, for example adequate and readily available training facilities for adult workers or special facilities needed as a result of technological development or new trends in employment. This provision contains several specific instructions for the member states. It is also explicitly mentioned that the respective states should encourage the full utilisation of the facilities provided by appropriate measures.

Also, all of the relevant acts issued by the ILO embrace expansion. Probably for reasons of binding effect, the specifications in the recommendations are much more precise than those in the conventions. Some of the former contain quite detailed and concrete requirements. For example, the **Human Resources Development Recommendation** determines that the national framework should include a

[67] Lock (2019), Art. 14 CFR Nr 3 sseq.

[68] Sigg (2024), Art. 14 CFR Nr 3 ff; Augsberg (2015), Art. 14 CFR Nr 10, 11.

[69] Art. 52 para 1 CFR.

[70] Kingreen (2022), Art. 14 CFR Nr 2.

credible system of certification which will ensure that skills are portable and recognised across sectors, industries, enterprises and educational institutions. The recommendation also highlights the necessity of research regarding lifelong learning.

Furthermore, **Principle 1 EPSR** calls for expansion. Specifications can be found in the respective Action Plan. The Action Plan on the EPSR is geared towards how working life should be organised in the future and can therefore also be seen as an appeal for the expansion of existing structures. The objectives and targets are quite comprehensive and predominantly represent overarching objectives as opposed to specific instructions for action. On the basis of the EPSR, the Commission is taking a number of steps and also encourages certain activities of the member states.

Consequently, there are several legal acts that call for the expansion of lifelong learning structures. These legal acts are predominantly non-binding. This is probably because states are reluctant to impose extensive obligations on themselves. At the same time, however, it shows that the expansion of lifelong learning structures is significant within Europe. The extent to which the respective member states will fulfil these tasks remains to be seen.

## 4 Lifelong Learning as a Fundamental and Human Right?

The analysis of the existing legal framework has shown that, with the ECHR and the CFR, there are even fundamental and human rights that protect lifelong learning. In this context, two questions arise: What is the relationship between these two provisions? Can one speak of lifelong learning as a fundamental and human right? This would certainly have strong political power.

Both provisions are intertwined. Art 14 CRF must be interpreted in accordance with Art 2 Protocol 1 ECHR. In comparison, further rights can be derived from Art 14 CFR. Art 14 para 2 CFR contains the opportunity to receive free compulsory education, which is not mentioned in Art 2 Protocol 1 ECHR. Also, Art 14 Abs 3 CFR determines a right to found educational establishments.[71] It is important to subject the existing legal framework to a holistic analysis and not to view them as completely separate legal acts.

A fundamental and human right to lifelong learning to the effect that individuals have an enforceable claim to the extensive availability of such facilities cannot be derived from these provisions. However, their importance for lifelong learning should not be underestimated. Art 2 Protocol 1 ECHR is of high significance regarding legal policy. The fact that such a right to education exists, which applies to different types of educational institutions and persons of different ages, emphasises the importance of education within the contracting states. Also, Art 14 CFR is to be used as a basis for interpreting Union and national law.[72] This means that the right

[71] Lock (2019), Art. 14 CFR Nr 1 sseq.

[72] Augsberg (2015), Art. 14 CFR Nr 9.

to education as an interpretation tool also has a certain steering function with regard to lifelong learning. The impact of the right to education on lifelong learning can also be viewed from a wider perspective. Art 14 CFR also shows that education does not end with school education. This provision concerns a longer period of life through further education, even if it is limited to working life. Learning beyond childhood is therefore a position protected by fundamental rights.

Because the relevant provisions do not fully cover the lifelong learning concept, it would probably be going too far to speak of a fundamental and human right to lifelong learning. Nevertheless, the mere existence of the right to education has an important function regarding lifelong learning. Every citizen of the European Union has a right to education. The education policy of the European Union promotes this right as a "civil right to transnational education". In this way, education policy unfolds its integration policy potential.[73] Ultimately, the very fact that there are human and fundamental rights to education shows that ensuring education and learning is of utmost importance within the European Union.

## 5 Conclusion: Lifelong Learning : The Casting of Political Initiatives into Legal Foundations

### *5.1 Entire Concept of Lifelong Learning is Protected*

The analysis shows that there are numerous legal bases with different legal statuses in the area of lifelong learning. The number of legal acts in force in this field demonstrate that the topic of lifelong learning is certainly receiving attention in Europe. Indeed, both the bodies of the European Union and international institutions are dealing with this issue. It is clear from their political initiatives and enacted legal acts that the core objective of lifelong learning endeavours is to develop the resilience of society and the economy to future challenges, such as the digital and green transformation. In addition, these aspirations also have a positive impact on individuals in terms of personal fulfilment and higher value on the labour market and also for companies regarding having a better-trained workforce. This strengthens the economy and society as a whole and makes it all the more important to safeguard the concept of lifelong learning legally.

It must be emphasised that almost the entire concept of lifelong learning, understood as "all learning activity undertaken throughout life, with the aim of improving knowledge, skills, and competences within a personal, civic, social, and/or employment-related perspective", is legally protected. On an **international law level**, the **ILO** in particular has been involved with lifelong learning for decades. It has issued legal acts regarding the development of human resources, paid educational leave and quality apprenticeships. These legal acts therefore affect important

[73] Ruffert (2022), Art. 165 TFEU Nr 4.

aspects of the concept of lifelong learning. However, the relevant requirements are rather vague and leave the states a great deal of room for manoeuvre. It should also be noted that many of the legal acts adopted by the ILO are not binding.

With **Art 2 Protocol 1 ECHR**, there is a binding individual right to education on an international law level. This protects lifelong learning by prohibiting discrimination in access to education. A right to the expansion of lifelong learning institutions cannot be inferred. This is therefore less suitable for promoting lifelong learning endeavours. Nevertheless, due to its binding effect, it secures the status quo and ensures equal treatment in educational endeavours. With the right to vocational training in accordance with **Art 10 ESC**, there is another binding legal act in international law. Many of the member states of the ESC have also opted into this provision. It has numerous contents that directly affect the concept of lifelong learning, albeit limited to continuing vocational training. However, the existing provisions are quite vague and, like the legal acts of the ILO, tend to leave a lot of leeway.

With regard to the relevant legal acts at the level of **European Union** law, it has to be stressed that the European Union only has a **coordination competence** based on Art 6 in conjunction with Art 165 and 166 TFEU. Harmonising legal acts can therefore not be issued. However, in specific cases, requirements can arise directly from other provisions of primary law, which can lead to de facto harmonisation. The extent to which existing competences are utilised also depends on the legal policy will of the institutions involved. Neither the institutions of the European Union nor the CJEU have exhausted these possibilities yet. Considering the existing primary law, more influence could be exerted from a purely legal perspective than has been the case to date.

Nevertheless, there are also several relevant legal acts at the level of **European Union law**. The most important are the following. Initially, the concept of lifelong learning was partially enshrined in fundamental law in Art **14 CFR**. This consists of the compulsory right to education, the right to access to vocational training and the right to free compulsory education. It therefore covers large parts of the lifelong learning concept but is limited to working life. **Principle 1 EPSR**, as an initiative by the European Commission, is of particular importance because it protects the entire concept of lifelong learning. According to the Action Plan, 60% of adults should participate in lifelong learning every year until the year 2030. In terms of content, it protects the core of lifelong learning. However, its de facto effect is limited by the absence of binding force. The endeavours of the **Council of the European Union** are along the same lines. It has issued several recommendations and resolutions on key competences, micro-credentials, adult learning, VET and vocational training. These legal acts also cover large parts of the lifelong learning concept, but are soft law, which limits their actual effect.

Also, there are numerous legal bases in European and international law that do not relate directly to education but have an indirect effect. Their effects and possibilities for lifelong learning have hardly been researched. Furthermore, since Art 14 CFR and Art 2 Protocol 1 ECHR are two fundamental or human rights relating to education, the question arises as to whether one can speak of a **fundamental and human right to lifelong learning**. This would go too far, because none of these provisions cover the entire concept of lifelong learning. However, both rights emphasise the importance of education in Europe and thus reinforce the concept of lifelong learning.

## *5.2 Protection on Two Levels*

If one considers all these existing legal acts in their entirety, one recognises that **the legal protection exists on two levels**: On the one hand, access to existing facilities is protected. On the other hand, there is an appeal to expand existing structures. Those legal acts that protect existing institutions are partly binding and tend to be concrete. It can therefore be said that the legal protection of existing educational institutions is quite pronounced. An overview shows that all players in Europe agree that lifelong learning facilities should be expanded. Those legal acts that have the expansion of structures as their objectives are generally non-binding and vague. As a result, there are hardly any obligations on states to expand existing networks and only some guidelines on how exactly this is to be done.

Future legislative activities should centre on this point. If Europe really wants to promote lifelong learning, there need to be more concrete obligations for realisation and expansion. This is particularly important for promoting uniform development within Europe. In view of the increased legislative activity in recent years, it is to be expected that this will continue to expand.

## *5.3 Research Needed in the Future*

This legislative activity is precisely where future research activities should focus. Overall, there are many legislative areas that touch on the concept of lifelong learning. To date, their effects and possibilities have not been researched in detail. The relationship between all these legal bases has also not yet been conclusively clarified in this area. Additionally, it would be worthwhile to explore to what extent general norms, such as fundamental freedoms, could be a basis for further legislative action. Also, the dynamic area of lifelong learning should be reviewed on an ongoing basis. In concrete terms, it would be of interest to investigate how the European and international legal requirements discussed in this chapter have been implemented in the respective member states. A comparative law study would be of particular interest here. In this way, best practices could be identified in pursuance of their implementation in other countries. A continuous exchange with practitioners is also particularly important for analysing the impact of legislative activities and political initiatives.

## References

Anderson K (2015) Social policy in the European Union. Bloomsbury, London
Augsberg S (2015) Art 14 CFR. In: von der Groeben H, Schwarze J, Hatje A (eds) Europäisches Unionsrecht, 7th edn. Nomos, Baden-Baden
Blanke H (2024) Art 166 AEUV. In: Grabitz E, Hilf M, Nettesheim M (eds) Das Recht der Europäischen Union: EUV/AEUV, 81st edn. Beck, München
Brameshuber E (2022) Die Europäische Säule Sozialer Rechte, Zur Konstitutionalisierung von Sozialen Rechten. In: Auer-Mayer S et al (eds) Festschrift Pfeil, 1st edn. Manz, Wien, pp 307–316
Budischowsky J (2023) Art 165 and 166 TFEU. In: Jaeger T, Stöger K (eds) EUV/AEUV, 1st edn. Manz Verlag
Council of the European Union (1963) Decision of 2 April 1963 laying down general principles for implementing a common vocational training policy. Official Journal 63/266/EEC
Council of the European Union (2018) Recommendation of 22 May 2018 on key competences for lifelong learning. Official Journal C-189/01
Council of the European Union (2020) Recommendation of 24 November 2020 on vocational education and training (VET) for sustainable competitiveness, social fairness and resilience. Official Journal C-417/01
Council of the European Union (2021) Resolution on a new European agenda for adult learning 2021-2030. Official Journal C-504/02
Council of the European Union (2022) Recommendation of 16 June 2022 on a European approach to micro-credentials for lifelong learning and employability. Official Journal C-243/02
Council of the European Union (2025) Digital transition: shaping the EU's digital future https://www.consilium.europa.eu/en/policies/digital-transition/. Accessed 02 Apr 2025
Deinert O (2022) Die europäische Säule sozialer Rechte: Rechtsnatur und Implikationen für das nationale Arbeitsrecht. DRdA 3:283–293
European Commission (2001) Communication from the commission, Making a European Area of Lifelong learning a reality, COM(2001) 678
European Commission (2019) Communication from the Commission to the European Parliament, the European Council, the Council, the European Economic and Social Committee and the Committee of the Regions, The European Green Deal, COM(2019) 640
European Commission, The European Green Deal https://commission.europa.eu/strategy-and-policy/priorities-2019-2024/european-green-deal_en. Accessed 02 Apr 2025
European Committee of Social Rights (2003) Conclusions 2003, France, Art 10 para 1, http://hudoc.esc.coe.int/eng?i=2003/def/FRA/10/1/EN. Accessed 02 Apr 2025
European Committee of Social Rights (2007) Conclusions 2007, Ireland, Art 10 para 1 http://hudoc.esc.coe.int/eng?i=2007/def/IRL/10/1/EN. Accessed 02 Apr 2025
Framework agreement on inclusive labour markets, https://ec.europa.eu/employment_social/2010againstpoverty/export/sites/default/downloads/Events/event_123_Framework_agreement_ILM_25.03.10.pdf. Accessed on 06 May 2025
Garben S (2019) Articles 165–166 TFEU. In: Kellerbauer M, Klamert M, Tomkin J (eds) The EU treaties and the charter of fundamental rights: a commentary, 1st edn. Oxford University Press, Oxford, pp 1424–1439
Granat K (2018) The principle of subsidiarity and its enforcement in the EU legal order: the role of national parliaments in the early warning system. Hart Publishing, Portland
ILO, Conventions, Protocols and Recommendations, https://www.ilo.org/international-labour-standards/conventions-protocols-and-recommendations. Accessed 02 Apr 2025
Kalteis M (2019) Art 14 CFR. In: Holoubek M, Lienbacher G (eds) GRC-Kommentar, 2nd edn. Manz, Wien, pp 299–329
Kempen B (2016) Art 14 CFR. In: Stern K, Sachs M (eds) Europäische Grundrechte-Charta: GRCh, 1st edn. Beck, München, pp 293–305

Kingreen T (2022) Art 14 CFR. In: Calliess C, Ruffert M (eds) EUV/AEUV, 6th edn. Beck, München, pp 2749–2751

Klamert M (2019) Articles 2–6 TFEU. In: Kellerbauer M, Klamert M, Tomkin J (eds) The EU treaties and the Charter of fundamental rights: a commentary, 1st edn. Oxford University Press, Oxford, pp 353–376

Léonard E, Perin E (2009) Lifelong learning and social partnership: a comparative overview of twelve European countries. IJCLLIR 25(3):283–300

Lock T (2019) Articles 6–19 CFR. In: Kellerbauer M, Klamert M, Tomkin J (eds) The EU treaties and the charter of fundamental rights: a commentary, 1st edn. OUP, Oxford, pp 2111–2157

Lukas K (2021) The revised European social charter. Edgar Elgar, Cheltenham

Obermaier AJ (2008) Fine-tuning the Jurisprudence: the ECJ's Judicial Activism and Self-restraint, Institute for European Integration Research Working Paper No. 02/2008, Vienna

Report on the implementation of the European framework agreement on inclusive labour markets from 2014., https://www.businesseurope.eu/wp-content/uploads/2025/02/2015-00260-E-07f-1.pdf. Accessed on 06 May 2025

Ruffert M (2022) Art 165 TFEU. In: Calliess C, Ruffert M (eds) EUV/AEUV, 6th edn. Beck, München, pp 1738–1746

Sigg D (2024) Art 14 CFR. In: Decker A, Bader J, Kothe P (eds) BeckOK Migrations- und Integrationsrecht, 18th edn. Beck, München

Thiele C (2023) Art 14 CFR. In: Pechstein M, Nowak C, Häde U (eds) Frankfurter Kommentar EUV/GRC/AEUV, 2nd edn. Mohr Siebeck, Tübingen

United Nations (1987) Report of the World Commission on Environment and Development from 04.08.1987, A/42/427

United Nations (2015) Resolution adopted by the general assembly, Transforming our world: the 2030 Agenda for Sustainable Development from 25.09.2015, A/RES/70/1

Volante L (2016) The European Union, education governance and international education surveys. Policy Fut Educ 14(7):988–1004

**Felicia Kain**, LL.M. (WU) is a scientific researcher (post doc) at the Institute for Labour and Social Law at the University of Vienna and a member of the Labour Law and Lifelong Learning Research Group.

# EU Recommendations on Micro-Credentials and Individual Learning Accounts: Soft (Law) Steps Towards Common EU Employment Markets?

**Matti Urpilainen**

## 1 Introduction

In this chapter, lifelong learning is analysed in connection with EU employment policy coordination. The chapter takes a closer look at two EU policy coordination measures[1] that are aimed at upskilling and reskilling the workforce by increasing incentives and motivation to participate in training:[2] *micro-credentials* and *individual learning accounts*. Micro-credentials is a system for formally recognising small-scale learning and incentivising individuals to acquire such training. Individual learning accounts provide individuals with learning entitlements that improve their access to training.

Micro-credentials and individual learning accounts are subject to two Council recommendations.[3] As part of the EU employment policy coordination, the Member States

[1] A key document in the EU employment policy coordination is the Council Decision on guidelines for the employment policies of the Member States, EU 2022/2296. Among other things, the guidelines provide recommendations on enhancing labour supply and improving access to lifelong acquisition of skills and competencies.

[2] Training—upskilling and reskilling—provides individuals with access to labour markets and abilities to progress within the labour markets, thus improving their employability. See, e.g. Council Recommendation on Upskilling Pathways: New Opportunities for Adults, 2016/C 484/01, Preamble 1.

[3] Council Recommendation on a European approach to micro-credentials for lifelong learning and employability, 2022/C 243/02, and Council Recommendation on individual learning accounts, 2022/C 242/03.

M. Urpilainen (✉)
Tampere University, Faculty of Management and Business, Tampere, Finland
e-mail: matti.urpilainen@tuni.fi



J. Murto, V. Franca (eds.), *Labour Law and Lifelong Learning*,
https://doi.org/10.1007/978-3-032-11035-0_5

are expected to support working adults' access to training. Upskilling, reskilling and employability are frequently mentioned in EU documents that seek to coordinate Member States' economic and employment policies.[4] One of the EU's headline targets to be achieved by 2030 is 60 per cent of adults participating in training every year.[5] Training benefits the working-age adults whose skills and competencies, and thus relative position in the employment markets, are improved. Training provides current and future employers access to a sufficiently skilled workforce essential for any business—especially for adapting to digitalised business environments.[6]

However, it is unclear how effective EU policy coordination can be attained through *soft law* in a field where the EU does not have regulatory competence[7] while considering the notable differences in theMember States' educational systems and employment markets.[8] Although soft law is formally non-binding upon the Member States and EU citizens, it has had a growing impact in the interplay of the EU and the national legal systems in many policy areas.[9] One explanation is provided by the discrepancy between the EU's ambitious policy agendas and its formal legislative competences: certain global policy challenges seem to urgently call for EU level measures, although the EU does not have specific legal competence to take such measures. This is also relevant for the current attempts to ensure the necessary upskilling and reskilling of workers across the EU.[10]

This chapter aims to understand why (and how) the two recommendations that are "merely" non-binding soft law instruments[11] can contribute to the ongoing legal integration in lifelong learning across the EU. For this purpose, the objectives and key provisions of the two recommendations are analysed to identify the "hardest edges" of soft law. The aim is to recognise those features of the recommendations that can be expected to have a meaningful impact on regulatory coordination across the EU despite their soft legal status.[12]

---

[4] The two are closely intertwined; a high employment rate is a key element of growth-inducing economic policy. See especially European Commission (2025).

[5] See "The European Pillar of Social Rights Action Plan", European Commission (2021), Section 2.

[6] The European Commission has labelled the current changes of the European economy *as twin transition* that includes green and digital transition. See European Commission (2022).

[7] On EU legal competencies at the crossroads of education and employment, see in this volume Kain F, Legal Foundations of lifelong learning and labour law in Europe, section 3.1.2.1.

[8] The absence of binding EU law creates a regulatory gap. However, the absence of EU regulatory competence creates a discrepancy between policy ambitions and what can be accomplished by legislation. Weiss (2017), pp. 111–121 notes that without legislative power, the EU cannot live up to the promises created by the European Charter of Fundamental Rights in the field of labour law.

[9] See, e.g. Andone and Coman-Kund (2022), pp. 22–47.

[10] The European Commission (2025) states that although Member States' efforts have increased, the challenges are too great and urgent to be left only to the Member States. This provides justification for the Commission's new initiatives and generally strengthens the EU's role in upskilling and reskilling. However, the Commission notes that it fully recognises the primary role of Member States under TFEU Articles 165 and 166 and that it will only act within its competencies.

[11] Article 288 TFEU stipulates that recommendations shall have no binding force.

[12] On the various types of EU soft law, see Hofman (2021), pp. 39–52.

Section 2 focuses on micro-credentials, and Sect. 3 on individual learning accounts. Section 4 compares the key features of the recommendations and discusses what kind of practical possibilities and limitations these soft law instruments may have in harmonising Member States' adult training systems. Section 5 concludes and reflects the findings of the analysis in the wider framework of the EU employment policy.

## 2 Micro-credentials

### *2.1 Micro-credentials and Lifelong Learning*

Micro-credentials provide individuals with the possibility to have their small-scale learning recognised and registered in various formal, informal and non-formal contexts.[13] Micro-credentials formalise the learning outcomes, which incentivise individuals to participate in qualifying training and to seek training opportunities that provide micro-credentials. A system of micro-credentials functions more effectively if individuals can combine micro-credentials and use them in different contexts. A key requirement is that they are based on standards that are sufficiently transparent for all stakeholders.[14]

The Council Recommendation on a European approach to micro-credentials for lifelong learning and employability 2022/C 242/03 (hereafter CRMC) defines a micro-credential as "the record of the learning outcomes that a learner has acquired following a small volume of learning".[15] The idea and concept of "micro-credentials" predates the EU recommendation, and other notable sources regard their design and potential besides the EU recommendation.[16] The OECD policy papers[17] on the topic are especially worth noting because notable similarities seemingly exist between the OECD policy recommendations and the EU recommendation.[18]

---

[13] Micro-credentials do not substitute "traditional" education and formal degrees but are complementary to them; see Poliou (2024), p. 39.

[14] Then, at best, micro-credentials can be turned into "trusted skills currency", see Poliou (2024), pp. 16–17.

[15] For differing but overlapping definitions of micro-credentials, see, e.g. OECD (2021a), p. 2.

[16] According to Poliou (2024), pp. 8–9, "different types of credential issuers are growing faster than our ability to make sense of them". Thus, micro-credentials can be considered a market-driven phenomenon, which calls for shared standards on their content and quality. It should be also noted that the Council has already in 2012 published a recommendation (2012/C 398/01) on the validation of non-formal and informal learning.

[17] E.g. OECD (2023a, b).

[18] Previously, some commentators have highlighted the significance of the OECD's expertise in setting agendas for EU welfare and labour market policies; see Dostal (2004). According to Dostal (2004) on p. 455, the OECD's influence should not be generalised but analysed separately in each field of policy.

Most EU Member States are members of the OECD (Organisation for Economic Co-operation and Development), and the EU participates in the work of the OECD under its own mandate. However, the OECD policy recommendations are strictly non-binding upon the EU and its Member States. Nevertheless, the OECD papers seemingly provide useful insights into the topic in the EU law context because the EU recommendation and the OECD papers on micro-credentials focus on the same policy challenges.

In a key OECD paper regarding micro-credentials,[19] the EU CRMC is mentioned as the first thing in the introduction, where it is connected to similar policy endeavours taken in other regions, particularly the Asia-Pacific and North America. It is apparent that the core understanding of what is meant by micro-credentials and of the key elements of the required policies are shared beyond the EU and almost globally.[20] Although the main title of the OECD paper mentions "lifelong learning", the text only mentions it in passing. According to the paper, micro-credentials "enable modularisation and offer different learning options to learners in initial education while also supporting *lifelong learning*, which is seen as important in the context of ageing populations". The discussion revolves more around the term *employability*—how to enhance labour market participation through micro-credentials. This is obvious even in how the paper's purpose is described, namely seeking evidence on how micro-credentials can help enhance employability, widen pathways to higher education and promote social inclusion among disadvantaged learners and workers. All are, of course, different aspects of lifelong learning.

The OECD has highlighted the need to create a facilitating framework called a *micro-credential ecosystem* through designing public policies. According to the OECD's view, this can be achieved by developing policies that support training providers and learners; integrating micro-credentials into education, training and labour market systems; and ensuring cooperation among relevant stakeholders.[21] The key stakeholders of such a micro-credential ecosystem include learners, education and training providers, public authorities and the broader environment including employers, social partners and other relevant organisations.

According to the OECD, the measures needed to create an "ecosystem" for micro-credentials include regulations and guidelines, public funding, quality assurance mechanisms and information systems. Each type contains measures that can be classified as softer recommendations, like utilising pilot projects or as direct policy recommendations that would require legislative changes or/and decisions on public resources. One of the direct measures in public funding is adopting individual learning accounts.[22]

The OECD's work on micro-credentials illustrates how wide an array of policy measures and stakeholders are lurking behind the seemingly simple definition of

[19] See OECD (2023a).

[20] For various definitions, see European Commission (2020a), pp. 10–12.

[21] See OECD (2023b).

[22] OECD (2023b), p. 11.

"micro-credential". In the OECD papers, the focus is not on general educational goals but on speeding up the employability of workers and inducing economic growth. Thus, of the various groups and learner types, an efficient "ecosystem" of micro-credentials would be needed primarily for incentivising the training of *working-age adults*. The OECD papers also remind us that building a whole "ecosystem" for micro-credentials requires legislative changes and, thus, involvement from national parliaments. This is worth noting because the full harmonisation of Member States' legislation in the fields of employment and educational policies is not possible under the current TFEU articles.

## 2.2 EU Soft Law on Micro-credentials

The CRMC outlines the "European approach" to micro-credentials. Whether any meaningful differences exist between the OECD's approach and the "European approach" can be asked. Both seemingly focus on the same policy considerations—improving the employability of working-age adults—and the elements of "ecosystem" for micro-credentials have much resemblance. If anything, the "European approach" is a soft law approach; CRMC does not propose direct legislative changes to Member States' legislation because harmonising educational and employment legislation is outside current EU competence. In this sense, the CRMC has a more restricted scope than the OECD's recommendations.

The introduction of CRMC refers to TFEU Articles 149, 165, and 166, which are in the TFEU's employment and education sections. Even before CRMC was published, several EU legal documents, most importantly in *The European Pillar of Social Rights Action Plan* (2021), mentioned and endorsed micro-credentials. The Action Plan states that micro-credentials are an innovative instrument that can facilitate flexible learning pathways and support workers on their job or during professional transitions.[23]

CRMC's preamble summarises the acute challenges European businesses and employers face and provides an outline of the recommended policies on micro-credentials. According to Preamble 4, "An effective culture of lifelong learning is key to ensuring that everyone has the knowledge, skills and competences they need to thrive in society, the labour market and their personal lives". CRMC further highlights the need to build trust in micro-credentials among providers and beneficiaries and recommends a wide array of measures to be taken for this purpose. According to Preamble 6, "Despite their increasing use, there is no common definition of, or standards for, micro-credentials in Europe". Micro-credentials are linked to *individual learning accounts* in the CRMC section "delivering on the potential of micro-credentials", where Member States are called to integrate micro-credentials into employment policies and active labour market policies, "including training

[23] European Commission (2021), Sect. 3.2. "Skills and equality".

leading to micro-credentials in recognised training opportunities that may be linked to individual learning accounts, where they exist". These kinds of statements clarify that CRMC cannot be read as a standalone initiative but should be understood in the broader context of EU policy measures aiming to improve economic output through better employability.

Below is a brief section-by-section overview of CRMC that illustrates what kind of "ecosystem" the recommendation seeks to attain across the EU.

*Objectives.* CRMC links the use of micro-credentials to one of the headline targets of the European Pillar of Social Rights Action Plan—that 60 per cent of all adults participate in training every year. As can be expected, increased participation in *lifelong learning* is mentioned as one of CRMC's objectives.

*Scope.* CRMC clarifies that the EU's recommendations do not aim to disrupt existing education systems or undermine or replace existing national qualifications and degrees. Thus, CRMC readily recognises the limits of EU regulatory competence in educational and employment policies.

*Definitions.* CRMC includes important definitions that constitute the key aspects of the wider micro-credential "ecosystem". The nine definitions consist of the following: (a) micro-credential, (b) providers of micro-credentials, (c) learning settings, (d) formal learning, (e) non-formal learning, (f) informal learning, (g) portability, (h) stackability and (i) assessment. According to CRMC, micro-credentials are portable if they are portable between and within education and training sectors, in the labour market *and across countries*. Surprisingly, this is the only point that refers to micro-credentials' potential in improving preconditions for the EU-wide employment market.

*Definition and European standard elements to describe a micro-credential.* CRMC requests the Member States to adopt the formal definition of micro-credential along with the standard elements that CRMC describes as *mandatory*, plus European principles for designing and issuing micro-credentials. The annex to CRMC describes the standard elements and European principles.

*Development of the ecosystem for micro-credentials.* CRMC describes multiple actions that the Member States should take to support and promote the development of micro-credentials in formal, non-formal and informal settings. According to CRMC, the Member States should support the quality and transparency of micro-credentials by integrating them into national qualifications frameworks and systems. Notably, CRMC uses the same term "ecosystem", which is what the OECD papers use regarding micro-credentials. Even here, CRMC is careful in pointing out that national authorities or institutions *in line with national circumstances* make such decisions, once again recognising the limits of formal EU competencies.

*Delivering on the potential of micro-credentials.* CRMC encourages Member States to integrate micro-credentials into education and training systems and skills policies, employment policies and active labour market policies. Micro-credentials are assigned a role in addressing skills mismatches and the upskilling and reskilling of workers in the context of digital and green transitions.

## 2.3 Standard-setting Functions of CRMC

Despite being soft law, CRMC formalises EU policies on micro-credentials: It explains why it is elevated in the EU political agenda, how it relates to other policy areas and what kind of outcomes the EU seeks to accomplish. Furthermore, CRMC extensively describes what kind of practical steps should be taken in the Member States to create an efficient "ecosystem" for micro-credentials. Many parts of the CRMC's text can be characterised as informative rather than juridical.[24] Some parts of CRMC highlight the need to consider local circumstances and that the concrete decisions are left at the discretion of local authorities in each Member State.[25] However, some parts of CRMC seek to set standards that can be assumed and taken into use across the EU.[26]

CRMC lists nine key definitions that are elemental for specifying what micro-credentials are, what features they have, and the contexts in which they are applicable. Even more important is the list (in Annex I) of the so-called mandatory elements of micro-credentials.[27] The list obviously aims to create a generally applicable conception of how small-scale learning is recognised and transformed as a formal micro-credential. This kind of shared understanding of micro-credentials is essential for their use in different contexts. Although standardisation increases stakeholders' trust in the usefulness of micro-credentials, standardisation makes it possible to expect that a variety of stakeholders mutually recognise micro-credentials.[28] The standardisation that CRMC seeks to accomplish partly arises from the ten European principles for designing and issuing micro-credentials (Annex II). The sixth principle states that the competent authorities recognise the micro-credentials based on the information provided according to the European standard elements and the principles for designing and issuing micro-credentials. It further states that when formal education providers issue micro-credentials, they are recognised based on standard recognition procedures used in recognising foreign qualifications and learning periods abroad.

[24] The CRMC does not use "rights-based" language. In comparison, using rights-based language in the European Pillar of Social Rights—also a soft law instrument—has increased the instrument's relevance and legitimacy. See Aranquiz (2018), pp. 341–363.

[25] According to Wheelahan and Moodie (2021), pp. 212–228, international policy flows around micro-credentials have been "embedded within national contexts".

[26] In practice, the need to formulate common definitions in the EU and beyond has arisen from the increased relevance of small-scale learning. See Berkling et al. (2023), p. 163.

[27] The full list of mandatory elements includes the following: Identification of the learner, Title of the micro-credential, Country(ies)/Region(s) of the issuer, Awarding body(ies), Date of issuing, Learning outcomes, Notional workload needed to achieve the learning outcomes (in ECTS credits, where possible), Level (and cycle, if applicable) of the learning experience leading to the micro-credential (EQF, QF-EHEA), if applicable, Type of assessment, Form of participation in the learning activity, and Type of quality assurance used to underpin the micro-credential.

[28] See, e.g. the European Commission (2024), where the problem of successful implementation of micro-credentials is framed as a question of trust on micro-credentials and between their multiple stakeholders.

The "hardest edge" of CRMC is obviously found in the common standards set for the use and recognition of micro-credentials. CRMC does not give rise to legal obligations that would guarantee that an efficient "ecosystem" of micro-credentials is set up in all Member States. CRMC notes that the standards should be followed "where appropriate", thus highlighting the practical differences between the educational and employment systems of the Member States. However, there are practical reasons to expect that when an "ecosystem" of micro-credentials is designed and taken into use in some Member State, it will be done along the standards set in CRMC and not by following some totally different path.[29]

Although CRMC is a non-binding soft law instrument, it may still function reasonably well in benchmarking the common standards for micro-credentials. This part of CRMC can be expected to work like many other types of soft law standards: If the standards are commonly known and reasonable, stakeholders should have strong practical reasons to follow them, irrespective of whether a legal obligation to do so exists.

However, it can be asked how sufficient a shared understanding of the key definitions and key operating standards is for constructing the whole "ecosystem" for micro-credentials in a roughly harmonised format across the EU. Notably, compared to the rather extensive list of measures that the OECD considers necessary for building an efficient "ecosystem" for micro-credentials,[30] the scope of CRMC is more restricted. The difference is naturally explained by the fact that enforcing changes to the Member States' existing educational systems and to Member States' relevant legislation is not within the EU powers.

CRMC is also vague regarding public funding and financial incentives because even these go beyond the EU's competencies. However, the OECD papers mention *individual learning accounts* as a source of public funding for micro-credentials. CRCM endorses these accounts, which are subject to another EU recommendation that will be analysed next.

---

[29] The idea that although following soft regulations is not obligatory, if they are followed, they should be followed in full has been voiced in other types of non-binding rules. For instance, the OECD's minimum tax rules (Pillar 2) follow a *common approach*: Countries have no obligation to use the OECD's minimum tax rules, but if they do, the rules must be implemented in the format the OECD has designed. See OECD (2021b). The common approach is irrelevant in the EU law context because Pillar 2 -rules have been incorporated into Council Directive (EU) 2022/2523 as of 14 December 2022 on ensuring a global minimum level of taxation for multinational enterprise groups and large-scale domestic groups in the Union. Thus, EU Member States cannot opt out of Pillar 2 rules.

[30] The OECD has conducted a detailed per-country analysis with recommendations; see, e.g. OECD (2020).

# 3 Individual Learning Accounts

## *3.1 Individual Learning Accounts and Lifelong Learning*

According to Council recommendation 2022/C/243/03 on individual learning accounts (hereafter CRILA),[31] an individual learning account is "a delivery mode for individual training entitlement that allows individuals to accumulate and preserve their entitlements over time, for whichever eligible training, guidance or validation opportunity they deem most useful and whenever they want to, in line with national rules".

CRILA emphasises the individual learner's viewpoint because it is further clarified that individual learning accounts provide *entitlements* "for which the individual has full ownership".[32] Also, freedom of choice is emphasised, as these accounts are expected to provide individuals access to necessary resources to acquire training "they deem most useful and whenever they want to". In this sense, individual learning accounts seek to incentivise learning and remove real-life obstacles for acquiring additional training at a very concrete level. However, individuals can only use these entitlements if sufficient private or public funding backs the system.

In comparison, the OECD policy papers use a somewhat broader concept of *individual learning schemes*, defined as training schemes attached to individuals and implemented by public authorities by mobilising public resources. Individual learning accounts are publicly financed, and although understood as individual entitlements, they are called "virtual" because the required resources are only mobilised when the training is undertaken.[33] The EU's recommendation and the OECD policy papers essentially describe the same system, be they called individual learning accounts or schemes. Thus, even here, the OECD materials may provide useful insights into how individual learning accounts relate to employment policy and lifelong learning in the context of EU law.

According to the OECD policy papers, individual learning schemes aim to increase individual educational autonomy and strengthen individuals' ownership of their choices and decisions regarding training. As such, their key focus is on workers and not on employers. Individual learning schemes can be expected to benefit especially those who do not have good access to training, such as low-skilled and low-income individuals, and, e.g. individuals employed in small firms or with non-standard (or part-time) employment contracts. At a more general level, individual learning schemes improve the employability of individuals by supporting necessary professional transitions and facilitating training that fits one's personal development

[31] Paragraph 4 also contains definitions of individual training entitlement, transferability and enabling framework.

[32] Individual learning accounts allocate public funding for upskilling and reskilling directly to the person receiving the qualifications, e.g. as micro-credentials, unlike funding models where the funding goes to training providers. See OECD (2023b), p. 20.

[33] OECD (2019), p. 9.

but which their employers may be reluctant to provide, e.g. because of fears that employees may leave after acquiring better qualifications.[34]

The potential benefits of individual learning accounts in promoting lifelong learning are rather obvious. An educational system that provides sufficient resources to acquire training when needed and facilitates more choices for individuals to obtain training that suits their circumstances is clearly preferred over a system without these features. Because individual learning accounts are not tied to certain predefined employment relationships or employment status, they can support and incentivise participation in training throughout working life. This aligns with the general goal of lifelong learning and the idea that upskilling and reskilling are necessary for successful transitions in the labour market, e.g. due to digitalisation.

However, the choices made in the design and at the level of practical implementation of individual learning accounts have much to do with whose learning they incentivise, what kind of learning they incentivise and what kind of resources back the system.[35] If the system covers a wide selection of individuals and does not set specific limitations of what kind of training the entitlement can be used for, it is mostly *neutral* towards individual choices. Conversely, if the system allows the entitlement to be strictly used for certain purposes, like efficient professional transformation, or limits its availability based on workforce demand in the relevant employment markets, it would be more *steering* regarding individual choices.

The OECD review of existing individual learning schemes has revealed, not unexpectedly, notable differences regarding coverage, financing and governance and what kind of training the individuals can take.[36] Notably, a system of individual learning accounts is mainly for pooling and allocating resources, but it is a different question what kind of training is generally available in the educational system or in the relevant "training markets" in which the individual is participating. It is unreasonable to expect that setting up individual learning accounts would guarantee that individuals gain access to just the kind of training that fits their specific needs. However, many individuals have the possibilities and incentives to acquire training even without a specific system of individual learning accounts. Thus, setting up a system of individual learning accounts does not guarantee that the training system functions fluently. In this sense, an individual learning account is just a "delivery mode", as the formal EU definition describes above, with resource allocation as its single most important feature. Thus, sufficient funding can be considered the existential question of individual learning accounts in all their variations. This sets some limitations on how efficiently individual learning accounts can be coordinated at the EU level because the EU does not have the legal competence to make binding decisions on allocating public resources.[37]

---

[34] OECD (2019), pp. 10–11.

[35] A further question is who ultimately benefits from the ILAs. See, e.g. Corazza and Filipucci (2022).

[36] OECD (2019), pp. 12–23.

[37] A system of individual learning accounts that is fully tax-financed is more redistributive than a system requiring contributions from the individual or other stakeholders. Because tax-financed

### 3.2 EU Soft Law on Individual Learning Accounts

The introduction of CRILA refers to TFEU Article 149. According to Article 149, the Council may support Member States in the field of employment through initiatives aimed at developing exchanges of information and best practices, but the measures shall not include the harmonisation of the laws and regulations of the Member States. Notably, CRILA does not refer to TFEU articles regarding education policy. Like micro-credentials, individual learning accounts are mentioned in several EU documents, e.g. in the European Skills Agenda.[38]

CRILA recommends that all Member States set up a system of individual learning accounts. CRILA outlines the features the systems should have. Supporting all working-age adults' access to training irrespective of their status and increasing incentives and motivation to seek training is the most important objective of such a system. The recommendation encourages Member States to set up individual learning accounts for every working-age adult legally residing in a Member States. Each account should provide adequate annual entitlement that can be accumulated and used over a longer period. Furthermore, those individuals most in need of reskilling and upskilling should receive additional entitlements.[39]

CRILA focuses on working-age adults and, thus, on improving their employability through continuous learning. CRILA does not elaborate on how this high-level objective should be attained in practice. CRILA does not provide detailed recommendations on what kind of training should be provided or how the resources should be allocated. Thus, CRILA is unambiguous in recommending that Member States should implement a system of individual learning accounts but not so much regarding the practical details of implementation. However, CRILA promises Commission-led EU support for the Member States in designing appropriate implementation measures.[40]

CRILA recommends that Member States should introduce awareness-raising campaigns with stakeholders with a special focus on those most in need of upskilling and reskilling. According to CRILA, individual learning accounts should be complemented with an enabling framework that provides career guidance and validation services, a national registry and a digital portal. The Member States should promote paid training leave so that individuals can use their training entitlements during working hours. This section of CRILA makes a reference to micro-credentials and CRMC.[41]

---

systems operate under budgetary constraints, they may be less predictable in the long run. See OECD (2019), p. 8.

[38] European Commission (2020b).

[39] See especially CRILA Sect. "Objectives" and "Individual learning accounts".

[40] See CRILA Sect. "Union support".

[41] "Where appropriate, Member States are recommended to encourage providers of formal and non-formal learning opportunities to develop and widen their offer based on identified needs, including, for example, by providing micro-credentials, in line with the Recommendation on

Regarding funding the individual learning accounts, CRILA just notes that Member States should provide adequate and sustainable funding for this purpose. The most concrete measure is an invitation to the Member States to take maximum advantage of available EU resources, e.g. the European Social Fund Plus, the European Regional Development Fund, the Just Transition Fund, the Recovery and Resilience Facility and the Technical Support Instrument.[42]

## 3.3 Standard-setting Functions of CRILA

The most important function of CRILA is seemingly to generally endorse the idea and conception of individual learning accounts at the EU level and introduce a coherent view of what individual learning accounts are. CRILA also documents the various aspects that should be considered in their practical implementation. CRILA does not provide clear-cut common standards of the features that individual learning accounts should contain, but most of the practical details are left to the discretion of Member States. This is already apparent from the formal definition that states that individuals should have freedom of choice regarding how the entitlements are used, but the choices are to be made "in line with the national rules".

CRILA is basically silent on the most important questions for all individual learning entitlements: What amount of funding should be considered adequate, and where should the funding of such a system be derived in practice? Setting up individual learning accounts and allocating resources should be considered an investment in education and skills, not merely a cost,[43] but this fact does not explain why individual learning accounts should be given priority among such investments. In terms of standard setting, vagueness in questions of funding is clearly CRILA's weakest point—even if it is noted that the EU's competence in these matters is limited.

In conclusion, CRILA seemingly lacks most of "hard" standard-setting functions recognised in Section 2 for EU soft law on micro-credentials. In this sense, CRILA can be considered a rather soft steering instrument, although it provides clear objectives, definitions and structure for individual learning accounts.

micro-credentials for lifelong learning and employability, and through the use of Union and national competence frameworks."

[42] See CRILA Sect. "Funding".

[43] European Commission (2025), p. 16.

# 4 Micro-credentials and Individual Learning Accounts in the Context of the EU Employment Policy

## *4.1 Soft Law Impacts in National Systems*

Introductions of CRMC and CRILA refer to various aspects of the EU employment policy. It is rather obvious why micro-credentials and individual learning accounts can be expected to advance these policy goals—not necessarily as key measures but at least as part of the overall policy coordination package. Micro-credentials and individual learning accounts are regulatory innovations which the Member States have not yet fully assumed in their domestic systems.[44] The measures cover working-age individuals with various skill levels within and outside the employment market. Both provide incentives to acquire the necessary training and facilitate more transparent recognition of the acquired skills and competencies. Thus, both help support better employability of individuals, which can be expected to support higher employment rates in national employment markets and, thus, across the EU.

In the current framework, the practical standard-setting impact of CRILA and CRMC should not be over- or underestimated. It has been noted above that the OECD has recently endorsed micro-credentials and individual learning accounts in several policy papers and that CRMC and CRILA seemingly contain many similarities with the OECD recommendations on the same topics. The overlaps between the OECD's and EU's recommendations are worth mentioning here because, for some reason, CRMC and CRILA do not explicitly mention the OECD's recommendations. CRMS and CRILA should not be studied as isolated EU efforts but as variations on a theme that is discussed almost globally. The inherent links between the OECD's and EU's employment policy recommendations have sometimes raised critical comments because the OECD's influence is seen as further diminishing the lacking social dimension of the EU's policies.[45] This kind of critical analysis may be necessary even for the EU's lifelong learning policies,[46] but CRMC and CRILA seem too technical and limited in scope to merit such discussion further here.[47]

---

[44] According to the European Commission (2025), pp. 10–11, a key challenge regarding micro-credentials is to increase their use in business recruitment and career promotion. Although many countries are piloting individual learning accounts, the Commission sees that more effort is needed in the coming years.

[45] See, e.g. Dostal (2004).

[46] Dehmel warned in 2006 that "Lifelong learning seems to be the slogan the EU chose to summarize, justify, publicize, and popularize its values and policies not only in the field of education and training, but also in other areas"; see Dehmel (2006), pp. 49–62.

[47] Ljungqvist and Sonesson (2023), pp. 153–188, have nevertheless approached CRMC with tools of critical discourse analysis. According to them, CRMC uses a set of discursive techniques that depoliticise issues of social inequality and prevent disagreement over educational issues that are fundamentally political.

CRMC makes several references to individual learning accounts, and CRILA makes references to micro-credentials.[48] Thus, CRMC and CRILA implicitly assume that the two systems coexist, although they operate at different levels of the educational system. Whereas micro-credentials are a way of recognising small-scale training, individual learning accounts are a way to allocate resources for individuals—as personal entitlements—to acquire the training to be recognised. It seems obvious that a system of micro-credentials can be successfully implemented as a standalone system, i.e. without setting up individual learning accounts. However, it is less clear whether setting up individual learning accounts as a standalone system would be at all reasonable. Individual learning accounts are more suitable for supporting small-scale training, unlike training with more extensive content and timeframe. In this sense, a system of individual learning accounts can be considered complementary to a system of micro-credentials, which is, in practice, the more important part.

Micro-credentials also stand out when the two recommendations are compared from the viewpoint of soft law policy coordination. CRILA successfully outlines the objectives and key features of individual learning accounts but remains silent on most of the practical details of implementation. Much is left to the discretion of each Member State where the practical decisions are taken. In comparison, CRMC is more elaborate in its norm-setting, especially in providing a standard EU definition of a micro-credential, its constitutive features and how the whole "ecosystem" of micro-credentials should be set up.

Because CRILA and CRMC are soft law instruments and, therefore, legally non-binding upon the Member States, they do not harmonise applicable rules on individual learning accounts and micro-credentials across the EU. This means basically two things. First, Member States do not have an unambiguous legal obligation to take individual learning accounts or micro-credentials in their national educational systems. Second, if a Member State decides to set up a system of micro-credentials, with or without individual learning accounts, it has much freedom in deciding how it is done in practice.

CRILA and CRMC contain several references to country-specific practices, needs and circumstances, thus conceding that significant differences exist between the Member States and that few "one size fits all" solutions could be readily implemented across the EU. The "soft" legal status of CRILA and CRMC has little to do with this feature of EU law. Differences between Member States' domestic legislation regarding education and the allocation of public resources set obvious limitations to what can be accomplished through EU coordination in this field. The practical challenges caused by such differences go far beyond the details of micro-credentials and individual learning accounts. In this way, CRILA and CRMC are probably capable of producing much of the regulatory coordination that can be realistically achieved at the EU level, considering the current regulatory framework.

---

[48] Micro-credentials and individual learning accounts are frequently mentioned together also in the OECD policy papers (2023b), p. 11, where individual learning accounts are listed as a method of public funding in the wider "ecosystem" of micro-credentials.

## 4.2 *Soft Law Impacts at the Level of EU-wide Educational and Employment Markets*

It also seems possible that (in the long run) the soft law impact of especially CRMC can be amplified by other, more binding norms and principles of EU law, especially those related to non-discrimination within the EU Single Market.[49] Without harmonised rules (like directives), market-building functions of EU law are usually taken up by non-discrimination case law.[50] Because CRMC contains a uniform definition of what micro-credentials are, the CRMC definition may evolve as a benchmark for establishing rules of interpretation on when domestically acquired training and training acquired in other Member States must be treated with equal footing. If training acquired abroad follows the same (CRMC-based) standards as domestic training, justifying the difference in treatment, e.g. in CJEU, should be difficult.[51] Thus, utilising (non-binding) CRMC definition of micro-credentials for purely domestic purposes may, in practice, set limitations to a Member-State's right to disregard comparable small-scale learning that has not been acquired domestically but in some other Member State.

Development towards a well-functioning (cross-border) employment market in the EU has been slow, providing the inevitable background to this kind of speculation. Currently, it seems likely there is still a long way to go, and there will be more small steps than giant leaps awaiting.[52] Be that as it may, for those interested in the EU employment policy and developing EU labour law, soft law instruments like CRILA and CRMC are certainly worth noting and analysing. The impact of two recommendations across the EU is unveiled gradually, and the future path of developments is not yet known.[53] Enhanced coordination in training of working-age

---

[49] TFEU Art. 45 stipulates that freedom of movement for workers entails abolishing any discrimination based on nationality between workers of the Member States regarding employment, remuneration and other conditions of work and employment. However, CJEU case law has not even mentioned the terms micro-credential and individual learning accounts.

[50] According to Andone and Coman-Kund (2022), p. 23, the "hardening" of soft law instruments means the capacity to produce (not negligible) legal and practical effects, despite soft law being legally non-binding.

[51] The CJEU's settled interpretation is that "the freedom of movement of persons would not be fully realized if the Member States were able to refuse to grant the benefit of the provisions of EU law to those of their nationals who had taken advantage of its provisions to acquire vocational qualifications in a Member State other than that of which they were nationals. The same consideration applies where a national of a Member State has obtained in another Member State a university qualification which supplements his basic education and training and of which he intends to make use after he returns to his country of origin." See, e.g. C-298/14 Brouillard, para 27.

[52] New initiatives may be coming soon. Among other things, the EU Commission is planning a legislative proposal to improve the acceptance of skills and qualifications to enhance the cross-border mobility of workers. See European Commission (2025), pp. 12–13. The Commission's Union of Skills document is ambitious and clarifies the EU strategy on upskilling and reskilling, providing a renewed policy framework and enhanced support for CRMC and CRILA.

[53] See, e.g. Sarcevic (2024), pp. 181–186.

adults can be considered one of the crucial ingredients for attaining functioning EU employment markets. In some cases, individuals might first need access to training arrangements that are recognised across the EU—such as the "ecosystem" of micro-credentials—before they have realistic opportunities to enter employment markets somewhere outside their current home country.[54]

## 5 Concluding Remarks

Lifelong learning is necessary for individuals and the markets. The changing digitalised economy requires employees with the abilities and possibilities to reskill and upskill during their careers as needed. Beyond that, training must be accessible even to those between jobs and those in a disadvantaged position in the employment market. Ideally, workers should be able to relocate abroad within the EU to seek employment matching their skill level and have their training recognised in the country of destination, putting them on equal footing with local domestic training.

The foregoing analysis has demonstrated that the EU's recommendations on individual learning accounts (CRILA) and micro-credentials (CRMC) have links to all the aspects of lifelong learning summarised above. Thus, it is not an overstatement to say that much of what lifelong learning should be taken to mean in the context of the EU employment policy can be read from the introduction and key provisions of these two recommendations.

Because the two recommendations are non-binding soft law instruments, they do not create enforceable legal rights for EU individuals. This seemingly underlines the recommendations' function as practical tools for promoting EU employment policy goals and, thus, for promoting lifelong learning, especially at the level of markets and to attain economic goals.[55] Similarities and overlaps with the OECD's materials on the same topic provide further evidence of this.

Some parts of CRILA and CRMC describe (somewhat idealistic) high-level goals for designing educational and employment systems for the Member States that go way beyond the EU's current regulatory competence. Nevertheless, in the foregoing analysis, identifying certain "hard edges", i.e. features that can be expected to have a meaningful standard-setting impact across the EU, was possible. The more important of the two recommendations is, arguably, CRMC, which lays down the detailed framework for the whole "ecosystem" of micro-credentials.

The EU's official endorsement of individual learning accounts and micro-credentials as part of its employment policy measures provides an important starting

[54] The relocation of workers can be understood as characteristic of so-called flexible employment markets. According to Casano (2016), p. 500, transferable skills may offset lower employment protection, but this trade-off only works if the acquired skills are validated and made transferable. An ecosystem of micro-credentials obviously facilitates this kind of trade-off.

[55] Generally, the EU approach to lifelong learning has been regarded as economistic and instrumental, unlike more humanistic views of lifelong education. Spolar and Holford (2014), pp. 38–39.

point for discussions and analyses regarding the national implementation of these systems. As noted, the Member States should be interested in developing individual learning accounts and micro-credentials for many reasons, even without any EU guidance. Furthermore, if the Member States decide to spend resources on these systems, there should not be too many convincing reasons, why they would not take CRILA and CRMC seriously and treat them as important and relevant benchmarks for implementing and governing the national systems. In the current regulatory framework, EU soft law coordination and measures like CRILA and CRMC may be the best available tools for pushing the idea of lifelong learning forward at the EU level. Thus, when CRILA and CRMC are analysed in the context of the EU employment policy and, as such, at the interface of EU law and national legal systems, their status as "merely" non-binding soft law does not feel like a fundamentally problematic feature.

Most of the decisions regarding the practical implementation of micro-credentials and individual learning accounts cannot be taken elsewhere than in each Member-State, considering local legislation and circumstances and features of local educational and employment markets. The level of national systems is where the optimal design and impacts of these systems should ultimately be evaluated and analysed. However, in this kind of analysis, the potential of EU soft law standard-setting should not be underestimated: CRMC and CRILA may provide useful insights on future developments when micro-credentials and individual learning accounts are analysed in each national law context. It is unclear how far targeted soft law instruments like CRMC and CRILA can advance the creation of EU-wide educational and employment markets. This dimension is worth noting in future analyses because the Commission has recently highlighted the need to increase EU-level actions at many levels to support "balanced cross-border mobility and free movement of knowledge and skills".[56]

## References

Andone C, Coman-Kund F (2022) Persuasive rather than 'binding' EU soft law? An argumentative perspective on the European Commission's soft law instruments in times of crisis. Theory Pract Legis 10(1):22–47

Aranquiz A (2018) Social mainstreaming through the European pillar of social rights: Shielding 'the social' from 'the economic' in EU policymaking. Eur J Soc Secur 20(4):341–363

Berkling K, Hänisch T, Schütz F (2023) Transforming CS Curricula into EU-standardized micro-credentials. Athens J Technol Eng 10(3):161–174

Casano L (2016) The future of European labour law and the right to employability. Which role for the validation of non-formal and informal learning? Eur Labour Law J 7(3):498–519

Corazza E, Filipucci F (2022) Who profits from training subsidies – evidence from a french individual learning account. Paris School of Economics Working Paper 2022-02

[56] European Commission (2025), p. 12.

Dehmel A (2006) Making a European area of lifelong learning a reality? Some critical reflections on the European Union's lifelong learning policies. Comp Educ 42(1):49–62
Dostal J (2004) Campaigning on expertise: how the OECD framed EU welfare and labour market policies – and why success could trigger failure. J Eur Public Policy 11(3):440–460
European Commission (2020a) Annex 1: A European approach to micro-credentials. Background paper for the first meeting of the consultation group on micro-credentials. Publications Office of the European Union, Luxembourg
European Commission (2020b) European Skills Agenda for sustainable competitiveness, social fairness and resilience. COM(2020) 274 final
European Commission (2021) The European Pillar of Social Rights Action Plan. COM(2021) 102 final
European Commission (2022) Towards a green, digital and resilient economy: our European Growth Model. COM(2022) 83 final
European Commission (2024) Building trust in micro-credentials for improving employability. Synthesis Report from the Peer Learning Activity 28-29 May 2024. Publications Office of the European Union, Luxembourg
European Commission (2025) The Union of Skills. Communication from the Commission to the European Parliament, the European Council, the Council, the European Economic and Social Committee and the Committee of the Regions. COM(2025) 90 final
Hofman A (2021) Types of EU soft law and their national impact. In: Eliantonio M, Korkea-aho E, Stefan O (eds) EU soft law in the member states. Theoretical findings and empirical evidence. Hart Publishing, Oxford, pp 39–58
Ljungqvist M, Sonesson A (2023) All that glitters is not gold: the depoliticization of social inequality in European education policy on 'microcredentials'. J Crit Educ Policy Stud 21(3):153–188
OECD (2019) Individual learning accounts: panacea or Pandora's box? OECD Publishing, Paris
OECD (2020) Continuous learning in working life in Finland, Getting Skills Right. OECD Publishing, Paris
OECD (2021a) "Micro-credential innovations in higher education: who, what and why? OECD Education Policy Perspectives No. 39
OECD (2021b) Statement on a two-pillar solution to address the tax challenges arising from the digitalisation of the economy, 8 October 2021
OECD (2023a) Micro-credentials for lifelong learning and employability: uses and possibilities. OECD Education Policy Perspectives No. 66
OECD (2023b) Public policies for effective micro-credential learning. OECD Education Policy Perspectives No. 85
Poliou A (2024) Exploring the emergence of microcredentials in vocational education and training (VET). Cedefop Working paper series No 22/June 2024. Publications Office of the European Union, Luxembourg
Sarcevic I (2024) A New Agenda on micro-credentials: filling the gaps in the European approach. J Learn Dev 11(1):181–186
Spolar VAM, Holford J (2014) Adult learning: from the margins to the mainstream. In: Milana M, Holford J (eds) Adult education policy and the European Union. Sense Publishers, pp 35–50
Weiss M (2017) European employment policies: a critical analysis of the legal framework. Eur Labour Law J 8(2):111–121
Wheelahan L, Moodie G (2021) Analysing micro-credentials in higher education: a Bernsteinian analysis. J Curric Stud 53(2):212–228

**Matti Urpilainen** (LL.D., Docent in Tax Law) is university lecturer of law at Tampere University, Finland, and author of more than 90 academic publications. His main research interest is on topics that surpass the narrow legal dogmatic view and that are linked to evolving state sovereignty and Europeanisation of the legal system.

# Apprenticeship in Europe: A Learning Hybrid Model Between Education and Work

## The Integration of Training and Employment Between Regulation, Opportunities, and Risks

**Giorgio Impellizzieri**

## 1 Introduction

Apprenticeship is one of the legal institutions that most effectively illustrate the interactions between training and work, providing a unique legal framework in which training rights and obligations are intertwined within the employer–employee relationship.

Its peculiarity lies in the fact that it integrates the learning process within labour law, highlighting structural tensions that arise when training becomes an integral part of the employment relationship. This centrality makes apprenticeship a privileged observation point for studying the dynamics between learning, labour law, employment, and labour market regulation.[1]

Traditionally, apprenticeship has been a key component of lifelong learning policies, primarily facilitating the transition from school to work for young individuals at the outset of their careers.[2] However, there is a growing recognition of its potential to serve as a valuable instrument for adult learning and upskilling throughout one's working life.[3] The increasing recognition of its role in the labour market is reflected in recent European initiatives, such as the 2018 Council Recommendation on a European Framework for Quality and Effective Apprenticeships, and the 2024

[1] See especially in this volume Murto J, Lifelong Learning and Labour Law—Mapping the new Phenomenon in the Systematics of Labour Law.

[2] OECD (2000).

[3] Cedefop (2019).

G. Impellizzieri (✉)
University of Modena and Reggio Emilia, Department of Economics "Marco Biagi", Modena, Italy
e-mail: giorgio.impellizzieri@unimore.it



J. Murto, V. Franca (eds.), *Labour Law and Lifelong Learning*,
https://doi.org/10.1007/978-3-032-11035-0_6

Proposal for a Directive on improving working conditions in traineeships, which aims to ensure fair conditions and training quality across Member States.

To fully understand the current role of apprenticeship, it is essential to consider its historical evolution, as its functions and legal nature have significantly changed over time. Originally, apprenticeship was the forerunner of the employment contract.[4] In the system of medieval guilds, which flourished between the twelfth and eighteenth centuries, it was the predominant legal and social mechanism that regulated work carried out under the supervision of a master.[5] The primary purpose of the apprenticeship contract was not the work carried out by the apprentice, but the transmission of knowledge and technical skills.[6] A young person was placed alongside a master to learn the secrets of a trade or an art, establishing a relationship that, while involving a form of 'formal' subordination, was primarily aimed at education and learning.[7] In fact, the apprentice did not receive any payment; on the contrary, he was often required to pay the master a sum of money as compensation for the teaching received.[8]

With the advent of the capitalist production system, apprenticeship underwent a profound transformation. The disappearance of artisan workshops, which guaranteed a high level of professionalism and direct control over the quality standards of the training process, led to a redefinition of the economic and social functions of the institution. Mass production, the introduction of machinery and the spread of low added-value work activities stripped apprenticeship of its original essence, reducing it to a tool for quantitatively regulating the matching of labour supply and demand. As a result, apprenticeship increasingly ceased to be a system for the transmission of knowledge and instead came to be seen, in many cases, as a form of low-cost employment relationship.[9]

From the late nineteenth century onwards, the first trade unions showed strong hostility towards the figure of the apprentice, fearing that this could take opportunities away from skilled workers and encourage a race to the bottom on wages.[10] On the other hand, employer associations were keen to maintain control over labour market dynamics and often resisted the monopolistic tendencies of trade unions, viewing apprenticeship as a means to ensure a study supply of trained workers while preserving flexibility in workforce management.[11]

Even then, some conceptual tensions were emerging that still characterise the debate on apprenticeship today. What is the main purpose of an apprenticeship: to train a young person, to teach a trade or simply to provide entry-level work for an

---

[4] Deakin (2001).

[5] De Munck (2011).

[6] Epstein and Prack (2009).

[7] De la Croix et al. (2016).

[8] Ogilvie (2020).

[9] Dunlop (1912).

[10] Webb and Webb (1896).

[11] Sikes (1894).

unemployed person?[12] What is the minimum training content that differentiates it from an ordinary employment contract?[13] Should the apprentice be guaranteed all the protections recognised for subordinate workers?[14] These questions reflect the challenges of integrating training and work that remain in the current European labour market. Apprenticeships, by their very nature, emphasise these issues, since training is not an accessory element, but the central object of the contract.

Throughout the twentieth century, apprenticeship gradually adapted to the changing to the changing economic and social landscape.[15] As industrial economies matured and education systems expanded, many countries introduced legal frameworks to regulate apprenticeship, aiming to balance its dual function as both an educational pathway and a form of employment. Public institutions, vocational training centres, and employers' association became increasingly involved in structuring apprenticeships, ensuring minimum training requirements and labour protections. At the same time, labour law has progressively expanded its focus on apprenticeship, addressing issues related to the rights of apprentices, working conditions, and the balance between training and productive work.[16] In parallel, international organisations, including the ILO and EU, started promoting quality standards to prevent the misuse of apprenticeship contracts as a source of cheap labour.[17]

This chapter sets out to investigate the current configuration of apprenticeships within European legal systems, with a view to assessing the capacity of EU regulation to mediate the inherent tension between their educational purpose and their character as employment relationships. It develops two interrelated research questions: First, how do national legal frameworks regulate apprenticeship schemes, and what principal challenges do they raise from a labour law perspective? Second, to what extent can EU legal instruments effectively address these challenges while safeguarding the pedagogical function of apprenticeships? These questions will be examined through a comparative analysis of national regulatory models,[18] an inquiry into the scope and limits of EU competences in this domain,[19] and a critical assessment of recent European initiatives, notably the 2018 Council Recommendation on Quality and Effective Apprenticeships,[20] and the 2024 Proposal for a Directive on improving working conditions in traineeships.[21]

---

[12] Bray (1909).

[13] Bemis (1891).

[14] Alexander (1921).

[15] Ainley and Rainbird (1999).

[16] Supiot (2001).

[17] McCann and Stewart (2024).

[18] See Sect. 2.

[19] See Sect. 3.

[20] See Sect. 4.

[21] See Sect. 5.

## 2 Apprenticeships Schemes in Europe: Heterogeneous Models and Cross-cutting Risks

In Europe, apprenticeship systems take various forms, shaped by the historical, economic, and cultural specificities of individual member states. Although the European Union has promoted the recognition of common standards to ensure quality apprenticeships and enhance young workers' mobility, significant differences persist among the models adopted.

### *2.1 Models of Apprenticeships*

Over time, several attempts have been made to classify apprenticeship models Ryan (2012), both at the institutional-governmental level and in academic literature (Deissinger 2008, Deissinger & Gonon 2021, Nyen & Tonder 2020, Veillard 2022). Recently, a study by the European Commission identified three main categories based on the regulatory framework governing apprenticeships in different member states.[22]

The first group includes countries where apprenticeships are regulated by specific legislation, with laws exclusively dedicated to this contractual arrangement. Examples include Belgium (Flemish and German-speaking communities), Denmark, and Ireland, where apprenticeship is governed by sectoral laws such as Denmark's *1937 Apprenticeship Act* and Ireland's *Apprenticeship Bill*. The second group consists of countries where apprenticeships are fully integrated into vocational training or education legislation, such as the Netherlands, Croatia, and Hungary. Here, apprenticeships are primarily conceived as educational pathways rather than employment relationships. The third group comprises countries where apprenticeships are regulated by a combination of education, vocational training, and labour laws. In Bulgaria, Lithuania, and Luxembourg, for instance, apprenticeship contracts are regulated separately within national labour codes, underscoring their occupational nature.[23]

Another classification was proposed by Cedefop,[24] which distinguishes between apprenticeships as a structured vocational education and training (VET) system, apprenticeships as a mode of VET delivery, and hybrid apprenticeship systems. In the first case, apprenticeships are fully embedded within the vocational education system and led to nationally recognised qualifications (e.g., Germany, Denmark, and Ireland). In the second case, apprenticeships serve as an alternative training pathway, often characterised by greater flexibility in delivery (e.g., Finland, Hungary, and the United Kingdom). Finally, in the third case, apprenticeships function as a social integration tool for disadvantaged groups or as a second-chance

[22] European Commission (2021).

[23] Ibid.

[24] Cedefop (2018).

route for young people who have not completed their education (e.g., Greece, Cyprus, and Belgium's French-speaking community).

Beyond these institutional classifications, the academic literature has proposed several theoretical frameworks for analysing apprenticeship systems. Within the field of political economy, the "skill formation regimes model" distinguishes between *state-centred* regimes, where the state plays a central role in regulating apprenticeships (e.g., France); *liberal regimes*, characterised by low public regulation and a high degree of employer discretion (e.g., the United Kingdom); *segmentalist regimes*, where companies manage training autonomously without a strong public coordination framework (e.g., Japan); and *collective regimes*, where apprenticeship regulation results from a balance between state intervention and social partners' involvement (e.g., Germany and Austria).[25]

In the vocational education and training (VET) field, different studies have classified apprenticeships based on their structure and training content. Some scholars distinguish between *integrated apprenticeships*, where classroom-based and *workplace-based training alternate* regularly (e.g., Germany), and *alternating* apprenticeships, where there is a clear separation between an initial school-based phase and a subsequent work-based training period (e.g., Denmark).[26] Others authors differentiate between *expansive apprenticeships*, designed to develop broad and transferable skills, and *restrictive apprenticeships*, which focus on company-specific competencies.[27] Similarly, some researchers propose a similar distinction between *holistic apprenticeships*, which provide a comprehensive training approach, and *modular apprenticeships*, which are more flexible and adaptable to individual needs.[28] A more recent approach was developed with the concept of "training logics," which integrates governance elements with training delivery models. This framework differentiates between apprenticeships aimed at forming a professional community (*professional education*), apprenticeships designed as in-company training schemes (*corporate training*), apprenticeships embedded within the education system (*school or university education*), and apprenticeships used as active labour market policy instruments (*public training schemes*).[29]

## 2.2 *Fragmented Protections and Common Challenges in Apprenticeship Regulation*

At present, no consolidated framework exists in labour law or labour market regulation to classify and standardise apprenticeships. However, this does not mean that the topic lacks relevance for these disciplines.

[25] Busemeyer and Trampusch (2012).

[26] Rayber and Smith (2010).

[27] Fuller and Unwin (2011).

[28] Pilz et al. (2018).

[29] Markowitsch and Witting (2020).

This regulatory gap directly impacts the critical issues surrounding apprenticeships. Although apprenticeships are a fundamental tool for facilitating the transition from school to work and reducing youth unemployment, their use is not free from risks and critical issues which, despite differences between countries, are common to all models. One of the main problems is the risk of exploitation of young workers. In some cases, apprenticeships are misused as a form of cheap labour, with apprentices being employed in repetitive and low-skilled tasks without receiving adequate training.[30] This phenomenon is more common in systems where controls on the quality of training are weak and where companies enjoy wide margins of discretion in the organisation of apprenticeship programmes.

However, recent labour market trends suggest a shift in dynamics. The ongoing shortage of skilled workers in many European countries is altering the traditional power balance in apprenticeship programmes.[31] Employers are increasingly struggling to attract and retain apprentices, particularly in high-demand sectors such as manufacturing, health care, and technology.[32] This shortage is leading some firms to offer better conditions, higher wages, and improved training programmes to make apprenticeships more attractive. While exploitation risks persist, particularly in less regulated sectors, the growing difficulty in recruiting apprentices is gradually shifting bargaining power towards young workers, especially in countries where demographic trends exacerbate labour shortages. In this context, a greater involvement of collective bargaining and social partners could enhance the attractiveness of apprenticeships, facilitating structured dialogue between companies, schools, and universities to improve training quality and labour market integration.[33]

A particularly significant risk is discrimination between apprentices and traditionally employed workers, which manifests itself through pay disparities, limited access to labour and social security rights, and fewer prospects for professional advancement. Apprentices, despite often contributing substantially to the productive activities of companies, receive significantly lower pay than ordinary workers.[34] Although this is justified by the training component of the contract, it becomes problematic when the training is insufficient or marginal and apprentices are mainly used as a low-cost workforce. Furthermore, in some jurisdictions, apprenticeships are not formally considered an employment contract, which can result in exclusion from essential protections such as social security contributions, paid leave and union rights. This situation not only creates disparities within the labour market but also makes apprentices particularly vulnerable to abuse and precariousness.[35]

The inconsistent quality of training is another critical issue.[36] In some systems, the lack of uniform training standards leads to apprenticeship programmes that do

[30] Smits (2005).

[31] Smith (2022).

[32] Kelly et al. (2022).

[33] Emmenegger and Seitzl (2020).

[34] Green (2015).

[35] Voitinius (2014).

[36] Göggel and Zwick (2009).

not guarantee the skills necessary for true integration into the labour market. This problem is particularly evident in more flexible models, where the quality of training can vary significantly between companies or sectors, generating frustration and poor employability among young people. Furthermore, the poor connection between training and the labour market can result in a misalignment between the skills learned by apprentices and those actually required by employers, making the programme less effective in combating unemployment. Moreover, the issue of skills mismatch further complicates the effectiveness of apprenticeships as a transition tool to stable employment. Many European countries are experiencing a growing gap between the skills provided through apprenticeship programmes and those actually demanded by employers. This misalignment is particularly evident in digital and technical professions, where rapid technological advancements outpace the training curricula offered within traditional apprenticeship schemes. However, greater involvement of employer associations in defining training standards and curricula could help mitigate the risk of skills shortages, ensuring better alignment between apprenticeship schemes and labour market needs.

Another critical issue concerns inequalities in access to apprenticeships. In some systems, access to training programmes is conditional on initial qualification levels or specific skills, excluding young people who are less prepared or come from disadvantaged backgrounds.[37] Similarly, territorial differences in the availability and quality of programmes can amplify inequalities, especially penalising rural or economically less developed regions.

Finally, dependence on public incentives poses a risk to the long-term sustainability of the apprenticeship system. In many countries, the participation of companies is motivated mainly by economic benefits rather than by a real commitment to training. This approach can lead to a fragile system, vulnerable to budget cuts or changes in government policies, compromising the stability of the model. Although a comprehensive discussion of funding structures falls outside the scope of this chapter, it is important to acknowledge that financial incentives and public subsidies remain a key variable influencing both the design and resilience of apprenticeship systems across the Member States.

## 3 EU Regulation of Apprenticeships Between Competence Constraints and Policy Ambitions

The heterogeneity of apprenticeship schemes across Europe, as discussed in the previous section, raises the question of whether the European legislator can play a role in fostering greater harmonisation while respecting national specificities. Given the hybrid nature of apprenticeships, which sit at the intersection of labour law and vocational education and training (VET), understanding the EU's competence in this area is crucial.[38]

[37] D'Agostino and Vaccaro (2023).

[38] See in this volume Kain F, Legal foundations of lifelong learning and labour law in Europe.

The regulatory complexity stems from the dual nature of apprenticeships: they function both as employment relationships, governed by workplace regulations, and as training pathways, subject to education and vocational training policies. This intersection between two legal domains means that the EU's ability to legislate on apprenticeships is constrained by the division of competences established in the Treaty on the Functioning of the European Union (TFEU). While Article 153(2)(b) TFEU allows the EU to adopt directives on working conditions, Articles 165(4) and 166(4) TFEU explicitly exclude the possibility of directives on education and vocational training. As a result, EU intervention is necessarily fragmented: it can set binding rules on aspects related to employment rights, but it lacks the authority to harmonise the training dimension of apprenticeships. Not surprisingly, the primary reference act for the EU in this area is currently a soft law instrument: the Council Recommendation of 15 March 2018 on a European Framework for Quality and Effective Apprenticeships (2018/C 153/01), which defines key quality criteria for apprenticeship schemes.[39]

Despite these limitations, the EU's involvement in apprenticeships must also be understood in the broader context of its commitment to full employment and employability, as reflected in its legal and policy framework. The European Pillar of Social Rights, which reaffirms the fundamental right to work, integrates the promotion of apprenticeships within its principles on active labour market policies (Principle No. 4). More specifically, Article 15 of the EU Charter of Fundamental Rights guarantees not only the right to engage in work but also the right to vocational training and access to labour market support, reinforcing the role of apprenticeships as an instrument for economic integration.[40] A stronger training framework is directly linked to better employment outcomes, as it enhances workers' skills and adaptability, thereby improving their long-term employability.

Another key aspect concerns the legal classification of apprentices under EU law, which directly affects the protections they are entitled to. While the employment status of apprentices varies across Member States, EU law adopts a functional definition of "worker" that is independent of national classifications.[41] According to the Court of Justice of the European Union (CJEU) in *Trojani*[42] and *Fenoll,*[43] an individual qualifies as a worker under EU law if they perform real and genuine activities under an employer's direction in exchange for remuneration. This interpretation is reinforced by Recital 6 of Directive 2019/1152 on Transparent and Predictable Working Conditions in the European Union, which states that apprentices may be considered as workers under EU law regardless of their classification under national law, provided they meet these criteria. Neither the level of productivity, the origin of remuneration, nor its limited amount excludes them from this status.[44]

---

[39] See Sect. 4 for a more detailed analysis of this recommendation.

[40] Deakin (2021).

[41] Menegatti (2019).

[42] Judgment of 7 September 2004, *Trojani*, C-456/02, EU:C:2004:488.

[43] Judgment of 26 March 2015, *Fenoll*, C-316/13, EU:C:2015:200.

[44] Giubboni (2018).

As a consequence, apprentices recognised as workers under EU law fall under the scope of multiple EU employment directives, such as Directive 98/59/EC on collective redundancies[45] and Directive 2000/78/EC on equal treatment in employment (e.g., in relation to social security benefits,[46] or protections for persons with disabilities).[47] This classification expands the EU's regulatory capacity over apprenticeships, particularly concerning working conditions and employment rights, even though their training component remains under the competence of Member States.

More recently, the EU has expanded its regulatory ambitions with the Proposal for a Directive on Improving the Working Conditions in Traineeships, presented by the European Commission on 20 March 2024 (COM (2024) 128 final).[48] Although this initiative is primarily focused on traineeships, it introduces binding obligations regarding training quality, contractual transparency, and fair remuneration, which also has a direct impact on apprenticeships. This reflects the EU's broader effort to balance flexibility, to meet employers' needs, with stronger protections for those engaged in work-based learning experiences. The potential consequences of this proposal for apprenticeship schemes will be examined in greater detail in the following section.

However, the EU's influence on apprenticeships is not limited to its legislative competence. Even in the absence of binding regulatory power over the training component, the EU actively shapes apprenticeship policies through financial instruments and strategic initiatives. EU funding programmes play an essential role in promoting apprenticeships. Erasmus+ fosters transnational mobility for apprentices, enhancing skills transfer across borders, while the European Social Fund Plus (ESF+) provides financial support to improve training accessibility at the national level.[49] Additionally, the Pact for Skills, launched in 2020, encourages collaboration between governments, businesses, and training institutions to align apprenticeship schemes with labour market needs.

A key EU priority is also to promote inclusiveness in apprenticeships, particularly for young people from disadvantaged backgrounds, rural areas, and those at risk of exclusion from the labour market. The Youth Guarantee plays a central role in this strategy, ensuring that young people in high-unemployment countries have access to training, apprenticeships, and employment opportunities.[50]

---

[45] Judgment of 9 July 2015, *Balkaya*, C-229/14, EU:C:2015:455.

[46] Judgment of 16 June 2016, *Lesar*, C-159/15, EU:C:2016:451.

[47] Judgment of 10 February 2022, *HR Rail*, C-485/20, EU:C:2022:85.

[48] See Sect. 5.

[49] Council of the European Union (2018) Recommendation (2018/C 153/01), Recital 22.

[50] Council of the European Union (2020) Recommendation (2020/C 372/01), Recital 21.

## 4 Harmonisation Without Obligation? The 2018 Council Recommendation on Apprenticeships

The Council Recommendation of 15 March 2018 on a European Framework for Quality and Effective Apprenticeships is part of the broader context of European Union policies aimed at improving the quality and effectiveness of apprenticeships in order to promote youth employment and the development of professional skills. From a legal point of view, the Recommendation is based on Article 166, paragraph 4, and Article 292 of the Treaty on the Functioning of the European Union, in conjunction with Article 153, paragraph 2, and Article 153, paragraph 1, letter b. It is therefore a non-binding act that establishes common guidelines and principles, but whose implementation is left to the discretion of the Member States.

### *4.1 Content*

In the definition contained in the Recommendation, apprenticeship is described as a vocational education and training programme that "combines learning in education or training institutions with substantial work-based learning in companies and other workplaces". This pathway must lead to nationally recognised qualifications and be regulated by an agreement between the apprentice, the employer and, if necessary, the education and training institutions. An essential element is the provision of a wage or compensation for the part of the training carried out in the company, thus emphasising the hybrid nature of the relationship that is established between the parties, halfway between training and subordinate work.

The measure establishes criteria to guarantee the quality of apprenticeships on two levels: (1) learning and working conditions and (2) framework conditions. On the first level, apprenticeships are regulated by a written agreement that clearly defines the rights and duties of all parties involved. The learning outcomes must also be identified, with a balance between specific professional skills and fundamental skills for lifelong learning. Adequate pedagogical support is required through the company tutor, who must collaborate with the training institutes to guarantee continuous feedback with the apprentice. At least 50 per cent of the training must be carried out in a work context, ensuring an effective connection with the needs of the market. Apprentices must receive remuneration in accordance with national and sectoral provisions or collective agreements and have access to social protection and benefit from safe working conditions that respect health and safety standards.

On the second level, with regard to the framework conditions, the Recommendation promotes the adoption of clear and coherent regulation, based on a structured dialogue between all stakeholders and on accreditation procedures for companies offering apprenticeships. A key aspect concerns the involvement of social partners in the design, management, and implementation of apprenticeship programmes, particularly at the sectoral level. This is a crucial labour law issue, as social partners play a fundamental role in balancing the interests of employers and apprentices, ensuring that training is not reduced to a mere form of precarious employment. The Recommendation highlights the need to establish a structured cooperation mechanism between trade unions, employer organisations, and public authorities to develop apprenticeship frameworks that guarantee both training quality and fair working conditions.

In addition, a system of financial and non-financial support is envisaged, with particular regard to micro, small, and medium-sized enterprises, so that they can offer cost-effective apprenticeships. Flexibility of training pathways is promoted, which must include the possibility of recognising informal and non-formal learning, include qualifications recognised in national and European frameworks and guarantee the transnational mobility of apprentices. The importance of providing career guidance and awareness raising, with mentoring and support services to reduce dropouts and promote apprenticeships as a valid educational choice is emphasised. It is necessary to ensure transparency in apprenticeship offers, including through EU tools such as EURES, and to implement quality assurance and continuous monitoring mechanisms based on the EQAVET framework.

### 4.2 *Persistent Fragmentation and the Need for Stronger EU Action*

Despite the Council Recommendation's attempt to provide a shared framework for quality and effective apprenticeships, its implementation remains uneven across Member States. The persistence of structural divergences in apprenticeship governance, contractual classification, and remuneration highlights the limitations of a non-binding instrument in fostering real convergence. These differences not only affect the functioning of apprenticeship schemes but also risk undermining their role as a tool for youth employment and skills development.

Mapping and analysis conducted by Cedefop[51] confirm that these discrepancies are particularly pronounced in three key areas: (1) the role of trade unions and employer organisations in apprenticeship governance; (2) the legal nature of apprenticeship contracts and the existence or absence of a formal employment relationship; and (3) the right to remuneration and the disparities it generates among apprentices.

First, significant differences exist regarding the role of trade unions and employer organisations in apprenticeship systems. In some countries (e.g., Bulgaria), social partners are only involved in consultative roles at the central/ministerial level, while in others (e.g., Germany), their participation is structural, occurring at both national and decentralised levels, including designing qualifications and playing an active role in certification and accreditation. In some systems (e.g., Netherlands, Poland), trade unions and employer organisations are involved in the final assessment and accreditation of training companies, as well as in monitoring in-company training.

[51] See the "Cedefop European database on apprenticeship schemes" on cedefop.europa.eu.

In other countries (e.g., France, Austria, Denmark), social partners play a significant role in shaping apprenticeship policies, ensuring alignment between training and labour market needs. Meanwhile, in some Eastern European countries (e.g., Romania, Slovakia), their influence remains limited to advisory roles, with less structured involvement in apprenticeship governance.[52]

A second area of divergence concerns the legal classification of apprenticeship contracts. In several countries (e.g., Italy, Latvia), apprenticeships do not constitute an ordinary employment contract but are instead a distinct contractual category (e.g., Germany, Croatia, France). In some cases (e.g., Portugal, Romania), apprenticeships are formalised through alternative agreements that do not qualify as employment contracts, leading to ambiguity in the legal status of apprentices. This uncertainty raises questions about the extent to which apprentices are entitled to the same labour protections as other workers.[53]

The third key issue involves the right to remuneration. While most jurisdictions grant apprentices a right to a salary, some countries still provide only an allowance that does not qualify as taxable income (e.g., Portugal, Hungary). This discrepancy creates inequalities in the treatment of apprentices and raises concerns about their financial stability and economic inclusion.[54]

These persisting inconsistencies suggest that relying solely on soft law measures is insufficient to ensure a coherent and equitable apprenticeship system across the EU. Without binding obligations, Member States retain excessive discretion in implementing apprenticeship policies, exacerbating fragmentation rather than reducing it. Given the clear disparities in governance, contractual protections, and financial conditions, the introduction of more robust regulatory mechanisms—such as a directive—appears increasingly necessary. A legally binding framework could establish minimum rights for apprentices, clarify their employment status, and reinforce the role of social partners, thereby preventing the risk of apprenticeships being used as a source of precarious employment rather than as a genuine learning pathway.

## 5 The Impact of the Proposed Internship Directive on Apprenticeships: Regulatory Overlaps and Legal Implications

The 2018 Recommendation on apprenticeships, despite its objectives, has proven insufficient in ensuring uniform protections across Member States. Its non-binding nature has allowed significant disparities in its implementation, leading to

[52] Ibid.

[53] Ibid.

[54] Ibid.

inconsistent protections for trainees. The absence of legal obligations has resulted in partial or ineffective applications, leaving gaps in regulation and enforcement.

In this context, there is ongoing discussion about the introduction of more binding instruments to strengthen protections in work-based learning schemes. A particularly relevant initiative in this regard is the Proposal for a Directive on Improving the Working Conditions in Traineeships, presented by the European Commission on 20 March 2024 (COM(2024) 128 final). This proposal aims to enhance the quality and protection of interns within the European Union by setting minimum standards to prevent exploitative practices and ensure adequate working conditions and social protection. It is based on two main objectives: improving the working conditions of trainees through the principle of equal treatment with comparable regular workers and preventing false traineeships, meaning jobs disguised as internships to circumvent labour protections and reduce costs.

However, the directive can only cover forms of internships that have an employment relationship, as its legal basis is Article 153 of the TFEU. This provision allows the European Union to intervene in matters of working conditions but does not extend to regulating the educational dimension of training.

Although formally aimed at internships, the directive is paradoxically set to have its most significant impact on apprenticeships rather than internships.[55] While it is presented as an instrument to regulate internships, it actually strengthens only those internships that are already considered employment relationships by national legislations, leaving the most precarious and unregulated forms of traineeships untouched. At the same time, however, it creates a regulatory spillover effect that makes apprenticeships the true focus of its legal consequences.

This is particularly evident in Article 2(b) of the proposal, which only qualifies as trainee "any person undertaking a traineeship who has an employment contract or employment relationship as defined by the law, collective agreements or practice in force in every Member State with consideration to the case law of the Court of Justice". Recital 17 also specifies "work-based learning programmes falling under the definition of traineeship vary significantly across Member States. Hence, apprenticeships may fall within the scope of this Directive, insofar as apprentices fall under the notion of 'worker' as defined by the law, collective agreements or practices in force in the Member States, with consideration to the case-law of the Court of Justice of the European Union". These provisions generate difficulties of interpretation,[56] especially in countries where the boundary between the two categories is blurred or where apprenticeships are characterised by lower pay and social protection conditions compared to standard employment contracts. The lack of a clear distinction between apprentices and trainees risks triggering regulatory inconsistencies, where apprentices—whose contracts already incorporate an employment component— are subjected to reinforced obligations, while the most unprotected internships remain largely unaffected by the directive's provisions.

---

[55] Helme (2024).

[56] See European Economic and Social Committee (2024).

Unlike internships, apprenticeships are frequently structured as employment contracts,[57] meaning that they fall squarely within the directive's regulatory scope. As a result, the directive will likely impose significant changes not in the realm of internships, but rather in the regulation of apprenticeships, which will end up being the main area of legislative impact. In legal systems where apprenticeship is primarily intended as both a training pathway and a form of work, the directive's implications could be substantial, particularly where the boundary between apprenticeship and internship is unclear.

## 5.1 *The Content of the Directive and Its Labour-Oriented Approach*

Considering this scenario, it is crucial to examine the provisions contained in the proposed directive and its potential impact on national apprenticeship frameworks.

The directive also aims to combat the misuse of internships as disguised employment relationships. To prevent such abuses, Member States must implement effective controls and inspections to identify and sanction employers who systematically replace regular jobs with internships.[58] Certain indicators, such as the lack of a meaningful training component, excessive internship duration, repetitive renewals with the same employer, and the assignment of tasks equivalent to those of regular employees, will be used to detect irregularities.[59] The directive mandates that employers provide detailed information to authorities regarding working conditions, contract duration, remuneration, and training content.[60]

Member States must guarantee that trainees have access to effective protection mechanisms, including dispute resolution procedures and compensation in cases of rights violations.[61] Protection against retaliation for interns reporting abuse or malpractice is also required, along with sanctions for non-compliant companies, which could include financial penalties or other regulatory actions.[62] The directive underscores the role of social partners, granting them the ability to intervene to uphold trainee protections and ensure compliance with the new legal framework.[63]

If effectively approved, the directive could represent a significant step forward in preventing forms of low-paid work that do not provide adequate protections for young people entering the labour market. However, its strong focus on working conditions—justified by its legal basis in Article 153 TFEU—risks further

57 As discussed in Sect. 4.2.

58 European Commission (2024), Art. 4.

59 European Commission (2024), Art. 5.

60 European Commission (2024), Art. 5, co. 2.

61 European Commission (2024), Art. 7.

62 European Commission (2024), Art. 9.

63 European Commission (2024), Art. 8.

exacerbating the labour-oriented dimension of apprenticeships, at the expense of their educational function. The very nature of the directive, which regulates work-based learning exclusively through the lens of employment protections, may contribute to shifting apprenticeships away from their formative purpose and towards a model in which they are treated primarily as subordinated employment relationships. This could lead to a situation where the educational value of apprenticeships is progressively sidelined in favour of an increasingly rigid and work-focused regulatory framework (§ 6, Conclusions).

## 6 Concluding Reflections on Regulatory Fragmentation and Functions Tensions

This chapter set out to investigate two closely related research questions. First, it examined the current state of apprenticeship in European labour law, assessing how the balance between training needs and employment protections is achieved in light of national differences and recent EU regulatory initiatives. Second, it explored how the case of apprenticeship helps to better understand the typical challenges that arise when labour law intersects with lifelong learning policies.

With respect to the first question, the analysis confirmed the existence of a highly fragmented European regulatory framework.[64] Although the EU attempted to introduce common quality criteria for apprenticeships through the 2018 Council Recommendation,[65] its non-binding nature has led to uneven implementation and persistent disparities between Member States. The measure that could potentially have the most significant impact—the proposed 2024 Directive on traineeships—was not originally designed as a tool for apprenticeship regulation but rather emerged as a collateral initiative with different objectives.[66] The absence of a clear and comprehensive EU strategy for apprenticeships is reflected in at least three critical issues concerning the effectiveness of legislative action.

First, the EU approach remains excessively focused on the individual dimension of apprenticeship, treating it primarily as a contractual framework governing the relationship between apprentices and employers. While this perspective is necessary, it is insufficient to capture the broader function of apprenticeship as a labour market regulation instrument. As highlighted,[67] apprenticeship is not merely an employment contract but also a mechanism for matching skills supply and demand. Any regulatory intervention should therefore go beyond defining the rights and obligations of individual parties and provide governance guidelines, involving key

---

[64] See Sect. 2.

[65] See Sect. 4.

[66] See Sect. 5.

[67] See Sect. 2.2.

stakeholders and establishing minimum quality standards. Apprenticeship is a matter not only of labour law but also of labour market regulation.

Second, the EU framework largely neglects the role of collective actors, particularly trade unions and employer associations, despite their historically central role in shaping apprenticeship systems. As previously discussed,[68] the most successful models— such as those in German-speaking countries—owe their effectiveness to the structured participation of social partners in the design, implementation, and oversight of training schemes. However, recent EU initiatives have paid little attention to this dimension, failing to acknowledge the crucial role that representative actors play in defining a more robust and effective system, with the exception of a few statements of intent which, to date, have not been fully reflected in binding legislative measures.[69]

Finally, a further limitation of the EU approach is the risk of an excessive shift towards employment protections, potentially undermining the educational function of apprenticeship. As pointed out (§ 5), the tendency to reinforce the safeguards typical of standard employment relationships could erode the specificity of apprenticeship, gradually transforming it into a regular employment contract. This issue is particularly evident in the debate over remuneration: aligning apprentice wages more closely with those of standard employees strengthens economic protections, but at the same time, it may incentivise employers to treat apprentices as ordinary workers, reducing the emphasis on their training. This tension reflects a broader dilemma: the stronger the apprentice's status as a worker, the more they risk being distanced from their role as a student in training.

With respect to the second research question, this chapter has shown that the intersection between training and employment presents significant challenges for EU policymakers due to the fragmentation of the relevant legal bases (§ 5). The EU's ability to enact hard law measures is confined to employment-related aspects, leaving the training dimension largely unaddressed. Moreover, the difficulty in integrating apprenticeship into the broader framework of lifelong learning reflects a deeper tension between labour law and lifelong learning policies: whereas the former is traditionally focused on worker protection, the latter emphasises flexibility and skill adaptability throughout life. Apprenticeship thus serves as an emblematic case of the challenges that arise when these two logics intersect, requiring a balancing act that, to date, the EU has struggled to define.

## References

Ainley P, Rainbird H (1999) Apprenticeship: Towards a new paradigm of learning. Routledge, London

[68] See Sect. 4.2.

[69] See Val Duchesse Social Partner Summit: Tripartite Declaration for a Thriving European Social Dialogue, signed on 31 January 2024.

Alexander MW (1921) Apprenticeship in the metal trades. In: Commons JR (ed) Trade Unions and labor problems. Ginn and Company, Boston, pp 233–247

Bemis EW (1891) Relation of Trade-Unions to apprentices. Quart Econ 6(1):76–93

Bray RA (1909) The apprenticeship question. Econ J 19(75):404–415

Busemeyer, Marius R., Christine Trampusch (eds.) (2012) The Political Economy of Collective Skill Formation. Oxford: Oxford University Press

Cedefop (2018) Apprenticeship schemes in countries. A cross-nation overview. Publications Office of the European Union, Luxembourg

Cedefop (2019) Apprenticeship for adults. Results of an explorative study. Publications Office of the European Union, Luxembourg

Council of the European Union (2018) Council recommendation of 15 March 2018 on a European Framework for Quality and Effective Apprenticeships. 2018/C 153/01

Council of the European Union (2020) Council Recommendation of 30 October 2020 on A Bridge to Jobs – Reinforcing the Youth Guarantee and replacing the Council Recommendation of 22 April 2013 on establishing a Youth Guarantee 2020/C 372/01. 2020/C 372/01

D'Agostino S, Vaccaro S (2023) Apprenticeships for promoting youth school-to-work transition: does it strengthen inclusion or the reproduction of inequalities? Inapp, Milano

De la Croix D, Doepke M, Mokyr J (2016) Clans, guilds and markets: apprenticeship institutions and growth in the pre-industrial economy. IZA Discussion Paper, No. 9828. Quart J Econ 133(1):1–70

De Munck B (2011) Gilding golden ages: perspectives from early modern Antwerp on the guild debate, c. 1450 – c. 1650. Eur Rev Econ Hist 15(2):221–253

Deakin S (2001) The contract of employment: a study in legal evolution. ESRC Centre for Business Research, University of Cambridge Working Paper No. 203

Deakin S (2021) Article 15 – freedom to choose an occupation and right to engage in work. In: Dorssemont F et al (eds) The charter of fundamental rights of the European Union and the employment relation. Hart Publishing, Oxford, pp 331–350

Deissinger T (2008) Cultural patterns underlying apprenticeship: Germany and the UK. In: Aarkrog V, Jorgensen C.H (eds) Divergence and governance in education and work. Peter Lang, Bern, pp 34–55

Deissinger T, Gonon P (2021) The development and cultural foundations of dual apprenticeship – a comparison of Germany and Switzerland. J Vocat Educ Training 73(4):197–216

Dunlop OJ (1912) English apprenticeship & child labour. A history. Macmillan

Emmenegger P, Seitzl L (2020) Social partner involvement in collective skill formation governance. A comparison of Austria, Denmark, Germany, the Netherlands and Switzerland. Transfer: Eur Rev Labour Res 26(1):27–42

Epstein SR, Prack M (eds) (2009) Guilds, Innovation and the European Economy. 1400-1800. CUP, Cambridge

European Commission (2021) Commission Staff Working Document: Putting into practice the European Framework for Quality and Effective Apprenticeship. SWD(2021) 230 final

European Commission (2024) Report from the Commission to the European Parliament and the Council on the delegation of power to adopt delegated acts conferred on the Commission pursuant to Regulation (EC) No 810/2009 of the European Parliament and of the Council of 13 July 2009 establishing a Community Code on Visas (Visa Code). COM (2024) 128 final

European Economic and Social Committee (2024) Opinion of the European Economic and Social Committee: Directive on Traineeships and Reinforced Quality Framework for Traineeships. SOC/805, adopted on 11 July 2024

Fuller, A. and Unwin, L. (2011) Apprenticeship as an Evolving Model of Learning. Journal of Vocational Education and Training, 63.

Giubboni S (2018) Being a worker in EU law. Eur Labour Law J 9(3):223–235

Göggel K, Zwick T (2009) Good occupation – bad occupation? The Quality of Apprenticeship Training. Zew, Centre for European Economic Research Discussion Paper No. 09-024

Green C (2015) UK apprenticeships: opportunity or exploitation? Open J Syst 1(1)

Helme J (2024) The problems and paradoxes with the EU's regulation of traineeships: a way forward. Ind Law J 53(4):679–710
Kelly M, Wilkinson L, Eyo-Idahor A, Williams L (2022) Improving the recruitment and retention of construction apprentices through Oregon's highway construction workforce development program. J Appl Soc Sci 16(2):459–481
Markowitsch J, Witting W (2020) Understanding differences between apprenticeship programmes in Europe: towards a new conceptual framework for the changing notion of apprenticeship. J Vocat Educ Train 74(4):597–618
McCann D, Stewart A (2024) Quality, formality and the evolution of international labor law: the new ILO quality apprenticeships standard. Ind Law J 53(4):638–678
Menegatti E (2019) Taking EU labour law beyond the employment contract: the role played by the European Court of Justice. Eur Labour Law J 11(1):26–47
Nyen T, Tonder AH (2020) Capacity for reform: the changing roles of apprenticeship in three Nordic countries. Transfer Eur Rev Labour Res 26(1):43–56
OECD (2000) From initial education to working life. Making Transitions Work. OECD, Paris
Ogilvie S (2020) The European guilds. An economic analysis. Princeton University Press
Pilz M, Li J, Canning R, Minty S (2018) Modularisation approaches in initial vocational education: evidence for policy convergence in Europe? J Vocat Educ Train 70(1):1–26
Rayber F, Smith E (ed) (2010) Rediscovering apprenticeship. Research findings of the international network on innovative apprenticeship. Springer
Ryan P (2012) Apprenticeship: between theory and practice, school and workplace. In: Pilz M (ed) The future of vocational education and training in a changing world. Springer, Hannover, pp 402–432
Sikes G (1894) The apprentice system in the building trades. J Polit Econ 6(1):76–93
Smith E (2022) Apprenticeships: the problem of attractiveness and the hindrance of heterogeneity. Int J Train Dev 27(1):18–38
Smits W (2005) The quality of apprenticeship training: conflicting interests of firms and apprentices. Maastricht University
Steedman H (2001) Benchmarking apprenticeship: UK and continental Europe compared. Centre for Economic Performance (LSE)
Supiot A (2001) Beyond employment: changes in work and the future of labor law in Europe. OUP, Oxford
Thelen K, Busemeyer MR (eds) (2012) The political economy of collective skill formation. OUP, Oxford
Veillard L (2022) Alternance training as a way to improve the Attractivity of vocational education programmes in France. In: Billet S et al (eds) The standing of vocational education and the occupations it serves. professional and practice-based learning 32. Springer
Voitinius JJ (2014) Young employees: securities, risk distribution and fundamental social rights. Eur. Labour Law J 5(3-4):366–389
Webb B, Webb S (1896) History of trade unionism. Longmans Green, London

**Giorgio Impellizzieri** is a research fellow in Labour Law at the University of Modena and Reggio Emilia. He holds a PhD in "Learning and Innovation in Work and Social Contexts," jointly coordinated by ADAPT (Association for International and Comparative Studies in Labour and Industrial Relations) and the University of Siena. His research focuses on collective bargaining, labour market regulation, vocational training, and occupational health and safety.

# Exploring the Collective Dimension of Lifelong Learning in Labour Law

# Social Dialogue and Lifelong Learning: The Difficult Interplay at EU Level and National Level

**Alexander De Becker and Valentina Franca**

## 1 Introduction

The chapter shall first focus on the development of the EU Social Dialogue in general. The EU Social Dialogue needs to be well understood in order to start the debate on lifelong learning in labour law.

The chapter shall than focus on the EU Social Dialogue and its roots. Once this concept is well understood, it becomes more evident to deal with the unique concept of lifelong learning in the larger context of labour law.

Theoretically, social legislation and a social dialogue were not included in the plan to develop an internal market. The creation of an internal market in 1957 did not include a large model for social cooperation.

Cooperation and the creation of an internal market included from the start some social aspects. Free movement of miners and steal workers was a fundament of the first European Communities (the European Community on Coal and Steal and the European Economic Community).[1]

However, the development of free movement of workers did not immediately include the development of a strong social dialogue at EU level.

[1] R.F (1953), pp. 497–504.

A. De Becker
Faculty of Law and Criminology, Ghent University, Belgium, Ghent
e-mail: alexander.debecker@ugent.be

V. Franca (✉)
Faculty of Public Administration, University of Ljubljana, Slovenia, Ljubljana
e-mail: valentina.franca@fu.uni-lj.si



J. Murto, V. Franca (eds.), *Labour Law and Lifelong Learning*,
https://doi.org/10.1007/978-3-032-11035-0_7

It took till 1987 before a social aspect at EC level was introduced. Article 130a of the Single European Act stipulated, for the first time, that the European Community shall develop and pursue its actions to strengthen its economic and social cohesion. Moreover, article 118b provided for the first time that the European Commission shall endeavour to develop the social dialogue between management and labour at the European level, which could lead, if the two sides consider it desirable, to relations based on agreements. This new article 118b had underwent quite a long debate before it entered into force.[2]

The most substantial debate took place at the summit of Fontainebleau which was a consequence of the French presential elections in 1981. François Mitterand, the new French president, had strongly stressed the social element of the Community. The Fontainebleau report of the European Council decided that the European Commission had to forge to take action on technological change and social adjustment.[3]

However, the European Commission did not really take a lot of initiatives with regard to social policy. Social Dialogue in the late 1980s and the beginning of the 1990s did not lead to full collective bargaining rounds. Some joint opinions were rendered but no real collective negotiations at EU level took place. Between 1985 and 1995, the social partners and the EU Commission generated 21 joint opinions and declarations, 2 key agreements and 7 high-level summits.

A real social policy was not established. It was considered that harmonization of social regulation was not needed because, according to the EU policy in general, free movement of capital would flourish without a harmonization of labour law. As a consequence, a race to the social bottom took place.[4] It took place until 1991 before this deadlock was broken.

The joint agreement of 31 October 1991 between Social Partners, meaning the Union of Industrial and Employers' Confederations of Europe (UNICE), the European Trade Union Confederation (ETUC) and the European Centre of Employers and Entreprises providing Public Services (CEEP), requested mandatory consultation of the social partners on regulation in the area of social affairs. The same joint agreement of 31 October 1991 provided that social partners can negotiate framework agreements at European level. These framework agreements can be initiated by the social partners, by the European Commission or by the European Council.

EU Member States honoured this joint agreement of 31 October 1991 by annexing it to the Maastricht Protocol on Social Policy, which thus provided for a constitutionally recognized role for the social partners in the European legislative process. At national level, social partners were given the opportunity to implement directives by way of collective agreement. The Social Policy Protocol, annexed to the Maastricht Treaty, allowed 11 EU member states (excluding the UK) to adopt

---

[2] Green Cowles (2013), pp. 107–120.

[3] Green Cowles (2013), pp. 107–120.

[4] Deakin (2017).

policies on employment and industrial relations. It created a "twin-track" approach to social policy, allowing these 11 states to take action while the United Kingdom remained outside the new procedures. This protocol also established a specific legal basis for EU legislation in employment and industrial relations and included the participation of European social partners in the legislative process.

The number of initiatives with regard to the Social Dialogue remained very limited. Framework agreements on parental leave (1996), part-time work (1997), and fixed-term contracts (1999) were implemented via Council Directives. These agreements, negotiated by social partners, were then adopted by the Council of the EU, becoming part of EU law.

The further development of the Social Dialogue will be analysed after the entry into force of the Treaty of Lisbon which has led to an increase of the Social Dialogue. The new millennium unleashed a bigger demand for a social Europe.[5]

The development of a more real social dialogue at EU level includes an enlargement of the subjects of the social dialogue. Lifelong learning as a topic could fit in this enlarged scope. However, the research question remains to what extent lifelong learning can be quoted as a topic which fits in the current competences which are granted to the EU and to the social partners at EU level or that it has to be tackled from a different angle. This chapter shall take a multilevel approach to this issue which is rather novel.

The methodology will be based on the analysis of the legislative framework, case law and legal scholarship with regard to the role of lifelong learning in the social dialogue. However, it also focuses on the interplay (based on the competences) between member states and the EU itself on social dialogue, EU and its Member States. In the second, third and fourth paragraph, the focus remains on a positivist approach indicating the evolution of social policy at EU level in relation to lifelong learning. For the fifth and sixth paragraphs, we adopt a constructivist approach, which analyses the impact of EU initiatives with a focus on their social interplay with initiatives at member-state level. The final chapters shall adopt a multilayered approach which can set up a novel and interesting interplay on the EU Social Dialogue, the Social Dialogue in different EU member states and lifelong learning.

## 2 The Basics of the EU Social Dialogue and Lifelong Learning

The development of a social dialogue did not influence social Europe to its heart. The EU did undertake some initiatives at the end of the twentieth and in the beginning of the twenty first century with regard to the collective redundancy,[6] transfer of

[5] Vandenbroucke et al. (2017).

[6] Directive 98/37 of 22 June 1998 on the approximation of laws of Member States relating to machinery.

undertakings,[7] health and safety,[8] part-time employment,[9] working time[10] and antidiscrimination.

The policy and behaviour of the EU institutions led to new queries with regard to the real development of social policy. An EU Social Dialogue had in principle created new opportunities as social partners were already involved in the process of the enactment of social policy regulatory framework. On paper, social partners were already involved in the enactment of certain legislation articles 138 and 139 European Economic Community which were set up through the Treaty of Maastricht in 1991. This did, however, not lead to a large impact of these social partners in the enactment of any regulatory framework.

Only six cross-industry frameworks and six sectoral framework agreements have been concluded till 2008.[11]

It was only at the beginning of the millennium that the role of labour law grew within the European Union. The role of the Viking and Laval cases therefore may not be underestimated. The Court recognized the fundamental right to collective action as a part of EU law, however, with limitations which can be deduced from the freedom of services and freedom of capital.[12]

Following the Viking and Laval-cases, the EU did not consider collective bargaining a fundamental human right. It is well known that the EU, and more specifically the ECB and the European Commission, did not really fully support the development of social rights during the austerity crisis. It was mentioned in numerous articles and contributions that the choices made by the so-called troika were not meant to be supporting the development of fundamental labour rights.[13] The Viking and Laval cases explicitly opened the debate for a more social Europe. Some authors even indicated that these judgements provoked the crisis in Europe as they indicated the social deficit of the EU.[14] The first, somehow bizarre, attempt was the so-called Monti II regulation on the regulation of the right to strike. This initiative got a yellow card with regard to the subsidiarity protocol.[15]

---

[7] Directive 2001/23/EC of 12 March 2001 on the approximation of the laws of the Member States relating to the safeguarding of employees' rights in the event of transfers of undertakings, businesses or parts of undertakings or businesses.

[8] Directive 89/391of 12 June 1989 on the introduction of measures to encourage improvements in the safety and health of workers at work—"Framework Directive".

[9] Directive 97/81/EC of 15 December 1997 concerning the Framework Agreement on part-time work concluded by UNICE, CEEP and the ETUC.

[10] Directive 93/104/EC of 23 November 1993 concerning certain aspects of the organization of working time.

[11] Welz (2008).

[12] ECJ, *Laval v Svenska Byggnadsarbetstareforbundet*, C-341/05, 18 December 2007 and ECJ, *International Transport Workers' Federation v Viking Line*, C-438/05, 11 December 2007.

[13] Schmitt (2014).

[14] Barnard (2014), pp. 205–206.

[15] Fromage and Kreilinger (2017), pp. 127–128.

Lifelong learning as topic within social policy also leads to a difficult qualification. Originally, within the European Union, lifelong learning was linked to competitiveness and a growing economy.[16] It took some time before lifelong learning was considered to be a part of a social market model.[17] Since the introduction of the European Pillar of Social Rights, the right on lifelong learning at the workplace is considered to be an individual right.

This is the consequence of an interesting development of social policy in the EU.

The EU Social Dialogue hampered in full in the first decade of the new millennium. During the Juncker presidency of the European Commission, the President often stated the relaunch of the EU Social Dialogue was key. He linked the EU Social Dialogue to the aim of setting up a common labour market in the EU.[18] To underpin this evolution, a quadripartite agreement was signed on the EU Social Dialogue. The European trade unions, the European employers, the European Commission and the Council of the EU promised each other in this agreement to respect the EU Social Dialogue, to set up cross-industry social dialogues and to let social dialogue and the enactment of legislative initiatives interact stronger than before.[19] It seemed that the EU Social Dialogue was going to finally obtain its position in the EU regulatory framework in full. The communication of the European Commission of 8 March 2016 provided the EU Social Dialogue would encounter the decline of the social policy in the EU.[20]

The Juncker Commission desired to develop a more Social Europe.[21] The development of the Pillar of Social Rights was therefore twinned with the development of a real EU Social Dialogue. The idea of an EU-Social Dialogue included the idea of the development of a real social policy within the EU framework. The Pillar of Social Rights was explicitly linked with the enactment of articles 153 and 154 of TFEU where it was stipulated that each initiative of the European Commission has to consult social partners before launching such a legislative proposal. The Pillar of Social Rights had to reinforce the idea of an EU Social Dialogue. It finally set out

---

[16] Volles (2014), pp. 1–21.

[17] Green (2006), pp. 307–308.

[18] Communication of the President of the EU-Commission, 8 March 2016 launching a consultation on a European Pillar of Social Rights, 1:

> We have to step up the work for a fair and truly pan-European labour market. (…) As part of these efforts, I will want to develop a European Pillar of Social Rights, which takes account of the changing realities of Europe's societies and the world of work. (…) The European Pillar of Social Rights should complement what we have already jointly achieved when it comes to the protection of workers in the EU. I will expect social partners to play a central role in this process.

[19] Statement of the Presidency of the Council of the EU, the European Commission and the European Social Partners, 16 June 2016, Statement of the ESP, EC, NL PRES on behalf of CNSL 27062016.pdf.

[20] Communication of the President of the EU-Commission, 8 March 2016 launching a consultation on a European Pillar of Social Rights, 2.

[21] They called it themselves a triple A for Social Europe.

the idea of the development of a real social policy within the EU framework in 2017. Article 1 of the Pillar of Social Rights recognizes lifelong learning as an individual right of the worker in the EU. This means that the right to lifelong learning has shifted from collective labour law to an individual employment right.

The focus on the EU Social Dialogue has to stay within the institutional framework of the EU. In reality, the competences of the EU with regard to social policy remained rather limited. Social policy actually remains a shared competence. This has been enacted in articles 151 till 154 TFEU.

Article 151 TFEU stipulates that the following objectives for social policy at EU level: promoting employment, improving working and living conditions, equal treatment of workers, adequate social protection according to need, social dialogue, developing human resources aimed at achieving a high and sustainable level of employment, as well as combating exclusion.

These goals cannot be reached without a collaboration between the EU institutions and the EU Member States. The goals of the EU Social Policy have to be reached by a unique collaboration between the EU institutions and Member States but simultaneously by a collaboration between EU Social Partners and Member-State Social Partners. It thus becomes a unique and interesting collaboration laboratory.

These articles do not explicitly mention lifelong learning. However, lifelong learning could be linked to all of the mentioned elements. The individual right to lifelong learning, however, can be linked to each of the subtopics of this shared competence. A basic individual right of workers has to be approached, according to article 5 of the Treaty on the European Union in accordance with the concept of referral. That means that the principles of subsidiarity and proportionality are key. The EU can only execute its competence in case the proposed action cannot be sufficiently achieved at national, regional or local level.

## 3 The Current Role of the EU Social Dialogue with Regard to lifelong Learning

Given the renewed Social Dialogue, the role of collective bargaining at EU level has increased significantly. Article 154 TFEU also stipulates that the Commission has the task to promote consultation of management and labour at Union level. This underlines the importance of collective bargaining.

This has led to the following situation in practice. The social partners may then choose to negotiate an agreement among themselves instead. They have nine months to negotiate, after which they may or (1) Conclude an agreement and jointly ask the Commission to propose a Council implementing decision; or (2) Conclude an agreement and implement it themselves, in accordance with their own specific procedures and practices and those of the Member States ('voluntary' or, later on, 'autonomous' agreements); or (3) Decide that they are unable to reach an agreement, in which case the Commission resumes work on the proposal in question.

The consequence thus is that many initiatives have been undertaken with regard to the competences which are explicitly mentioned to be shared competence. One may think of the framework agreements on active ageing and an intergenerational approach (2017) and on digitalization (2020). Some Directives also explicitly transposed EU framework agreements of social partners. This was the case with the Council Directive 2018/131 of 18 January 2018 which made a sectoral agreement on transport in the maritime sector directly applicable through a directive. However, not all framework agreements were to be accepted by the Commission in case social partners asked to implement their framework agreements. For instance, the public sector's framework agreements to inform and consult in public administration were not transposed into Directives by the European Commission. This led to a procedure before the European Court of Justice wherein the Court decided that the European Commission has no legal duty to transpose the framework agreements in case the social partners request to do so.[22] From a legal point of view, the judgement of the European Court of Justice finds its sources in the current existing legal framework.

The weakness of the EU Social Dialogue therefore remains. It seems that the evolution towards a stronger EU Social Dialogue has still not yet developed full fledgedly. The difficulties which Copeland identified, remain, namely the difficulties between free movement of capital and social dialogue but mainly the hinders which social partners create at EU level themselves and furthermore the distinct approach of Member States with regard to the EU Social Dialogue.[23]

The slow development of the EU Social Dialogue also is embedded in the EU institutional framework. The TFEU excludes a major part of the substance of a full Social Dialogue. Article 153 TFEU stipulates that it aims to promote employment, improve living and working conditions, by making their harmonization possible while the improvement is being maintained, and a proper social protection, dialogue between management and labour, the development of human resources with a view to lasting high employment and the combating of exclusion are aimed for.

However, and simultaneously, article 153 (5) TFEU has often been used to limit social dialogue. This paragraph stipulates the following:

> The provisions of this article shall not apply to pay, the right of association, the right to strike or the right to impose lockouts.

The case law of the European Court of Justice is still critical with regard to the competence of the EU in social policy. One may think of the case law with regard to the Viking and Laval cases which limited the right to collective action in case it infringed the free movement of goods and of services. This case law of the European Court of

[22] ECJ, *EPSU v Commission*, C-928/19, 2 September 2021. A lot of authors defended that the EU, once again, did not take collective rights in labour law seriously. Even if this can be understood and politically defend, it does not fit into the current legal framework. Read on this topic: Dorssemont (2022), pp. 52–66.

[23] Copeland (2021), pp. 133–144.

Justice goes intertwined with the advice of the Advocate General with regard to the Directive (EU) 2022/2041 on adequate minimum wages in the European Union ('the AMW Directive').[24] This case once again shows the difficult balance between labour law and social policy as set out in the constitutional framework of the EU. The Advocate General assesses that the AMW Directive is violating article 153 (5) TFEU. Even if this advice can be criticized due to the fact that the concept of pay always is relevant in labour relations,[25] article 153 (5) TFEU has already been the subject of a long debate with regard to the principle of subsidiarity.[26]

In order to find a way out of the difficult interplay between the case law of the ECJ, legal scholarship and the development of real social policy lie exactly in the role of the principle of subsidiarity. The development of the right to lifelong learning does not (always) have to be achieved at EU level. It is really fundamental to use the multilevel approach of this principle within the specific multilevel governance that identifies the EU precisely.[27] The reluctant approach of the ECJ in its case law can best be tackled by the use of the principle of subsidiarity.

## 4 Lifelong Learning, EU Social Dialogue and the Principle of Subsidiarity

The position of lifelong learning in the spectrum of competences of the EU is difficult to assess. Lifelong at the workplace is not a clear competence. The only possibility to link the individual right to lifelong learning at the workplace to a real social dialogue has to be meticulously analysed.

The concept of lifelong learning knows a specific evolution. Within the European Pillar of Social Rights, the first principle of the 20 key principles is education, training and lifelong learning. The aim of the EU is to have at least 60 % of the workers involved in training at least once a year.[28] It seems to be a strong ambition. However, it is not really novel. The concept of lifelong learning dates back to 2006 within the scope of the EU.[29]

At this stage, the role of the EU Social Dialogue with regard to lifelong learning has not yet led to important steps to develop a full right to lifelong learning on the work floor nor to binding regulations on this topic.

---

[24] Opinion of Advocate-General Emiliou on 14 January 2025. https://curia.europa.eu/juris/document/document.jsf;jsessionid=764D0DB60BF22243AAC8947F87C4BD66?text=&docid=294192&pageIndex=0&doclang=EN&mode=req&dir=&occ=first&part=1&cid=19121528.

[25] Menegatti (2025).

[26] Panara (2022), pp. 269–296.

[27] Panara (2015).

[28] Cedefop (2024).

[29] See in this volume Claus F, Exploring the Future of Lifelong Learning through the Tapestry of European Policy History and Kain F, Legal foundations of lifelong learning and labour law in Europe, Sect. 4.3.

This is partially linked to the limited results of the EU Social Dialogue in general. At cross sector level, 11 autonomous agreements have been concluded at cross-industry level between 2002 (EU Telework Framework Agreement of 16 July 2002) and 2021 (EU Social Partners Agreement on Women in Rail of 16 November 2021). Some more achievements have been concluded at sectoral level. The EU Social Dialogue knows at this moment 44 sectors for a social dialogue. A lot of joint declarations and joint actions have launched but real agreements remain limited. However, the outcome of the social dialogue at a sectoral level remained limited with regard to the creation of a new regulatory framework.

The development of a good sectoral social dialogue might be useful for the development of lifelong learning in the larger EU context. The concept of lifelong learning as an individual right on the work floor has not yet been underpinned in a vast regulatory framework. Harmonization of existing legislation could and will be useful but therefore the social partners at EU level need to map what the current regulatory framework within the different Member States is. At this stage, even at Member States' level, the substance of the right to lifelong learning remains to be discovered.

The current regulatory framework at EU level, however, does not lead to a full and fruitful regulatory framework with regard to the lifelong learning. The key principle therefore remains the use and the adoption of the principle of subsidiarity. While this principle is very often detested, a good use of this principle might lead to a better development of lifelong learning and labour law, both at EU level and at national level.

## 5 The Role of the Principle of Subsidiarity as a Useful Tool for the Development of a Regulatory Framework in the EU

The EU Social Dialogue can only be understood if it is linked to the principle of subsidiarity. Major changes can be made at the Member-State level. Member States can deal with lifelong learning issues.[30] The principle of subsidiarity is a key principle of EU law. However, it is often mentioned to weaken to a certain level the development of EU (labour) law.[31] The principle tried and still tries to overcome the fear within some Member States to overcome the centralization of EU law.[32] The principle of subsidiarity has, according to the preparatory documents, to be understood as a dynamic principle which allows the EU to exercise its powers in case it is judged necessary. This makes the principle of subsidiarity a principle which is very

[30] See in this volume Sipka P, Lifelong Learning: An Obligation for the Employer or an Empty Right?, section 5; Zwolińska A, Lifelong learning as a worker right - Lifelong learning within the context of employment relationship: the worker's perspective and Johansson C, Regulating life-long-learning in collective agreement, section 4.

[31] Read on this topic Davies (2006), p. 63.

[32] Fabbrini (2016).

difficult to grasp. Some authors have already described it as a legal principle with very unclear legal content.[33] Even if this may be the case, labour law has undergone the consequences of the application of the principle of subsidiarity. As mentioned, article 153 (5) TFEU established a shared competence with regard to social policy, however indicating explicit boundaries for the application of the exercise of this competence. The boundaries were mentioned before:

> Pay, the right of association, the right to strike or the right to impose lockouts.

Therefore, given these important limitations, it seems really useful to develop simultaneously a regulatory framework at national level which is linked to a larger harmonization of EU labour law wherein the development of lifelong learning and labour law both at national and EU level can take place.

It is important to underline that precisely with regard to labour law, the principle of subsidiarity limits the development of a regulatory framework. The Monti II regulation tried to overcome the consequences of the case law of Viking and [34] Laval[35] cases.

However, the principle of subsidiarity almost immediately blocked the adoption of the Monti II directive by using the subsidiarity control mechanism. The Monti II directive tried to find a balance between the fundamental right to collective action and the economic freedoms within the EU. However, article 153 (5) TFEU stipulated and still stipulates that the right to strike and the right to association cannot be regulated by the EU. Therefore, the Monti II regulation did not pass the subsidiarity test, as is foreseen in Protocol number 2 on the principles of Subsidiarity and Proportionality.

With regard to social dialogue and lifelong learning, the principle of subsidiarity and of proportionality can be a useful tool. Social dialogue at EU level with regard to a very vague concept remains a difficult issue. Lifelong learning as a term is only used in general terms within the framework of the EU. It remains a goal which was set up without a clear legal definition of the concept of lifelong learning. In order to be able to set up a legal harmonization of the existing regulatory framework within the EU, the existing substance of the right to lifelong learning has to be mapped.

Mapping the existing regulatory framework can be used as a first step to identify similarities and differences within the Member States. Starting from the principle of subsidiarity, this knowledge offers the social partners to identify to what extent they can play a role in the development of regulations with regard to the right to lifelong learning as a fundamental right for workers.

---

[33] Schutze (2009), p. 450 and Estella (2002), p. 75.

[34] ECJ, *International Transport Workers' Federation v Viking Line*, C-438/05, 11 December 2007.

[35] ECJ, *Laval v Svenska Byggnadsarbetstareforbundet*, C-341-05, 18 December 2007.

## 6 Starting Point of the Lifelong Learning and the Principle of Subsidiarity

The Monti II disaster may not remain the only memory of labour law with regard to the principle of subsidiarity.

The EU has tried to set out a harmonized basis for education within the EU but the focus on the individual right to lifelong learning is lacking behind. That is not surprising as the right to lifelong learning has not yet been underpinned by a thorough legal framework.

It seems therefore useful to grant an overview of the ongoing regulatory frameworks in all different EU Member States in order to deduce the remaining gaps which could be filled in by the EU Social Dialogue. In order to understand which joint statements can be made or which initiatives in general can be undertaken, it is useful to map the existing regulatory framework in the different EU Member States. The comparison shall also be focused on the role which collective bargaining agreements play at Member-State level. Mapping these elements facilitates the good interplay between the Member States' level and the EU level for the necessary EU Social Dialogue.

## 7 Existing Regulatory Framework in the Different EU Member States

Within the different member states, the concept of lifelong learning has been introduced in a large part of the EU Member States. However, the substance of the concept differs as does the procedural aspects of how to obtain results for it. Some consider it fully right while others remain vague about the concept.

The following table indicates whether any regulation with regard to lifelong learning exists in all of the 27 EU Member States and whether it is developed in regulation by the State or the substate. The last column indicates whether collective bargaining agreements do exist within the framework of the existing regulation or that social dialogue is even the primary source of regulation. In some Member States, such as Denmark and Sweden, collective bargaining agreements are considered to be the primary source of labour law. In other countries, collective bargaining agreements are not considered as crucial but rather as an additional regulation.

Table 1 indicates whether there exists a formal right to lifelong learning on the work floor (column 2), it also indicates to what extent the Member-State has enacted legislation with regard to the right to lifelong learning on the work floor. In other words, has Parliament taken any initiative (column 3)? The last two columns deal with collective bargaining agreements: Does there exist any collective bargaining agreement (column 4) and if so, is that collective bargaining agreement the primary source of regulation (column 5)?

**Table 1** Existence of a formal right to lifelong learning

| Table 1 | Right to lifelong learning | Regulatory framework by the (sub)State | CBA | Social Dialogue primary source |
|---|---|---|---|---|
| Austria | No full right but a recognition of the concept in the Anerkennung des Qualitätsrahmens für die Erwachsenenbildung Ö-Cert (The recognition of the Quality framework for the education of adults) | No real regulatory framework with regard to the right | No collective bargaining agreements yet | No collective bargaining agreements yet |
| Belgium | Act of 3 October 2022 provides a right to lifelong learning (education) for all employees (5 education days a year) | The right is general, but the Act of 3 October 2022 only provides a general framework for companies with at least 20 employees | Collective bargaining agreements can develop at sectoral level certain conditions and the framework | Collective bargaining agreements at company level (with less than 20 employees) can be developed but are not a primary source of law |
| Bulgaria | The Employment Promotion Act stipulates that the Ministry of Labour and the Ministry of Education have the duty to set up a regulatory framework for adult training | Part of the regulatory framework is adapted to develop the idea of lifelong learning, but it does not become an execution of a fully granted basic right | Collective bargaining with regard to lifelong learning does not take place at national nor at company level.[a] | Collective bargaining with regard to lifelong learning does not take place at national nor at company level. |
| Croatia | Article 57 of the Labour Act stipulates the right to paid leave in case of absence for general or employed-related education, but this does not imply a real right to lifelong learning | Article 32 of the Labour Act stipulates a right to education for each worker in accordance with his/her abilities and the need of the work | At sectoral level some important initiatives have been taken to develop collective bargaining agreements on lifelong learning[b] | Plays a role at decentralized (company and sectoral) level but is not a primary source of law |

(continued)

**Table 1** (continued)

| Table 1 | Right to lifelong learning | Regulatory framework by the (sub)State | CBA | Social Dialogue primary source |
|---|---|---|---|---|
| Czech Republic | No full right on lifelong learning exists | Articles 108 till 110 of the Act 435/2004 on Employment stipulate the possibility to retrain jobless people and employees to prepare them for new challenges | Sectoral and company level collective bargaining agreements are concluded on education and vocation of employees | Plays a role at company and sectoral level but is not a primary source of law |
| Denmark | No basic right to lifelong learning | No real Act dealing with | Numerous collective bargaining agreements on sectoral level to develop the right to lifelong learning | Plays a role at sectoral and company level and is the primary source of law |
| Estonia | No full right on lifelong learning | Adult Education Act organizes the right on lifelong learning at the work spot. It also introduces the concept of micro credentials. | Collective bargaining agreement at sectoral level develops the basics set out in the Act | Plays a role on sectoral and company level but is not the primary source of law |
| Finland | Right to lifelong learning | In different acts, spread out over education and labour, right to lifelong guidance are ensured | Collective bargaining agreements are key to developing this right | Plays a role on sectoral and company level and can be the primary source of law. |
| France | Article L6111-1 provides a right to lifelong learning as an individual right of the employee. | The Labour Code provides two articles to this right which are linked to the Educational Code | National, sectoral and company collective bargaining agreements exist | Collective bargaining agreements develop the fundamental right which is in general wordings founded. |

(continued)

**Table 1** (continued)

| Table 1 | Right to lifelong learning | Regulatory framework by the (sub)State | CBA | Social Dialogue primary source |
|---|---|---|---|---|
| Germany | The Federal State does not deal with the fundamental right to lifelong learning. The Länder have enacted a lot of Acts with regard to this topic | Many Länder recognize the right to lifelong learning in their Administrative and Constitutional Acts | Collective bargaining at sectoral and company level fills in the regulatory framework | Collective bargaining agreements at sectoral and company level play an important role but they are not the primary source of law |
| Greece | Article 1 of the Act 3369/2005 on the Systematization of Lifelong Learning and other provisions provides a right to lifelong learning | The same Act stipulates the elements with regard to education, organization and the work floor needed to develop the right to lifelong learning. | Collective bargaining agreements remain limited | Collective bargaining agreements are not the primary source of law. |
| Hungary | No full right on lifelong learning | No fully developed regulatory framework on lifelong learning | No till very limited collective bargaining agreements on the topic | Collective bargaining agreements are not the primary source of law |
| Ireland | Article 4 of the Qualifications (Training and Education) Act provides that the Act aims to facilitate lifelong learning, but no real right is recognized | Article 4 of the Qualifications (Training and Education) Act can be considered to grant a certain but vague basis | Collective bargaining agreements are numerous trying to recognize it as an individual right | Collective bargaining agreements are not considered to be a primary source of law, but they play a bottom-up role. |
| Italy | Act 92/2012 stipulates a right to lifelong learning Article 35 of the Constitution stipulates a duty for the State to help in a vocational training, article 38 stipulates the same for disabled workers. | The right provided in the Act 92/2012 is not set out in a full regulatory framework | The State stipulates that funding can be found for initiatives but setting out real collective bargaining agreements are limited | Sectoral and company level have collective bargaining agreements, but they are not a primary source of law |

(continued)

**Table 1** (continued)

| Table 1 | Right to lifelong learning | Regulatory framework by the (sub)State | CBA | Social Dialogue primary source |
|---|---|---|---|---|
| Latvia | No real right on lifelong learning | Right to education is recognized in the Constitution but the regulatory framework is limited | Limited number of collective bargaining agreements | Limited number of collective bargaining agreements and they are not the primary source of law |
| Lithuania | No recognition of the right to lifelong learning | Right to education is recognized but not really a right to lifelong learning | Limited number of collective bargaining agreements | The collective bargaining agreements are not a primary source of law |
| Luxembourg | No full recognition of the right to lifelong learning | The Act of 19 December 2008 provides a framework for lifelong learning for an organizational perspective but not with regard to the substance | Collective bargaining agreements at sectoral and company level | The collective bargaining agreements are crucial to fill in practicalities but do not bound the right to lifelong learning |
| Malta | No full right to lifelong learning but article 12 (2) of the Maltese Constitution stipulates that Malta as a state provides professional and vocational training for employees | The Education Act (chapter 327 of the Laws of Malta) provides a basis for lifelong learning but does not grant a full right | Sectoral and company agreements exist on this topic | The collective bargaining agreements are not the primary source of law. |
| The Netherlands | No fundamental right to lifelong learning | NLFQ-Act of 2024 provides a framework for lifelong learning | Sectoral and company collective bargaining agreements are numerous | Sectoral and company collective bargaining agreements are not a primary source of law |

(continued)

**Table 1** (continued)

| Table 1 | Right to lifelong learning | Regulatory framework by the (sub)State | CBA | Social Dialogue primary source |
|---|---|---|---|---|
| Poland | Article 70 of the Polish Constitution provides a right to education which is considered to imply a right on lifelong learning | The Act on Promotion of Employment and Institutions of the Labour Market of 2004 provides training for unemployed persons and the Act on Higher Education of 2005 provides continuous education | Very limited number | The limited number of collective bargaining agreements are not a primary source of law |
| Portugal | The Education Act 46/86 provides continuous education but no right on lifelong learning is provided | The Education Act does not provide specific elements with regard to lifelong learning | Very limited up to none | The limited number of collective bargaining agreements leads to the fact they cannot be considered as a primary source of law. |
| Romania | Article 13 of the National Education Act provides a right on lifelong education | The National Education Act provides in the articles 171 till 173 conditions for postgraduate education | Collective bargaining remains a difficult topic in Romania although recent legislative measures (in 2022) have been undertaken | Collective bargaining agreements, if any, are not a primary source of law |
| Slovakia | The Act 568/2009 on lifelong learning does not provide an individual right to lifelong learning | Act 292/2024 on lifelong learning provides a whole framework on the right to lifelong learning and how it needs to be organized | The coordination is set out by state and not by social partners | Collective bargaining agreements, if any, are not a primary source of law |

(continued)

**Table 1** (continued)

| Table 1 | Right to lifelong learning | Regulatory framework by the (sub)State | CBA | Social Dialogue primary source |
|---|---|---|---|---|
| Slovenia | No full right on lifelong learning | Employment Relation Act: right and duty to education and training | Limited number of collective bargaining agreements | Collective bargaining agreements at sectoral and company level but they are not a primary source of law |
| Spain | Article 5.1. of the Organic 2/ 2006 of the Act on Education stipulates a right on lifelong learning | The Royal Decree 86/2025 of 11 February 2025 provides the recognition of competences obtained through vocational training | At the national level a collective bargaining agreement was concluded in 2023 | Collective bargaining agreements fill in the regulatory framework and are therefore an additional source of law |
| Sweden | No fundamental right to lifelong learning | Very splintered regulation but not focused on lifelong learning specifically | National collective bargaining agreement in 2022 set up a labour reform and included lifelong learning | The collective bargaining agreements were and still are the primary source of law |

[a]Kirov (2019)
[b]Butkovic (2017), pp. 50–51

It may be clear from this table that the role of the EU Social Dialogue with regard to lifelong learning remains a very difficult one. Lifelong learning has not yet been considered by many EU Member States as a fundamental right. To the extent that this is desired by the EU institutions or by the Social Partners, they could set up a joint opinion on the necessity to improve health and safety of the workers or to improve the working conditions. These are interesting and challenging topics which could gain from a good and fundamental breakthrough at EU level.

The development of this fundamental right and the substance can better be granted at national level. This interplay would be a perfect example of a good application of the principle of subsidiarity and proportionality. Instead of obliging the Member States to develop in full regulations on the organization and the carrying out in practice of the right on lifelong learning, this outcome would be a lot stronger.

A good and well-balanced interplay between EU institutions (meaning in this case the social partners of the EU Social Dialogue) and Member States (meaning in this case the social partners in different EU Member States) have a major opportunity to use in practice and correctly the multilevel governance which used to be the basis of the EU: unity in diversity.

## 8 Conclusion

The EU Social Dialogue has needed a lot of time to develop in full. After the first mention in the European Single Act of 1987, it actually took till the beginning of the new millennium before the EU Social Dialogue could really play its role in full.

The setting up of a real EU Social Dialogue has currently been promoted by the last two EU Commissions. They same to be willing to use the means which are provided by the TEU and the TFEU in order to establish a more social Europe where social partners can play a role in full.

However, the concept of lifelong learning remains a vague concept at EU level. Even if it is fully recognized as an individual (and fundamental) right in the Pillar of Social Rights, it remains to be discussed what the precise content of this right. Social Partners at EU level could play a role in demystifying this fundamental right.

It is our conviction that such a demystification has to take place in cooperation and constant interplay between the EU and its Member States. It is therefore of utmost importance to map how each of the EU Member States currently deals with the so-called right on lifelong learning. A first analysis guides us to the conclusion that most of the EU Member States have not yet fully recognized this right of the Pillar of Social Rights into their legal constellation.

Given this background, it seems useful that the EU Social Dialogue on lifelong learning does not forget to take the necessary intermediate steps. The principal subsidiarity can therefore be a useful tool. Constant dialogue between social partners at EU level and at Member States level may lead to more intensive results of the social dialogue on lifelong learning in the Member States itself.

The only initiative which may not lose the Member States and can help them on a short-term basis, is to recognize the right to lifelong learning at EU level. EU Social Dialogue can therefore be crucial to set the first step to harmonization.

## References

Barnard C (2014) EU employment law and the European social model: the past, the present and the future. Curr Leg Probl 67(1):199–237

Butkovic H (2017) Innovative practices of Croatian trade unions: is there sufficient ground for optimism? In: Bernaciak M, Kahancová M (eds) Innovative union practices in Central-Eastern Europe. ETUI, Brussels, pp 39–56

Cedefop (2024) The imperative of lifelong learning. https://www.cedefop.europa.eu/en/news/imperative-lifelong-learning

Communication of the President of the EU-Commission, 8 March 2016 launching a consultation on a European Pillar of Social Rights

Copeland P (2021) The politics of the EU social dialogue. In ter Haar B, Kun A (eds) EU collective labour law. Edward Elgar, Cheltenham, pp 132–144
Davies G (2006) Subsidiarity: the wrong idea, in the wrong place at the wrong time. Common Mark Law Rev 43(1):66–84
Deakin S (2017) What follows austerity from social pillars to new deal. In: Vandenbroucke F, Barnard C, De Baere G (eds) A European social Union after the crisis. CUP, Cambridge, pp 160–191
Dorssemont F (2022) Some observations on the EPSU case: a bad judgment for democracy and subsidiarity, alias a textbook example of not promoting the European Social Dialogue. In: Hartzen A-C, Iossa A, Karageorgiou E (eds) Law, solidarity and the limits of social Europe. Edward Elgar, Cheltenham, pp 43–61
Estella M (2002) The principle of subsidiarity and its critique. OUP, Oxford
Fabbrini F (2016) The principle of subsidiarity. In: Trimidas T, Schutze R (eds) Oxford principles of EU law. iCourts Working Paper Series No. 66. OUP, Oxford
Fromage D, Kreilinger V (2017) National parliaments third yellow card and the struggle over the revision of the posted workers' directive. Eur J Leg Stud 10(1):125–160
Green A (2006) Models of lifelong learning and the 'knowledge society'. COMPARE 36(3):307–325
Green Cowles M (2013) The single European act. In: Jones E, Menon A, Weatherill S (eds) The Oxford handbook on EU law. OUP, Oxford, pp 107–120
Kirov V (2019) Bulgaria: collective bargaining eroding but still existing. In: Müller T, Vandaele K, Waddington J (eds) Collective bargaining in Europe: towards an endgame, vol III. ETUI, Brussels, pp 77–92
Menegatti E (2025) Why the Directive on Adequate Minimum Wage Does Fit in the EU Competence: A Response to the Advocate's General Opinion. Menegatti, Emanuele, Why the Directive on Adequate Minimum Wages does Fit within EU competence: A Response to the Advocate General's Opinion (April 14, 2025). ETUI Research Paper - Policy Brief 2025.02, ETUI, Brussels. https://papers.ssrn.com/sol3/papers.cfm?abstract_id=5227333
Opinion of Advocate-General Emiliou on 14 January 2025. https://curia.europa.eu/juris/document/document.jsf;jsessionid=764D0DB60BF22243AAC8947F87C4BD66?text=&docid=294192&pageIndex=0&doclang=EN&mode=req&dir=&occ=first&part=1&cid=19121528
Panara C (2015) The sub-national dimension of the EU: a legal study of multilevel governance. Springer-Verlag, Heidelberg
Panara C (2022) Subsidiarity vs. autonomy in the EU. Eur Pub Law 28(2):269–296
R.F (1953) Labour under the European coal and steal community. World Today 9(11):497–504
Schmitt M (2014) Evaluation of European Union responses to the crisis having regard to primary legislation. In: Bruun N, Lörcher K, Schömann I (eds) The economic and financial crisis and collective labour law in Europe. Hart Publishing, Oxford, pp 195–241
Schutze R (2009) From dual to cooperative federalism: the changing structure of cooperative federalism. OUP, Oxford
Statement of the Presidency of the Council of the EU, the European Commission and the European Social Partners, 16 June 2016
Vandenbroucke F, Barnard C, De Baere G (eds) (2017) A European Social Union after the crisis. CUP, Cambridge
Volles N (2014) Lifelong learning in the EU: changing conceptualisations, actors, and policies. Stud High Educ 41(2):343–363
Welz C (2008) The European Social Union under the articles 138 and 139 of the EC Treaty. Wolters Kluwer Law International, Alphen aan den Rijn

**Alexander De Becker** is professor of labour law at Ghent University. He has held numerous visiting professorships and the following Chairs: The State as Employer (University of Amsterdam, 2010–2015; University of Leiden, 2015–2017); Excellence Chair University of Turin, 2022;

Bologna Chari, University of Bologna, 2025. He has widely published and is recognized as a leading expert in the field of The State as Employer.

**Valentina Franca**, PhD, works as an associate professor and researcher of labour law and social security law at the Faculty of Public Administration, University of Ljubljana, Slovenia. Her research includes numerous studies, books, and articles in the field of collective labour relations, digitalization in labour relations, and new forms of work. She is a member of the editorial boards of scientific journals and participates as a national expert in international associations such as the Worker Participation Network at the ETUI Institute in Brussels and CEELEX at the International Labor Organization. She is also an active researcher in national and international projects for various organizations, such as Eurofound, ILO, EIGE, OECD, EC, and the like, and lecturer at various professional and scientific conferences.

# Regulating Lifelong Learning Under Collective Agreements

**Caroline Johansson**

## 1 Introduction

This chapter explores the advantages and disadvantages of regulating lifelong learning under collective agreements. If lifelong learning is to be structured as part of the system of labour law, it is important to examine the premises for its regulation under collective agreements, which with collective bargaining is one of the primary tools for regulating labour.[1] Collective agreements form an important part of labour market regulation in several European countries, albeit there are different industrial relations models that lead to differences in how bargaining is conducted, on what level it is done, and the content of the agreements. Furthermore, regulating the labour market through collective agreement is both encouraged and protected by international law and the EU.[2]

The collective dimension of labour law is one of the two dimensions that constitute classic labour law. It is explained as a way to redeem the weak position of the worker.[3] Collective bargaining and the regulation of wages under collective agreements reduce competition between workers and ensure fair wages for those who are covered. Wages are not the only working conditions established in collective agree-

[1] See in this volume Murto J, Lifelong Learning and Labour Law – Mapping the new Phenomenon in the Systematics of Labour Law.

[2] See in this volume Claus F, Exploring the Future of Lifelong Learning through the Tapestry of European Policy History and Kain F, Legal Foundations of Lifelong Learning and Labour Law in Europe.

[3] Ahlberg and Bruun (2017), pp. 17–20; Jacobs (2011), Davies and Freedland (1983).

C. Johansson (✉)
Department of Law, Uppsala, Sweden
e-mail: caroline.johansson@jur.uu.se



J. Murto, V. Franca (eds.), *Labour Law and Lifelong Learning*,
https://doi.org/10.1007/978-3-032-11035-0_8

ments: vacation time, work environment, occupational benefits, and also the right to training and education have long been subject to collective bargaining.[4] Many of the more highly qualified blue-collar professions have a tradition of workplace training and apprenticeships that can be traced back to the guild system.[5]

Regulation under collective agreements should not be viewed in a vacuum. Even in the most autonomous industrial relations model, there are collaborations with the state, or economic, or legal incentives that derive from it. Public policy aspects are dealt with in other chapters of this contribution.[6] In this chapter, the actions of social partners will be stressed, and state measures in connection with social dialogue will only be mentioned briefly. The same goes for the social partners' involvement in education and training policies that fall outside collective bargaining. The social partners may play other roles in the regulation of lifelong learning, especially on national level. They may, for example, play a consultative role in the law-making process or advocate for certain policies.[7] Such initiatives will not be dealt with here.

The chapter outline is as follows. After the introduction comes two main sections. The first focuses on thematic aspects of regulating lifelong learning under collective agreements and the second gives an account of the advantages and disadvantages of regulating lifelong learning under collective agreements, depending on what level—local, sectoral, or cross-sectoral—the agreement is concluded. This section connects to different European industrial relation models and provides examples from various countries. The chapter ends with some concluding remarks.

## 2 Thematic Aspects of Regulating Lifelong Learning in Collective Agreements

This section focuses on certain aspects that follow from the contractual traits of collective agreements and what impact such traits may have on the regulation of lifelong learning under collective agreements.

[4] Jacobs (2009) and Johansson (2020).

[5] Carlson (2018), Jacobs (1986), Adlercreutz (1954).

[6] See e.g. in this volume Murto J, Lifelong Learning and Labour Law – Mapping the new Phenomenon in the Systematics of Labour Law, section 4.3. and Urpilainen M. Micro-credentials and individual learning accounts – Promoting lifelong learning in the EU' employment policy?

[7] Winterton (2007).

## 2.1 *Collective Agreements and Their Contractual Traits*

Collective bargaining and collective agreements sprang from the development of contract law and the inequality in bargaining power that contracts between individual workers and employers entail.[8] Collective agreements may have more or less in common with other forms of contracts, depending on the industrial relations model in play. Nonetheless, there are some contractual traits that are inherent to regulation under collective agreements. Most importantly, the content of the agreement is negotiated by the social partners, and during this process, the social partners own the collective agreement.[9] The autonomy of the social partners and the right to collective bargaining are protected both as civil rights[10] and as labour rights,[11] indicating that these contractual aspects are inseparable from regulation under collective agreements. This implies that the content of collective agreements depends on the interests of the social partners and the power balance between them. Both the interest of the social partners and the power balance between them are affected by the level on which bargaining takes place and on the coordination between levels.[12] Furthermore, public incentives affect how inclined the social partners are to include lifelong learning and can also steer the content of learning activities on all levels of bargaining.

While the initial stage—bargaining and content of the agreement—is close to contract law in all industrial relations models, other aspects tend to be more differentiated. For example, the scope of a collective agreement and its enforcement vary considerably between different models. In many countries on the European continent, collective agreements gain their mandatory effect through public intervention.[13] This makes enforcement of labour rights more inclined to be a public matter than a contract matter.[14] In the Nordic countries, on the other hand, the collective agreements' legal status derives from them being enforceable contracts, valid between the parties and their members. Their scope is usually based on which social partners have concluded the agreement, the number of employers who are members, and the wording of the contract. The main form of enforcement of collective agree-

---

[8] See for example Gardner (2018), Jacobs (1986), Chap. 5 and Kahn-Freund (1967).

[9] However, many states have during different periods exercised or made attempts to exercise formal or informal control over the regulation of working conditions, especially wages. See Jacobs (2009), pp. 204–207.

[10] Article 11 in the European Convention on Human Rights.

[11] Right to Organise and Collective Bargaining Convention (No. 98) and article 28 of the EU Charter of Fundamental Rights.

[12] See Sect. 3 in this chapter.

[13] Collective agreements are made generally applicable in a certain sector through public decision. See for example Jacobs (2009), pp. 209–210.

[14] Malmberg (2009), pp. 273–279. By "public matter" I refer to inspections by labour inspectorates and individual judicial procedures. The latter has become more prominent in all European countries, partly due to the influence of EU law and the European Court of Human Rights, see pp. 280–283.

ments is through trade union supervision and negotiation between the parties in combination with individual court proceedings, where the social partners often take part in the proceedings, representing both workers and employers, respectively.[15]

## 2.2 The Definition of Lifelong Learning in Relation to Collective Agreements

The definition of lifelong learning used here and in the EU is very broad.[16] It entails formal, non-formal, and informal learning. It is not necessary to draw a clear distinction between the subcategories, but for the purpose of this chapter, the main focus will be on the first two, since they entail intentional learning. Learning needs to be intentional and have some sort of firmness in order to constitute content of an agreement, at least content that can be enforced. Informal learning can, however, be relevant, in the sense that everyday learning from activities at the workplace can be formalised through validation measures. How validation measures are outlined, to whom they are accessible, and by whom they are developed are issues that can be regulated under collective agreements.[17]

It is important to acknowledge that the concept "lifelong learning" is often not used by the social partners. Instead, they might use different concepts that are more common in their national context and that are more in line with the policies for learning activities that exist nationally or in their sector. Such concepts may have a narrower meaning than lifelong learning.[18] Lifelong learning is, however, used in this chapter as an umbrella conception encompassing various forms of training, education, and other learning activities established in collective agreements, independent of whether the activity as such primarily benefits the individual worker, the employer, the labour market, or society as a whole.

## 2.3 A Contractual Right or an Aspiration?

Clauses in collective agreements can be formulated as contractual rights or as aspirations.[19] This is also true for lifelong learning. Furthermore, learning is a form of activity in which the worker needs to take initiative and perform in order for the

[15] Malmberg (2009), pp. 270–272.

[16] See in this volume Introduction and Claus F, Exploring the Future of Lifelong Learning through the Tapestry of European Policy History.

[17] Martínez Lucio et al. (2007), pp. 227–228.

[18] Léonard and Perin (2009), pp. 291–293; Cedefop (2010), Sect. 4.1.

[19] The same goes for other contracts; See in this volume Sipka P, Lifelong Learning: An Obligation for the Employer or an Empty Right?, section 3.3.

activity to have the desired quality and result.[20] It can also be in the interests of the employer that the worker learns and that the investment made at least indirectly benefits the employer. In that sense, there might be streaks of obligation inherent in learning activities. In addition, learning can be part of social partner policy, rather than rights and obligations between worker and employer. This entails that the clauses on lifelong learning can be directed at the individual or at the social partners on lower bargaining levels.

The wording of clauses on learning and training can be more or less strict. When it is less strict, it is not farfetched to view it more as a policy statement or a sign of mutual understanding of a desired direction, than a right. In the collective agreement between the Swedish Teachers Union and Almega, the term "professional development" is used. It is stated that

> The partners' joint view is that educational work with children presumes… professional development.[21]

Such a statement does not indicate how professional development is to be organised or what it entails. It does not contain any specific rights or duties for the individual worker. Its only function is to express a mutual opinion of the partners that needs to be further elaborated. This can be done in other parts of the agreement or on a lower level, such as in a local collective agreement or in an individual employment contract.

In Belgium, the content of collective agreements is often formulated as rights for workers. This is also true regarding learning activities. For example, in the collective agreement covering blue-collar workers who are not covered by a specific sectoral agreement, it is stated that it is an individual right for workers

> … in companies with more than 5 but less than 10 employees to receive a collective training right of an average of 2 days per employee every 2 years...[22]

Hence, important aspects to consider when analysing regulation in collective agreements are the wording, to whom the content of the agreement is directed, and for whom the wording creates rights and obligations. This has implications for the ability to enforce a collective agreement: both form the worker's and the employer's perspective. If the agreement does not contain any individual rights or obligations, it will not be possible to enforce it through individual judicial proceedings. On the other hand, from an industrial relations approach to enforcement, such agreements give the social partners tools and arguments for subsequent negotiations and/or follow-up on whether and to what extent employers must actually provide learning

---

[20] Tuschling and Engemann (2006), pp. 457–459.

[21] Friskoleavtalet 2023-09-01 to 2025-08-31, concluded by Almega Tjänsteföretagen and Sveriges lärare, annex 7.

[22] Commission Paritaire Auxiliaire pour les ouvriers (CP 100), Accord sectoriel du 24 octobre 2023 pour la période 2023–2024, art 10.

activities.[23] Subsequent negotiations can also lead to individual rights in collective agreements on lower bargaining levels.[24]

### 2.4 Lifelong Learning as a Contractual Right: Remuneration or Something Else?

When a collective agreement establishes contractual rights for an individual worker, it leads to the question of how to formulate such rights. Should lifelong learning be viewed as remuneration? The most common form of remuneration is monetary. Remuneration can also be in the form of long-term benefits such as occupational pensions and supplementary sick leave benefits.[25] Even if this form of remuneration differs from ordinary pay, it consists of monetary contributions that will be disbursed in the future or in case of certain events, such as sickness. Lifelong learning, on the other hand, encompasses more aspects than monetary remuneration. At the same time, learning needs to be broken down into concrete content that the employer can offer and the worker can claim a right to. One way to describe this transformation is that the premises for learning are what can be put in a contract. Examples of such premises can be to be granted the economic conditions to learn, the time to learn, and access to learning infrastructure such as courses and programmes.

The right to lifelong learning can first of all be translated into money. In the Swedish sheet metal and ventilation work agreement, it is established that apprentices have a right to receive their salary during the hours they study and train. Similar regulations can be found in French sectoral agreements. Furthermore, the Swedish transition agreements contain different forms of study allowances with the aim of making it economically feasible for an individual worker to take both longer and shorter periods of studies.[26]

Second, to facilitate training and studies, the employer needs to ensure that the worker has time to study. Several collective agreements include the right to take time off to study, such as the Belgian example in Sect. 2.3 above. In another Swedish example, the employee has the right to take time off work to study or train, or to validate skills. The time off can be limited or denied if it constitutes a serious disruption to the employer's activities. The meaning of serious disruption is clarified as the employer's business not being able to continue in a reasonable manner or the

[23] Such approach to enforcement is still common, albeit not as dominant as before, in the Nordic countries and the UK, Malmberg (2009), pp. 270–272.

[24] See footnote 66 below for an illustrative example.

[25] Comandé and Giubboni (2020), Lurie (2020), Votinius Julén (2020) and Johansson (2020).

[26] These agreements are dealt with in Sects. 3.3 and 3.4.1 respectively.

time off leading to greater increases in costs. That a worker's time off entails disruption or inconvenience is something that the employer has to accept.[27]

Third, apart from pay or allowance and time off for education or training, a collective agreement can require that an employer organises in-work training or gives access to certain training and education organised or commissioned by the social partners. The employer's obligation to ensure that education and training are in place can be combined with an individual right for each worker to access in-work training in an organised manner in order to upskill and maintain relevance in the workplace. Examples of internal activities of less formal character is the opportunity to take part in project schemes and produce reports. It can also consist of job rotation or the opportunity for employees to try on other tasks in the company.[28] This form of internal training can be made relevant outside the current employer's realm if the right to receive in-work training is combined with a right to get it formally validated.

Finally, free auxiliary services such as educational guidance, mentors, or access to certain third-party institutions constitute other possible rights established in collective agreements.

## *2.5 Learning for Life and Limited Contract Periods*

Rights and obligations stemming from a contract are usually limited to the period when the contract is in force. This is also true for collective agreements. The duration of a collective agreement may vary with the type of industrial relations model in play. In most countries, collective agreements differ from other agreements in how their content is applicable not only to the parties but also to third parties in the form of workers. The Swedish social partners and their members are directly bound and the employer is further obliged to apply the terms in the collective agreement to all workers within its scope. Otherwise, the employer breaches the contract and can be liable to pay damages to the trade union. In many other countries, the applicability comes with a public decision making the agreement generally applicable, often in a certain sector. The latter tends to detach the applicability from the contract logic. However, the contract logic is present in one way or another in all industrial relation models. Three aspects will be mentioned here.

---

[27] The collective agreement on skills and transition for the Swedish municipality sector, KOM-KR Kompetens och omställningsavtal i lydelse 2022-10-01, concluded by Sveriges Kommuner och Regioner and Sobona – Kommunala företagens arbetsgivarorganisation and Svenska Kommunalarbetareförbundet, OFR, Lärarförbundets och Lärarnas Riksförbunds Samverkansråd and AkademikerAlliansen, chapter 4.

[28] Examples taken from the agreement concerning training and development in the company, 2023-04-02–2025-03-31, concluded between Teknikföretagen, Sveriges ingenjörer, Unionen, and Ledarna.

The first aspect has to do with the social partners' autonomy. Bargaining always entails a give and take that is dependent on the power of each party. Depending on the industrial relations model and on the level at which the agreement is negotiated, it is more or less easy to terminate or renegotiate a collective agreement. When lifelong learning is a contractual right, its content and scope lies in the hands of the social partners. The more local such an agreement is, the more exposed such a right is to the economic reality of the employer in question and the power dynamic between the local social partners.

Second, if the worker changes employers and the learning activities are connected to a local collective agreement, or if the worker changes sector, the worker will no longer fall within the scope of the collective agreement. This limits the time during which the worker can enjoy learning activities, and hence the period during which such activities can be enforced on a certain employer. However, such issues can be bridged by, for example, moving the learning activities to a third party that is financed by current contributions during the worker's period of employment. Study allowance can, for example, be put aside for each worker in a manner similar to occupational benefits, to use when the worker needs, or wants, to study or learn a new skill.[29] Access to third-party education or training institutions could also constitute an acquired right for a former worker.[30]

This leads us to the final aspect. The social partners may include vesting periods or waiting periods in order for a worker to enjoy learning activities. Parallels can be drawn to occupational benefits such as occupational pensions.[31] Vesting periods or waiting periods can be motivated when the financial burden of a worker's education and vocational training falls on an individual employer. From the employer's perspective, the shorter the time period the worker has been employed, the lesser their incentive to pay for rights that can be claimed after the employment ends. Instead, it is in the employer's interests that the worker has been at the workplace for a longer period in order for the employer to invest further in his or her training. However, such arguments carry less weight if the financial burden is divided between employers in a sector. If learning activities are established in collective agreements that cover several employers, a branch, or even several branches, the incentive for each employer increases—partly because the cost can be divided between a collective of employers, partly because it is possible to profit from investments in workers' training that other employers have made.

To conclude, the scope of the collective agreement is vital for workers' access to learning activities. This leads us to the issue of what level collective agreements are concluded on, since the higher the level, the wider the scope.

---

[29] Johansson (2020).

[30] See Sect. 3.4.1 and the Swedish transition agreements for an illustrative example.

[31] In the case of occupational pensions, the EU has limited the use of such periods by adopting Directive 2014/50/EU of the European parliament and of the council of 16 April 2014 on minimum requirements for enhancing worker mobility between Member States by improving the acquisition and preservation of supplementary pension rights.

# 3 Lifelong Learning and the Levels of Collective Bargaining

This section focuses on the advantages and disadvantages of regulating lifelong learning under collective agreements, depending on the level on which the agreement is concluded. It is clear that there are clusters of countries where the main regulation is on a certain level. Hence, which of the levels is dominant varies between European countries, and not all levels exist in all countries. How well coordinated the levels are differ as well.

## *3.1 The Levels of Collective Bargaining and the Move Towards Decentralisation*

Both in literature and in practice, one way to systematise collective bargaining is to use levels.[32] First, there is the local or company level, where collective agreements are concluded between individual employers and local trade unions or local branches of trade unions. Second, there is the sectoral level, where collective agreements are concluded for a sector or a branch. These are in general concluded on the national level, but in some countries such agreements can be regional.[33] Finally, there is a higher level which can consist of either all relevant social partners (national level) or several sectors that are more or less coordinated (cross-sectoral or confederate level).

The level on which collective agreements are concluded may affect the types of learning activities that are included in the agreement. The more local an agreement is, and the less coordinated it is with collective agreements on higher levels, the more likely it is that the learning activity is primarily beneficial for a specific employer's undertaking. Workers, on the other hand, may obtain greater benefits from training and education that can be applied across a branch or are useful in the labour market as a whole.[34] It also affect the scope of the collective agreement (see Sect. 2.5).

A common European trend over recent decades is a shift towards decentralised bargaining.[35] The decentralisation has different characteristics depending on the industrial relations model. In Sweden, for example, decentralisation has taken place within the institutional structure of the social partners, in the sense that negotiations on wages and other working conditions first moved from the confederate level to the sectoral level. In most sectors, the agreements are formulated in such a way that they leave the local partners ample room for manoeuvre. In many cases, wage

---

[32] Cedefop (2010); European Commission, Directorate-General for Employment, Social Affairs and Inclusion (2008) and Heyes (2007) to mention some examples.

[33] This is true for Germany, Cedefop (2010), p. 73; Martínez Lucio et al. (2007).

[34] Heyes (2007).

[35] Tros (2023), Koukiadaki et al. (2016), Baccaro and Howell (2011).

negotiation has turned into a concern for the individual worker. This development, although affected by external pressures, was regulated by the social partners. It has been called a form of organised decentralisation.[36] In relation to lifelong learning, however, an opposite development can be traced since more issues on learning have been regulated on the confederate level.[37]

A different example is Italy, which was recentralised during the same time period as Sweden started its organised decentralisation.[38] However, Italy underwent a decentralisation process in the aftermath of the European economic crisis. The tendency during the crisis was even more evident in other European countries within the eurozone. A shift towards decentralised bargaining was often recommended by the EU.[39]

## 3.2 *Regulating Lifelong Learning at the Company Level*

In some European countries, predominantly in the eastern part of Europe, collective bargaining is conducted mainly on company level.[40] There may be many explanations for this. Trade union density is low, which can be explained by the role that trade unions played during the communist era.[41] After the communist era, the organisation level among employers has been low. Low organisation levels do not offer fertile ground for coordination, leading to decentralised bargaining models. Furthermore, in East Europe, lifelong learning and training in general is often dealt with outside collective bargaining, sometimes between the social partners on the company level without concluding an agreement, sometimes between employers and individual workers or as a company matter decided by the employer or among a group of employers.[42]

While local collective agreements may exhibit egalitarian features in providing the same conditions for workers employed by the same employer, they share some common features with individual contracts. Local collective agreements, unlike employment contracts, have the benefit that the conditions are negotiated by a trade union. This often entails a better bargaining position for the workers' side: A trade

---

[36] Johansson (2020), p. 344; Baccaro and Howell (2011), pp. 543–545.

[37] See Sect. 3.4.1.

[38] Baccaro and Howell (2011), pp. 541–534.

[39] Koukiadaki et al. (2016).

[40] This is true in, for example, Poland, Romania, and Lithuania. Cedefop (2010), p. 81. The widespread use of company-level bargaining in the eastern part of the EU and its impact on sectoral bargaining on the EU level is discussed in Marginson (2005).

[41] European Commission, Directorate-General for Employment, Social Affairs and Inclusion (2008), p. 74.

[42] Lithuania, Poland, Hungary, and Slovakia are mentioned as examples, Cedefop (2010), p. 73. As in all countries, this is also combined with public initiatives, see for example Eurofound (2023b, 2024b).

union usually has more insight into the sector concerned, which reduces information asymmetry. Furthermore, competition between workers at the workplace is reduced. Additionally, company-wide regulation facilitates in-house organisation of education and training. Even when sectoral collective agreements do not guarantee concrete rights (see Sect. 2.3), local trade unions might be able to negotiate more successfully with companies where the economic margin is wider.[43] This facilitates enforcement of the rights of individual workers. Company collective agreements may function as good examples or forerunners and inspire other companies or even sectoral bargaining on lifelong learning.[44]

When a collective agreement is concluded at the company level, however, there is a risk of lock-in effects. The conditions are limited to the contract period and the company in question. Workers will normally lose access to the learning opportunities connected to the workplace in question if they choose to change employers. There may also be less incentive for the employer to offer training and education that is of more general use, since such investments may instead benefit another employer if the worker leaves.[45] This indicates that company-level agreements may discourage workers from moving from a company with a good learning benefit, and it may also put a strain on the variety of learning activities (see Sect. 2.5).

When the masters of the agreement in question are at the company level, there is little to stop them from renegotiating the terms if they find it fitting or necessary. In harsher economic times, when training and education are at least as important, there is a risk that trade unions sacrifice learning in favour of retained wage levels. There is also an interrelation between weak social partners and decentralisation, indicating that the trade unions in this case do not have a strong bargaining position.[46] There is, of course, the possibility to ensure that costs for education and training are evenly spread by making monthly contributions for each employee, similar to occupational benefits (see Sect. 2.4). However, such systems can be difficult to organise on the company level. They often presuppose a more coordinated industrial relation model or some form of public–private hybrid or other form of public interventions where the state sets the framework in which the social partners negotiate, or provide incentives that make it economically sound for companies to choose to conclude agreements on, for example, learning activities.

---

[43] A combination of bargaining on different levels seem to be successful for collective agreement coverage, European Commission, Directorate-General for Employment, Social Affairs and Inclusion (2008), p. 79.

[44] Comandé and Giubboni (2020), pp. 329–330. A similar example of how forerunner agreements can work is how some Swedish trade unions managed to push for flex-pension—a form of part-time pension—in some sectors, which then was followed by other sectors in subsequent negotiation rounds. See Johansson (2020), p. 349. For an empirical and theoretical discussion on wage imitation and pattern bargaining, see Kaufman (2002) and De la Croix (1994).

[45] Research, however, shows that employers do tend to offer general training, see Brunello and Wruuck (2020), p. 4. It may also be difficult to draw a sharp line between general training and company-specific training in many sectors.

[46] European Commission, Directorate-General for Employment, Social Affairs and Inclusion (2008), p. 79.

Lifelong learning regulated at the company level tend to be unevenly distributed over regions, sectors, and workers.[47] In countries with local collective bargaining and no public interventions regarding lifelong learning, there are only a few sectors where it is fairly common. In Poland, for example, lifelong learning has been subject to negotiations in the chemical sector.[48] This might be explained by the fact that the chemical sector is knowledge-based and exposed to international competition.[49] The uneven distribution can also be seen in countries that have gone from centralised collective agreements to more decentralised collective bargaining, such as Italy. Even though the Italian industrial relations model still includes bargaining on higher levels, there has been an increase in negotiations on the company level. In the aftermath of the European economic crisis, the move towards decentralised bargaining accelerated.[50] Many local agreements contain benefits that can be placed under the umbrella notion of company welfare (welfare aziendale), which covers a range of monetary and non-monetary benefits, including education and training.[51] Comandé and Giubboni refer to empirical research that shows that only a small portion of the companies offer company welfare and few workers have access to it. The majority of such collective agreements have been concluded in the north of Italy.[52] The uneven distribution of local collective agreements indicates that learning activities offered in such context are not a question of long-term need and general labour market strategy, but rather a business strategy for companies with the economic means to offer occupational welfare.[53]

## *3.3 Regulating Lifelong Learning at the Sectoral Level*

Sectoral collective bargaining is a common feature in many industrial relations models. For Western European countries, negotiation on wages is primarily done at the sectoral level.[54] The sectoral social partners have a common interest in workers' skills being up to date in order to ensure the competitiveness of the sector. An example of such a joint position can be found in the Agreement concerning training and development concluded between the Swedish engineering sector's companies, the Engineers of Sweden, Unionen, and Ledarna.

---

[47] European Commission, Directorate-General for Employment, Social Affairs and Inclusion (2008), p. 78; Winterton (2007).

[48] Cedefop (2010), p. 74.

[49] Bechter et al. (2012).

[50] For a more extensive account in English, see Iossa (2017), pp. 208–219.

[51] Comandé and Giubboni (2020), p. 326.

[52] Comandé and Giubboni (2020), p. 327. See ADAPT (2024).

[53] Iossa draws similar conclusions framing it as an instrument adopted by single companies to compete on the market. Iossa (2017), p. 212.

[54] For example, Germany, Italy, Sweden and Spain, Cedefop (2010), pp. 80–81. See Jacobs (2009), pp. 224–225.

> Companies within the engineering industry are operating in conditions of increasingly tough national and international competition. Possession of the required skills is important in order for companies to be able to run their operations. This requires the development of work methods and organisation and that the knowledge of all personnel is renewed and strengthened.[55]

Hence, the sector-specific challenges can make fertile ground for negotiations on lifelong learning.

Sectoral bargaining reduces lock-in effects since the same conditions are applicable to all employers in the sector that are bound by the agreement. Hence, workers can move freely between employers without losing their rights to learning activities. However, like local agreements, sectoral agreements may be more focused on the training and education needed for the specific profession and less on general knowledge or the needs of the labour market as a whole. There is ample variety of regulation on sectoral level—from a detailed regulation that does not need to be fleshed out on the company level to framework agreements that require specification on the local level, and finally sectoral agreements that supplement national regulations. Depending on the type of agreement, it may be more or less feasible for an individual worker to claim any rights deriving from the agreement.

As mentioned in the introduction to this chapter, there was detailed regulation of training and apprenticeship in the guild system. In Sweden, the tradition of regulating training in certain blue-collar professions went from public regulation during the guild era to being regulated under sectoral collective agreements.[56] A modern example of how such collective agreements can be outlined is the sheet metal and ventilation work agreement. Annexed to the agreement on wages and working conditions is a separate education agreement focusing on the different steps of the education to become, among other things, a fully trained sheet metal worker. The agreement imposes obligations mainly on the employer but also on the apprentice. In the agreement, it is stated that

> The employer shall as soon as possible, but at least within 8 weeks, register the apprentice in PVYN's (the Sheet and ventilation professional board) apprentice register (KUB). When the registration is done the worker becomes an apprentice and the employer binds itself to give the basic and qualified training according to this agreement.[57]

The education is supposed to fulfil the standards established by the organisations in the sector. Apart from the social partners themselves, there is the sheet and ventilation professional board, which supervises the training. This is an organisation established by the social partners and not a public body. Fulfilling the standards is often a requirement to be able to continue working within the profession. An important feature is that it is the social partners that have the primary influence in both setting

[55] Agreement concerning training and development, 2023-04-02–2025-03-31 concluded between Teknikföretagen, Sveriges ingenjörer, Unionen and Ledarna.

[56] Olofsson and Wadensjö (2020), p. 56.

[57] Plåt- och ventilationsavtalet 2023-05-01-2025-04-30 concluded by Plåt & Ventföretagen and Svenska Byggnadsarbetareförbundet, Utbildningsavtalet, clause 4.

the standards and assessing whether individual workers fulfil the requirements. Similar systems exist in Germany, for example.[58]

Agreements on lifelong learning are also common in white-collar sectors. The above-mentioned Agreement concerning training and development in the engineering sector sets a framework for professional development in the sector, but the idea is that the concrete measures are elaborated further on the company level in so-called agreements on professional development. The sectoral agreement indicates that the local parties shall cooperate to facilitate training and education.[59] The sectoral agreement also states the priorities of the "Engineering industry skills development council", which is set up by the sectoral parties. Amongst other things, it shall encourage the local social partners and follow up on the needs in the sector. In conclusion, the sectoral agreement sets a framework and offers an infrastructure to support the local social partners. This means that no individual rights are established in the sectoral agreement. The closest the agreement gets to addressing the rights of a certain group of workers is that special attention should be paid to those workers who have short and insufficient training for the tasks performed within the company and to those who return to work after a longer period of parental leave or sick leave. This is stated after the general proclamation that all workers should be given an opportunity for personal development at work, which shows that the social partners are aware that in practice certain groups are at risk of falling behind.[60] The clause regulates a typical trade union interest.[61]

Sectoral agreements of the kind mentioned above are focused on education that enables the worker to continue working for a certain employer or in a certain sector. The limitation to the sector can be redeemed by concluding collective agreements on a higher level, i.e. either the confederate or national level. It can also be redeemed with various forms of private/public hybrids. In France, public regulation gives workers a right to training (droit individuel à la formation). The right to training was initiated by the national intersectoral agreement of 2003 on workers' access to lifelong learning, which was then introduced in the labour code by the law of 2004 on lifelong learning and social dialogue. According to the law, every worker who fulfils certain criteria is entitled to 20 hours of training per year, with a maximum of 120 hours training in 6 years, on his or her own initiative.[62] An interesting feature is that sectoral agreements can supplement the statutory rights of the worker. A sectoral agreement can provide that training takes place during working hours, but in the

[58] Cedefop (2010), p. 69 and Heyes (2007), pp. 251–252. See in this volume Ruhwedel K – Stein J, Works councils as promoters of lifelong learning – opportunities and challenges.

[59] A comparison can be made with German company training mentors. - See in this volume Ruhwedel K – Stein J, Works councils as promoters of lifelong learning – opportunities and challenges, section 3.3.

[60] Unqualified or low skilled workers and older workers have been identified as the groups that are the most disadvantaged in receiving or undertaking formal training, Subramanian and Zimmermann (2020), p. 302.

[61] Heyes (2007).

[62] There have been recent changes in the system, see Eurofound (2023a, 2024a).

absence of such an agreement, the employee will train after working hours, with a benefit paid by the employer that corresponds to 50% of the salary. Hence, a sectoral agreement can regulate both whose time is used—the worker's spare time or working hours—and the remuneration— wages or a benefit calculated from the wages.[63] The French example constitutes a mix of intersectoral and sectoral agreements combined with legislation. The sectoral agreement enforces the worker's position regarding both the balance between working life and private life, and who bears the monetary cost.

### 3.4 Regulate Lifelong Learning on Cross-sectoral or National Level

Several, primarily Western, European countries have a tradition of collective bargaining on the cross-sectoral or national level.[64] In Spain, national agreements have been important in how the national training system is outlined, and in Belgium, training is part of the intersectoral negotiations that result in collective agreements.[65] There are also examples of cross-sectoral bargaining from Italy, Ireland, and France.[66] In Sweden, most trade unions and employers' associations are members of confederations. The confederations conclude agreements on various topics such as negotiation procedures, occupational benefits, and learning activities.

There are advantages with regulation on the confederate or national level. Inevitably, such negotiations come closer to the public discussion on education and learning, irrespective of whether the industrial relations model has formal ties to public decision-making or not.[67] It is common for the social partners in Belgium, Spain, and Sweden to take part in national discussions on education and learning. This constitutes an advantage since the agreements then form part of a general strategy which may give the agreements a larger impact. The content of such agreements does not primarily target the interests of a certain employer or a certain sector, but those of the labour market as a whole. Furthermore, the agreements on confederate or national level are applicable to broader groups of workers, which is of value in

[63] Subramanian and Zimmermann (2020), p. 301; Cedefop (2010), box 20.

[64] Collective bargaining on learning activities is scarce in many Eastern European countries, especially on the national or confederate level. Cedefop (2010), see particularly pp. 73–74.

[65] Cedefop (2010), p. 67.

[66] Cedefop (2010), p. 72. A more recent example from Italy is the cross-sectoral agreement of the manufacturing industry from 2018 ('Patto della fabbrica'). The agreement indicated, among other subjects to be negotiated at sectoral level, the vocational training of workers. Subsequently, some sectoral collective agreements introduced a subjective right to training (e.g. in the metal and electrical sector) or training pacts (e.g. in the food sector, there is an obligation for the worker who has received training not to resign for three years, in order to protect the employer's investment). This illustrates the interplay between the sectoral and cross-sectoral levels. See ADAPT (2024).

[67] Cedefop (2010), pp. 81–84.

itself, since it promotes equality between different workers. It also reduces the risk of lock-in effects and enables flexibility. When both large groups of workers and employers are covered, costs and risks are divided among a larger collective.

However, agreements on confederate or national level do not guarantee individual workers enforceable rights. As with all agreements, it depends on the wording and purpose of the collective agreement. The Swedish development agreement mentions, for example development of professional skills but addresses the member organisations and request that they in turn negotiate on lower levels.[68] A contrary example from the same country is, however, the renegotiated transition agreements that indicate a move from decentralisation to centralisation regarding learning activities and employment protection. The content of the agreements is directed both to social partners on the sectoral and local levels and to individual employers and workers. In order to give a more in-depth example of a development that can be explained as a move towards lifelong learning regulated under collective agreements, the transition agreements will be further elaborated on below.

### 3.4.1 The Renegotiated Swedish Transition Agreements: From Transition in Case of Redundancy to Lifelong Learning

Sweden has a long history of regulating some form of learning activities in collective agreements on confederate level, albeit only as a transition measure in case of redundancy.[69] Since 2022, a new system has been put in place. The new system is a hybrid of private and public law, as well as a hybrid of collective agreements on the confederate level and public law administered by public bodies. The legislation process in itself was interesting from a Swedish point of view. The large confederations in the private sector were not only the actors in negotiating the collective agreements that regulate their sectors but also in how the public components were outlined. Hence, these social partners have played a decisive role for the content of general regulation, affecting other sectors of the labour market.[70] After the system was put in place, other confederations renegotiated their agreements, indicating that the major part of the Swedish labour market is covered by collective agreements with similar contents. The new system does not only cover transition in redundancy situations but has components that are more in line with a lifelong learning perspective.

First, the new agreements do not apply only after an employment has ended but also during an ongoing contract. Hence, workers with open-ended contracts can apply for support in order to strengthen their position in the labour market in

[68] Utvecklingsavtalet 1985-09-09, concluded by Svenskt näringsliv, LO and PTK, § 5 mom 4. See also Olofsson and Wadensjö (2020), p. 55.

[69] For further reading regarding the layout of the former transition agreements, see Johansson (2020).

[70] The transition regulations form part of a larger package that includes employment protection. For the legislative procedure see Ulander-Wänman (2022) and Herzfeld Olsson (2022). For comments on the content of the package, mainly employment protection, see Selberg and Sjödin (2024).

general.[71] This has led to a renegotiation of sectoral agreements where learning activities on the sectoral level have been coordinated with the new agreements on the confederate level and with the new legislation.[72] All in all, this facilitates continuous learning.

Second, the overall personal scope has been broadened compared with the old transition agreements. Apart from the opportunity to receive support during an ongoing employment, the new agreements also cover larger groups of workers facing unemployment. They cover not only certain workers dismissed due to management decisions but also fixed-term workers whose contracts have expired without renewal and workers whose employment ceases due to sickness, indicating that more vulnerable groups in the labour market receive access to study allowance, guidance, and other forms of support. Another difference compared to preceding agreements is that there are no lower age limits.[73] In this way, the new agreements grant access to learning for younger generations. There is, however, still a condition that the worker should have worked a certain amount of time in order to receive benefits, which entail that persons with no or a weak connection to the labour market do not have access to the rights according to the agreements.

Third, the support provided under the new agreements is broader. The support could, for example, be to have contact with a mentor that helps a worker to map out what skills he or she has and give recommendations regarding relevant training to supplement existing skills. Validation of skills and tailored education/training are other common measures.[74] The support is organised by organisations connected to the social partners with decades of experience regarding support in connection to vocational training.[75] These organisations decide the content and the scope of, and priorities in, the support. Hence, the collective agreements do not contain any detailed regulation of the support, apart from the fourth and final point mentioned here—the supplementary study allowance. The supplementary study allowance supplements a public study allowance. The public study allowance is supposed to cover 80 per cent of the monthly salary, but the cap is set fairly low, indicating that most workers will receive a lower sum.[76] The supplementary study allowance

[71] Huvudavtal om trygghet, omställning och anställningsskydd, concluded by Svenskt Näringsliv and PTK, Chap. 2 Sect. 2 § 3; Huvudavtal om trygghet, omställning och anställningsskydd, concluded by Svenskt Näringsliv and LO, Chap. 2 Sect. 2 § 4.

[72] See for example HÖK 24 concluded by concluded by Sveriges Kommuner och Regioner and Sobona – Kommunala företagens arbetsgivarorganisation and OFR teachers' section.

[73] According to the older agreements, the worker had to have turned 40 years old in order to have the right to economic support, see ISF (2018), p. 40 (white-collar workers) and p. 50 (blue-collar workers).

[74] Huvudavtal om trygghet, omställning och anställningsskydd, concluded by Svenskt Näringsliv and PTK, Chap. 2 Sect. 2 § 2 and Huvudavtal om trygghet, omställning och anställningsskydd, concluded by Svenskt Näringsliv and LO, Chap. 2 Sect. 2 § 2.

[75] Regarding the two large agreements used as an example here the relevant organisations are Trygghetsfonden (TSL) and TRR Trygghetsrådet.

[76] For a brief overview of the public allowance, see Eurofound (2023c), p. 10.

redeems that to a certain level since its cap is set much higher.[77] Hence, together they are supposed to offer an income-based benefit for full-time studies lasting up to two years.[78] For individuals over 40, there is no time limit.[79] Consequently, despite the limitation on education and training earlier in one's career, there are opportunities to completely change profession at a later stage.

In conclusion, the shift towards a focus on lifelong learning in the new transition agreements can be seen in an increased personal scope, making it possible for more workers to access the benefits, not only when made redundant but also during ongoing employment. The focus of the learning activities in question is not on the needs of a specific employer or sector but on the labour market as a whole, which makes it easier for the individual worker to act in his or her own interests. The opportunity to receive an enhanced study allowance over a longer period of time also makes it possible to study without too great economic disadvantage during the studies.

There are, however, disadvantages with the layout of the Swedish transition system. Even though the parts of the system that are established under collective agreements are privately funded through contributions paid by the employers to organisations owned by the social partners, the supplementary study allowance is dependent on the worker receiving approval for public study allowance. The criteria are the same, but there are issues that limit access to the public system. First, the system is not rights-based, but contributions are paid to the extent that there are budgeted means.[80] Second, the popularity of the system and the lack of budgeted means for administering the applications has caused the system to be ineffective at the initial stage. Hence, if the state does not prioritise the effectiveness of the public allowance, it puts a hold on the supplementary part financed by the social partners.

From the worker's perspective, the purpose of the learning activities in question can also be an issue. The study allowance is only approved for education and training that is presumed to strengthen the individual's position in the labour market. It is the public body administering the public study allowance that make the decision. However, the transition organisations owned by the social partners may release a statement that a certain form of education strengthens the individual's position in the labour market. This right is motivated by the organisations' knowledge of the individual worker's situation and of their long experience of labour market issues.[81]

---

[77] Huvudavtal om trygghet, omställning och anställningsskydd, concluded by Svenskt näringsliv and PTK, Chap. 2 § 6–8. The same wording is found in the main agreement between Svenskt näringsliv and LO.

[78] It is calculated as 80 percent of the worker's yearly wage income, but there is a cap first on the public allowances and second on the collectively bargained allowance, albeit the cap is set higher on the latter. For workers with high salaries, there is an opportunity to take a public loan in order to reach the actual level of 80 percent.

[79] Prop. 2021/22:176, Flexibilitet, omställningsförmåga och trygghet på arbetsmarknaden (Swedish Government bill), p. 198.

[80] Prop. 2021/22:176, Flexibilitet, omställningsförmåga och trygghet på arbetsmarknaden (Swedish Government bill), p. 284.

[81] Prop. 2021/22:176, Flexibilitet, omställningsförmåga och trygghet på arbetsmarknaden (Swedish Government bill), p. 206.

The individual worker, on the other hand, does not have a say in the assessment of the relevance of the education or training.[82] The connection to the strengthening of the individual's position in the labour market taps into a broader question on how lifelong learning is to be defined: Is it a good for the labour market or for the individual?[83]

## 4 Concluding Remarks

In contrast to individual employment contracts, collective agreements have a better basis for regulating lifelong learning that stretches beyond the employer's interests. This connects both to the more even bargaining power of the social partners and to a shift of interest from the individual employer to the collective of employers. Many of the examples given above indicate that collective agreements of various types offer opportunities to improve skills in order to better one's chances in a certain profession or sector. Trade unions' influence means that the workers' collective voice is considered in issues that concern them. Thus, there is also a democratic aspect of regulation under collective agreements that cannot be met in regulation under employment contracts. The democratic aspect is present at all levels of collective bargaining, but the equality aspect is stronger than the higher the level of regulation.

There are advantages and disadvantages with regulating lifelong learning exclusively on a specific level. Even if regulation on the cross-sectoral or sectoral level offers greater equality between various groups of workers and a more equal power balance between trade unions and employers' associations, there is a larger distance between those affected by the regulation, the individual worker and employer, and those deciding the terms. On the other hand, regulation exclusively on the local level tends to create uneven coverage and disfavour weaker groups. Instead, for lifelong learning as for other form of content in collective agreements, regulation on different levels seems to be the most efficient form of regulation. It enables framework regulation on higher levels and more detailed regulations on lower levels, placing concrete decisions closer to those affected by them. This also connects to an advantage that regulation of lifelong learning under collective agreement have in relation to statutory regulation—the social partners have knowledge regarding the needs in their sector and at their workplace, and the competence to organise the education and training needed, which can lead to more appropriate content. An additional aspect is that regulation under collective agreements offers flexibility.

The social partners are organisations created to protect workers' and employers' interests, respectively. Lifelong learning from a labour law perspective will

[82] The same goes for the individual employer since the relevance for the current workplace is not of importance.

[83] See in this volume Haar B ter, Lifelong Learning and Work in the Future.

therefore inevitably be rooted in the needs and interests of workers and employers. From a narrow perspective, the workers' interests could be explained as having the right to train and upskill at the current workplace in order to not become redundant to the employer's activities and be replaced by another worker. From a broader perspective, a worker's interests could be explained as acquiring competences and skills that are relevant to other employers in the same branch or when changing profession altogether. That might not be beneficial for the individual employer but it is good for the collective of employers. Even the broader perspective reveals one of the disadvantages of regulation under collective agreements, it risks too strong a focus on the needs of the labour market compared to the needs of the workers. Furthermore, access to learning activities may be restricted to the workers covered by the collective agreement, which can result in an uneven distribution of opportunities.

Finally, a worker might, as a person, want to study or train for personal interest and to grow as a human being. The last interest falls outside the scope of a direct labour market interest, but could still be regulated under collective agreements, depending on the will of the social partners and their respective bargaining strength. There are examples of benefits that go beyond labour market issues being regulated under collective agreements.[84] Even if such examples can be explained as employment perks rather than general social partner policy, they show that the social partners are capable of negotiating issues that aim primarily at improving general wellbeing and development as human beings and not only increasing workers' employability.

## References

ADAPT (2024) La Contrattazione Collettiva in Italia (2024), XI Rapporto ADAPT. ADAPT University Press

Adlercreutz A (1954) Kollektivavtalet – Studier över dess tillkomsthistoria. CWK Gleerup, Lund

Ahlberg K, Bruun N (eds) (2017) The new foundations of labour law. Peter Lang AG, Frankfurt am Main

Baccaro L, Howell C (2011) A common neoliberal trajectory: the transformation of industrial relations in advanced capitalism. Polit Soc 39(4):521–563

Bechter B, Brandl B, Meardi G (2012) Sectors or countries? Typologies and levels of analysis in comparative industrial relations. Eur J Ind Relat 18(3):185–202

Brunello G, Wruuck P (2020) Employer Provided Training in Europe: Determinants and Obstacles. IZA Discussion Papers, No. 12981, Institute of Labor Economics (IZA), Bonn

Carlson L (2018) Workers, collectivism and the law: grappling with democracy. Edward Elgar Publishing, Cheltenham

Cedefop (2010) The social dialogue on education and training in the Copenhagen process – study on the social partner's work perspectives and perceptions to contribute to enhanced European cooperation in VET and LLL. Cedefop working paper no 5, Publications Office of the European Union, Luxembourg

[84] Comandé and Giubboni (2020).

Comandé D, Giubboni S (2020) The social partners in the welfare system in Italy: from coordination to fragmentation. Int J Comp LLIR 36(3):315–338
Davies P, Freedland M (1983) Kahn-Freund's labour and the law. Stevens & Sons, London
De la Croix P (1994) Wage interdependence through decentralized bargaining. J Econ Surv 8(4):371–403
Eurofound (2023a) Industrial Relations and Social Dialogue France: Developments in working life 2022. Eurofound working paper, No. WPEF23012
Eurofound (2023b) Industrial Relations and Social Dialogue Poland: Developments in working life 2022. Eurofound working paper, No. WPEF23023
Eurofound (2023c) Industrial Relations and Social Dialogue Sweden: Developments in working life 2022. Eurofound working paper, No. WPEF23029
Eurofound (2024a) Industrial Relations and Social Dialogue France: Developments in working life 2023. Eurofound working paper, No. WPEF24045
Eurofound (2024b) Industrial Relations and Social Dialogue Poland: Developments in working life 2023. Eurofound working paper, No. WPEF24056
European Commission, Directorate-General for Employment, Social Affairs and Inclusion (2008) Industrial Relations in Europe. Publications Office of the European Union, Luxembourg
Gardner J (2018) The contractualisation of labour law. In: Collins H, Lester G, Mantouvalou V (eds) Philosophical foundations of labour law. OUP, Oxford
Herzfeld Olsson P (2022) Den svenska modellen i en ny era. Juridisk Tidskrift 2021/22(3):783–798
Heyes J (2007) Training, social dialogue and collective bargaining in Western Europe. Econ Ind Democr 28(2):239–258
Iossa A (2017) Collective autonomy in the European Union – theoretical, comparative and cross-border perspectives on the legal regulation of collective bargaining. Lund University
ISF (2018) Utvecklingen av kollektivavtalade ersättningar sedan 2000-talets början - En redovisning av kollektivavtalade ersättningar som kompletterar den allmänna socialförsäkringen och arbetslöshetsförsäkringen. ISF 2018:14, Stockholm
Jacobs A (1986) In: Hepple B (ed) The making of labour law in Europe – a comparative study of nine countries up to 1945. Hart Publishing, Oxford
Jacobs A (2009) Collective labour relations. In: Hepple B, Veneziani B (eds) The transformation of labour law in Europe – a comparative study of 15 countries 1945–2004. Hart Publishing, Oxford, pp 201–231
Jacobs A (2011) Labour and the law in Europe – a satellite view on labour law and social security law in Europe. Wolf Legal Publishers, Oisterwijk
Johansson C (2020) Occupational pensions and unemployment benefits in Sweden. Int J Comp LLIR 36(3):339–366
Kahn-Freund O (1967) A note on status and contract in labour law. Mod Law Rev 30(6):635–644
Kaufman B (2002) Models of union wage determination: what have we learned since Dunlop and Ross? Ind Relat 41(1):110–158
Koukiadaki A, Távora I, Martínez Lucio M (2016) Joint regulation and labour market policy in Europe during the crisis. ETUI, Brussels
Léonard E, Perin E (2009) Lifelong learning and social partnership: a comparative overview of twelve European countries. Int J Comp Labour Law Ind Relat
Lurie L (2020) Occupational welfare in Israel: a study of collective agreements and benefits. Int J Comp Labour Law Ind Relat
Malmberg J (2009) Enforcement of labour law. In: Hepple B, Veneziani B (eds) The transformation of labour law in Europe – a comparative study of 15 countries 1945–2004. Hart Publishing, Oxford, pp 263–287
Marginson P (2005) Industrial relations at European sector level: the weak link? Economic and Industrial Democracy
Martínez Lucio M, Skule S, Kruse W, Trappmann V (2007) Regulating skill formation in Europe: German, Norwegian and Spanish policies on transferable skills. Eur J Ind Relat 13(3):323–340

Olofsson J, Wadensjö E (2020) Vuxenutbildning för arbetsmarknaden. Underlagsrapport till Utredningen om en moderniserad arbetsrätt
Selberg N, Sjödin E (2024) Det nya anställningsskyddet: Rättsvetenskapliga perspektiv på Trygghetsöverenskommelsen 2022. Juristförlaget i Lund
Subramanian D, Zimmermann B (2020) Voice in French corporate training: a critical issue in developing employee capability. Economic and Industrial Democracy
Tros F (2023) Pathways in decentralised collective bargaining in Europe. Amsterdam University Press
Tuschling A, Engemann C (2006) From education to lifelong learning: the emerging regime of learning in the European Union. Educational Philosophy and Theory
Ulander-Wänman C (2022) The social partners as actors in new labour law legislation in Sweden. Eur Labour Law J
Votinius Julén J (2020) Collective bargaining for working parents in Sweden and its interaction with the statutory benefit system. Int J Comp Labour Law Ind Relat
Winterton J (2007) Building social dialogue over training and learning: European and National Developments. Eur J Ind Relat

## *Collective Agreements*

Agreement concerning training and development in the company, 2023-04-02–2025-03-31 concluded between Teknikföretagen, Sveriges ingenjörer, Unionen and Ledarna
Commission Paritaire Auxiliaire pour les ouvriers (CP 100), Accord sectorial du 24 octobre 2023 pour la période 2023–2024
Friskoleavtalet 2023-09-01 to 2025-08-31, concluded by Almega Tjänsteföretagen and Sveriges lärare
HÖK 24 concluded by concluded by Sveriges Kommuner och Regioner and Sobona – Kommunala företagens arbetsgivarorganisation and OFR teachers section
Huvudavtal om trygghet, omställning och anställningsskydd, concluded by Svenskt Näringsliv and LO
Huvudavtal om trygghet, omställning och anställningsskydd, concluded by Svenskt Näringsliv and PTK
KOM-KR Kompetens och omställningsavtal i lydelse 2022-10-01, concluded by Sveriges Kommuner och Regioner and Sobona – Kommunala företagens arbetsgivarorganisation and Svenska Kommunalarbetareförbundet, OFR, Lärarförbundets och Lärarnas Riksförbunds Samverkansråd and AkademikerAlliansen
Plåt- och ventilationsavtalet 2023-05-01-2025-04-30 concluded by Plåt & Ventföretagen and Svenska Byggnadsarbetareförbundet, Utbildningsavtalet
Utvecklingsavtalet 1985-09-09, concluded by Svenskt näringsliv, LO and PTK

**Caroline Johansson** is associate professor in private law and holds a position as lecturer at the Law Faculty, Uppsala University. Her research focus on collective labour law, with emphasis on occupational benefits and the social partners as welfare creators.

# Works Councils as Promoters of Lifelong Learning: Opportunities and Challenges

**Katharina Ruhwedel and Jaqueline Stein**

## 1 Introduction

In the face of upcoming and ongoing structural changes—on a digital, economic and demographic level—that lead to the need of transforming nearly all industries, new and different skills from workers are required permanently. It is crucial that a country's continuing education and training (CET) system—the employment-related perspective of the concept of lifelong learning[1]—functions well for this challenge.

It must be emphasised that the term "lifelong learning" is neither used by the German law nor by the company parties, but instead specific terms for different vocational training formats. Examples are: reskilling and further education measures,[2] compulsory professional training,[3] training, further training and additional training and vocational advancement,[4] and improvement of employee

[1] See in this volume, Introduction.

[2] Sect. 1§2 of the Unfair Dismissal Protection Act (KSchG), "Umschulungs- oder Fortbildungsmaßnahmen".

[3] Sect. 111 of the Trade Regulation Act (GewO), "Pflichtfortbildungen".

[4] Sect. 80§1 Nr. 2a WCA, "Aus-, Fort- und Weiterbildung".

K. Ruhwedel
Hugo Sinzheimer Institute for Labour and Social Security Law (HSI),
Frankfurt (Main), Germany
e-mail: katharina-ruhwedel@boeckler.de

J. Stein (✉)
Institute for Labour Law and Industrial Relations in the European Union (IAAEU),
Trier, Germany
e-mail: stein@iaaeu.de



J. Murto, V. Franca (eds.), *Labour Law and Lifelong Learning*,
https://doi.org/10.1007/978-3-032-11035-0_9

qualifications.[5] In this chapter, the term "lifelong learning" will be used for more general observations on the participation of works councils, whereas for the specific instruments provided by the law the term "vocational training"[6] is applied. This is because it is the dominant term in the Works Councils Act (WCA) and the Social Code Book III (SCB III), which are the most important points of reference for the works councils' instruments considered here.

First, the main goal of this chapter is to shed light on the role that works councils play in the CET in the European countries that have a two-channel-system (unions and works councils as the employees' stakeholders).[7] Acting as intermediaries between employers and employees on a company level, the rights and the structure of these committees differ from country to country. The focus is on the German system as it has one of the most essential works council regulations in Europe. Consequently, it can take on a pioneering role concerning the significance of works councils in the area of lifelong learning.[8]

Another objective of this chapter is to identify the advantages as well as the possible challenges that arise from the role of works councils regarding lifelong learning. Additionally, new legal approaches by Germany that can be transferred to other two-channel countries will be depicted.

To achieve these goals, the chapter is structured as follows: After the introduction, Sect. 2 deals with the basic concept of works councils and their role in representing the interests of the employees on a company level, in contrast to the role of trade unions. Based on this, Sect. 3 contains the main, most detailed legal part of this chapter in which certain rights—or "tools" —of the works councils related to vocational training are introduced and cursorily depicted. Section 4 analyses the various challenges works councils face when participating in the regulation of CET. Finally, Sect. 5 gives an outlook on how the extension of the works councils' rights would benefit the cause of mastering the structural change due to the promotion of CET and lifelong learning in general.

[5] Sect. 92a§1 WCA, "Qualifizierung".

[6] In German: "Berufsbildung".

[7] More on the different types of company-level representation: Oesingmann (2015).

[8] For the role of trade unions on a company level see in this volume Johansson C, Regulating lifelong-learning in collective agreements, section 3.

## 2 Works Councils: Basic Concept and Their Role in Regulating Lifelong Learning

While trade unions exist in most EU member states and beyond Europe, works councils are less common. However, works councils constitute an essential and important corporate-level phenomenon of modern labour law.[9] For that reason, this section serves as a short overview over the concept of works councils, their occurrence in different countries, and most importantly their role as promoters of lifelong learning.[10]

With trade unions serving as sector-based or even nation-wide bodies for representative communication between employees and employers, works councils fulfil this representation and communication function on the company level.[11] What distinguishes them from unions is that they are company-specific, represent all employees of a company (not only union members), and focus on management co-decision making rather than bargaining about wages and broader working conditions.[12]

Company-level representation varies between different European countries. Only a few[13] have strong representative features like works councils which guarantee participation and co-determination rights in legislation, while in many countries, employees only have limited opportunities to influence lifelong learning and further training opportunities at their workplace.[14] Germany's works council system is one of the former.

Nevertheless, only 43% of German employees were represented by works councils in 2023, and only 36% of employees in the private sector, which is most likely to undergo structural challenges caused by the twin transformation.[15][16] In addition, there are also notable regional and sectoral disparities in Germany.[17] At the same time, there is a significantly higher rate of participation in further training in larger

[9] Augustin (2020), p. 27f.; Nienhüser (2020), p. 267f.; Arrigo and Casale (2010); Rogers and Streeck (1995).

[10] For a detailed account of this see Sect. 3.

[11] Rogers and Streeck (1995), p. 6; Nienhüser (2020), p. 260f; on the historical background see Augustin (2020), p. 13f.

[12] Rogers and Streeck (1995), p. 6ff.; Nienhüser (2020), p. 260; see in this volume Johansson C, Regulating lifelong-learning in collective agreements, Sect. 4.2 for further insight on company-level trade union representation.

[13] E.g. Austria, Germany, the Netherlands; for a detailed overview: Mohrenweiser (2022), p. 2 and Nienhüser (2020), p. 261; on the implementation of works councils in Eastern Europe: Waas (2014).

[14] E.g. Sweden. In some of these countries, company-level employee representation rights are usually exercised by unions.

[15] Graf-Drasch et al. (2023).

[16] Statistisches Bundesamt (2024).

[17] Works council representation is still lower in the federal states of former Eastern Germany compared to those of Western Germany, most likely due to the higher percentage of small(er) companies in the East, Statistisches Bundesamt (2024).

companies (75% of employees in 2020) than in smaller companies (51% of employees in 2020).[18]

Complementary to the analysis of collective agreements on lifelong learning in Chapter 6, the role of works councils as company-specific actors in shaping lifelong learning for employees will be examined in this chapter. Their role is noteworthy as they can actively mediate between the sometimes-conflicting interests of employers and employees and thus shape the transformations in the companies "for the benefit of the employees and the company".[19] As a part of this transformation process, works councils play a central role in the organisation of company-level training,[20] provided that the necessary structures, resources, and support are available.[21]

## 3 Opportunities: Works Councils' Instruments to Address Lifelong Learning

Works councils have various opportunities to address, regulate, or even introduce vocational training and training-related topics in the establishment. In most cases, this can only be done in cooperation with the respective employer. The instruments available to the works council regarding vocational training can be divided into preventive instruments, on the one hand, and reactive instruments, on the other.[22]

In the case of preventive measures, the initiative to address, introduce, or design lifelong learning comes before unemployment is imminent. For this chapter, preventive instruments are understood to be measures that are supposed to increase the security of employment at the initial company through the promotion of qualification within the (comparatively safe) employment (Sect. 3.1). Reactive instruments, on the other hand, only come into play when the employer is forced to react at short notice and decided to change the company or establishment, for example to reduce staff. An immediate, personnel-friendly solution must then be found; from the employees' and works council's point of view, only damage limitation can ultimately be carried out in these cases (Sect. 3.2).

[18] Bundesministerium für Bildung und Forschung (2020), p. 33.

[19] According to Sect. 2§1 WCA, Erol (2024), p. 429; Stegmaier (2012); Cantner et al. (2014), p. 20f.; Bellmann et al. (2019), p. 15; Lammers et al. (2022), p. 3f.

[20] Lammers et al. (2022), p. 28 find that the presence of works councils increases training activities.

[21] Erol (2024), p. 439; Stegmaier (2012); Cantner et al. (2014), p. 20f.; Bellmann et al. (2019), p. 15.

[22] The co-determination and participation rights in particular are closely related and can be applied by the works council in combination. The strict distinction between preventive and reactive instruments is therefore more of a theoretical nature.

## *3.1 Preventive Measures: Forward-looking Planning as Part of the Transformation Processes*

Preventive measures are the more far-sighted instruments, as they enable long-term, forward-looking planning as part of the transformation processes. The works council has a few participation rights that give it the right to inform, propose to, and advise the employer. It is also possible for the parties to conclude works agreements[23] relating to vocational training. In social law, there are some new, welcome incentives for the parties to conclude such training-related works agreements.

### 3.1.1 Limited Influence: The Works Council's Participation Rights

In the WCA, there are some regulations that provide the works councils with (limited) information rights, the right to submit proposals and to demand the employer's determination of the need for vocational training.[24] What they all have in common is that they are not enforceable co-determination rights of the works council, but merely participation rights. In practice, this means: None of these rights can be used to unilaterally introduce vocational training measures without the willingness of the employer.

The first example is the works council's right to information, consultation, and proposals on manpower planning.[25] It refers to the involvement of the works council in the establishment's personnel (development) and issues relating to the professional development of employees.[26] The aim of the provision is therefore not to manage personnel planning as mere corporate planning, but rather to integrate the interests of the works council, including career advancement opportunities and vocational training measures, (far-sightedly) into the employer's concrete personnel planning.[27] The right to information offers an opportunity to make qualification requirements transparent for the works councils, i.e. to make them capable of acting. Together, these rights give works councils the opportunity to provide their own impetus for personnel planning within a narrow framework.[28]

Directly related to the works council's involvement in the establishment's personnel development is the works council's right to submit proposals about securing and promoting employment.[29] According to this, the works council may at any

---

[23] A works agreement is an agreement between employer and the works council that establishes the rights and obligations of these parties and formulates binding standards for all employees in a company. It works in a similar way to a collective agreement, but at company level.

[24] Sect. 92, 92a, 96 and 97§1 WCA.

[25] Sect. 92 WCA.

[26] Homburg (2024), Sect. 92 recital 31.

[27] Homburg (2024), Sect. 92 recital 6.

[28] For further information on this see Arpaci and Tolke (2025), (in publication).

[29] Sect. 92a § 1 WCA; Homburg (2024), Sect. 92 recital 1.

time[30] submit proposals in this regard, especially regarding vocational training. The works council can use this right of proposal to take the initiative to provide impetus.

Additionally, the works council's right to participate in the promotion of vocational training[31] offers various (but limited) opportunities for preventative influence. First, it contains the general obligation for the two parties to promote vocational training of the staff within the framework of the manpower planning for the establishment.[32] Second, the employer must determine the need for vocational training and consult it on matters relating to staff training, if requested by the works council. Third, the works council may make relevant proposals regarding vocational training.

Another (at least potentially) preventive measure is provided by the consultation rights regarding vocational training facilities and programmes.[33] In Germany, employers must consult the works council on the establishment and equipment of in-plant training facilities,[34] the introduction of vocational training programmes in the establishment,[35] and participation in external vocational training programmes.[36]

### 3.1.2 Incentives in Social Law: Promotion of Vocational Training[37] and Qualification Money[38]

The company parties can also conclude works agreements relating to vocational training.[39] Their uniform regulations are then binding for all employees in the establishment. A works agreement can be concluded explicitly relating only to vocational training or individual provisions relating to it can be included in a general works agreement.[40] In principle, the works agreement can include an entitlement for employees to further training, but also (within legal and collectively agreed limits) an obligation to participate in training measures.[41]

In 2023, the German legislature established and reformed some tools in social law to support both employers and works councils regarding vocational

[30] Däubler (2024), Sect. 92a recital 13.

[31] Sect. 96 WCA.

[32] Buschmann (2024), Sect. 96 recital 4.

[33] Sect. 97 § 1 WCA.

[34] For example, training workshops, company training centers, transfer companies, see Buschmann (2024), Sect. 97 recital 3.

[35] For example, advanced training courses, master craftsman courses, technician courses, measures to introduce new technical processes, or trainee programmes, see Buschmann (2024), Sect. 97 recital 5.

[36] For example, carried out by private sponsors, chambers or employment offices, see Buschmann, (2024), Sect. 97 recital 6.

[37] Sect. 82 § 1 and 3 SCB III.

[38] Sect. 82a Social Code Book III.

[39] For further information on this see Arpaci and Tolke (2025), pp. 56–68 (in publication).

[40] Arpaci and Tolke (2025), pp. 56–57 (in publication).

[41] In detail see Arpaci and Tolke (2025), p. 61 (in publication).

training—in particular, the Continuing Education Act (CEA, "Weiterbildungsgesetz") aims to provide new incentives.[42] The legislature has recognised that continuous, preventative vocational training—or lifelong learning—of employees is necessary, particularly in view of structural change and the shortage of skilled workers.[43] Consequently, the CEA makes changes in the part of the Social Code Book III (SCB III) that deals with the promotion of vocational training. Most relevant in this context are the reforms of Sections 82 and 82a that privilege companies with works agreements on vocational training. Employers and works councils are rewarded for taking joint responsibility on this matter. The idea is that vocational training will be included in works agreements to a greater extent than before.

The promotion of vocational training[44] provides two combinable benefits for vocational training for employees. If all eligibility requirements are met, the employment agency grants full or partial coverage of the training or (additionally) of the wage subsidies.[45] A major change that came with the CEA is that it is no longer necessary for "structural change-related qualification needs" to exist in a company to receive this funding. This is because the legislator now correctly assumes that there is a need for vocational training in almost all sectors of the economy because of structural change.[46] The subsidies are also possible without a collective agreement. However, if a collective agreement concerning vocational training exists, certain privileges apply.[47]

In addition to that, the qualification money was introduced by the CEA in 2023 and came into effect on 1 April 2024. It supports both employees and companies in the process of the economy's transformation. Under certain conditions,[48] employees can receive qualification money from the employment agency while they are participating in vocational training. The target group are employees who are at risk of losing their jobs due to structural change, but for whom vocational training can enable future-proof employment in the same company or establishment. In contrast to the promotion of vocational training,[49] the eligibility requirements here still include the structural change-related qualification requirements. This is not immediately comprehensible due to the legislator's justification for the deletion of the

[42] For further information see Ruhwedel and Simon (2023) and Ruhwedel and Simon (2024), pp. 241–252.

[43] BT-Drs. 20/6518, pp. 23, 41.

[44] Sect. 82 SCB III.

[45] The eligibility requirements cannot be discussed further in this article. For further information see Ruhwedel and Simon (2023), pp. 16 ff.

[46] BT-Drs. 20/6518, pp. 24 and 38.

[47] The employer's contribution to the training course costs is reduced by 5% regardless of the size of the company or establishment. Additionally, the subsidies to the funding benefit from the employment agency can be increased by 5%.

[48] These conditions cannot be discussed further in this article. For further information see Ruhwedel and Simon, (2023), pp. 29–35 ff.

[49] Sect. 82 § 1 SCB III.

feature in the context of section 82 SCB III.[50] The granting of qualification money requires a collective agreement.[51] According to this, the agreement must contain company-specific regulations stating that (a) there is a need for qualification due to structural change,[52] (b) there are associated prospects for employees for sustainable employment in the establishment, and (c) the parties claim the qualification allowance.

## 3.2 *Reactive Measures*

If a change in operations—caused by the structural changes mentioned above—is imminent, both parties have various options at their disposal to react to this. The WCA provides participation and co-determination rights associated with vocational training (Sect. 3.2.1). In addition to that, transfer social plans are a way for the two parties to react to staff reductions (Sect. 3.2.2).

### 3.2.1 Limited Influence of the Works Council Through Participation and Co-determination Rights

The rights of the works council to respond to specific plans of the employer have varying degrees of effect.

Thus, the works councils' information and consultation rights[53] offer only a limited influence on the regulation of lifelong learning at the company level, but are often the first opportunity for the works council to become aware of impending changes. It is mandatory to inform and consult the works council if the employer has (advanced) plans concerning, e.g. the (re)construction of offices, the working procedures or the workplace. These plans may also result in a need for vocational training for employees. The employer is obliged to inform the works council of this without being asked and in a timely manner, i.e. as early as possible and still at the planning stage.[54] This is intended to enable the works council to influence the planning process initiated by the employer with its own ideas.[55]

In contrast to this, the right to participate in the decisions relating to the implementation of vocational training programmes in the establishment is the works

---

[50] Ruhwedel and Simon (2023), p. 30.

[51] With the exception of micro-enterprises with fewer than ten employees. In this case, a written declaration from the employer is sufficient, Sect. 82a (2) sentence 6 SCB III.

[52] However, the requirements for the presentation are relatively low: General statements on the nature of the specific impact are sufficient, see Fachliche Weisung der BA (2024), pp. 12 f.

[53] Sect. 90 WCA.

[54] Klebe (2024), Sect. 90 recital 19 and 23.

[55] Klebe (2024), Sect. 90 recital 20.

council's most powerful instrument for vocational training.[56] If the employer has planned or implemented measures that change the work of the employees concerned and their professional knowledge and skills are no longer sufficient to perform their tasks,[57] the works council must be involved in decisions on the introduction of vocational training measures in the establishment. The works council can achieve the introduction of the measures unilaterally—without the support of the employer—with the help of the conciliation committee. However, these measures can only ever be introduced in the context of acute risk of job loss and only for the group of employees concerned—in this context far-sighted planning is not possible.

In addition to the latter, the works council has a co-determination right to participate in the decisions relating to the implementation of vocational training in the establishment.[58] This right is limited: Only when a decision is already taken by the employer that vocational training will be conducted, the works council participates in the manner of the specific implementation. In this case, too, the decision of the conciliation committee can replace the lack of agreement between the company parties.[59]

#### 3.2.2 Transfer Social Plans[60]: Vocational Training Promoted by the Employment Agency

The transfer social plan—a special social plan that operates at the interface between WCA and social law and is not solely based on compensation payment—offers the two parties a further opportunity to have vocational training promoted by the employment agency.[61] This instrument has developed from company practice.[62] Its aim is the employees' transition to a new employment relationship primarily through vocational training. The prerequisites for a transfer social plan are an already planned operational change,[63] for example through staff reductions, and the threat of unemployment for the employees. If these and other eligibility requirements are met, the employment agency can promote participation in transfer measures[64] for

[56] Sect. 97 § 2 WCA.

[57] It is disputed in which cases this requirement is fulfilled, Arpaci and Tolke (2025), p. 46 f (in publication).

[58] Sect. 98 WCA.

[59] Buschmann (2024), Sect. 98 recital 1.

[60] Sect. 112 WCA.

[61] As an introduction to the topic of the transfer social plan see Däubler (2024), Sect. 112, 112a recitals 227–230.

[62] It is controversial whether such a transfer social plan can only be concluded in cooperation between the two parties or whether it can also be enforced by a decision of the conciliation committee. This is due to the controversial legal qualification of the tool regarding the differences between social plans and transfer social plans. In detail see Schütte (2013), p. 249.

[63] In accordance with Sect. 111 WCA.

[64] Sect. 110 SCB III.

integration into the labour market and can pay transfer short-time allowance.[65] The latter partially compensates for the loss of earnings. While receiving it, support can also be provided by covering the costs of vocational training.[66]

Overall, the provision is intended to encourage the two parties to make greater use of social plan funds for measures that serve to prevent unemployment instead of compensating for unemployment through compensation payments.[67]

### 3.3 *Company Training Mentors: Proposition of a New Type of Personnel Representative*

As shown, co-determination and participation rights, but also the social law support options offer a lot of potential. However, the complexity of the legislation and the subject in general make it difficult for those affected to keep track of. The works council often lacks the time and the resources to deal intensively with vocational training opportunities and personnel planning (see Sect. 4.2). Particularly when there is no imminent crisis that requires rapid action to secure employment, intensive familiarisation is difficult due to the general day-to-day business.

To counter this problem, the unions of IG Metall, Ver.di, NGG, and IGBCE (and the employers' federation for the chemical industries) put the project of the Company Training Mentors (CTMs) into practice as part of the National Further Training Strategy (Nationale Weiterbildungsstrategie, NWS).[68] It is funded by the Federal Ministry of Education and Research, but has not yet been enshrined in law.[69]

The aim is to qualify employees, works council, or trade union representatives to be familiar with the funding opportunities, to determine the need for vocational training in the company and to motivate and advise colleagues on the topic. In addition, they are trained to reach out to disadvantaged groups of employees, to support them, and increase their participation. Ultimately, they should also become experts in the company's transformation strategy, preparing works agreements, and collective agreements specific to vocational training.

According to the Federal Ministry of Education and Research (BMBF) there are more than 460 CTMs in around 170 companies and administrations in Germany.[70] Unfortunately, initial studies on the approach do not go beyond field reports and do

---

[65] Sect. 111 SCB III.

[66] See Sect. 111a SCB III.

[67] BT-Drs. 13/4941, pp. 197f and BT-Drs. 14/5741, p. 52.

[68] For more information see https://www.bmbf.de/bmbf/de/bildung/berufliche-bildung/foerderinitiativen-und-programme/weiterbildungsmentoren/weiterbildungsmentoren_node.html.

[69] A new BMBF funding guideline extends the previous project funding, see https://www.bmbf.de/bmbf/shareddocs/bekanntmachungen/de/2024/11/2024-11-14-bekanntmachung-weiterbildungsmentoren.html.

[70] As you can see on this interactive map https://www.bmbf.de/SiteGlobals/Forms/Karte/interaktive-landkarte/interaktive-landkarte_formular.html?nn=1075772.

not provide general statements on its effectiveness.[71] However, the lack of a legal anchoring stands in the way of their effectiveness, especially in the face of the many pressing structural changes: CTMs are neither entitled to paid time off to carry out their duties nor do they have special protection against dismissal.[72] As a result, currently it only makes sense for works council members—who were originally supposed to be relieved of their duties—to take on the task. Therefore, a lot of potential of the initial concept is being squandered.

## 4 Challenges of Works Council Participation in Lifelong Learning

The analysis of the works councils' role has shown its importance in shaping lifelong learning opportunities for employees. However, some challenges have also become evident. As most European countries do not yet feature elaborate legal regulations for company-level co-decision making as Germany, the following detailed analysis of the apparent limitations is intended to inform the design of such regulations, specifically regarding lifelong learning. The limits of employee participation on company-wide lifelong learning measures can be classified in three different categories: (1) structural and legal limitations, (2) professional limitations, and (3) limitations of representation.

### *4.1 Structural and Legal Limitations*

The structural limitations are probably the most fundamental category. They are set by the WCA and the social law. Therefore, they can also be qualified as legal limitations.

When it comes to lifelong learning and company training programmes in the preventive stage, works councils have very few co-determination rights (see Sect. 3). Without their own right of initiative, they can only influence the form of professional training if the employer decides to provide it (see Sect. 3). This is a problem because the employees (who are represented by the works councils) are the ones who are directly affected by the consequences of a lack of qualification and further training and whose employment is at stake. The strongest tool in this stage is the works council's right to request the employer to determine the need for vocational training (see Sect. 3). This is the only way in which a works council can force an employer to take action at this stage. Even so, the employer is only obliged to determine training needs— not necessarily provide training.

[71] See mendi.net (2024) and Calmez and Winkler (2024).

[72] mendi.net (2024), p. 51.

Consequently, the employer has the unilateral right to make decisions on company-based lifelong learning to a wide extent, as it sets the amount of funding and determines its purpose.[73] The works council can participate in the organisation of the training, i.e. on the content and duration of the knowledge and skills to be imparted, on the methods of knowledge transfer, on the duration and location of the measure, and on the question of whether an in-company assessment is provided and how this is structured.[74] However, these options are dependent on the employer deciding to provide training. Additionally, co-determination is limited by the budget allocated to the training by the employer.

The structural position of the works council is strengthened when concrete restructuring or redundancies in the establishment are imminent. This is because works councils in Germany have the right to co-determine redundancies.[75] Accordingly, this right is extended to measures that serve to prevent or supplement redundancies.

Another structural limitation exists related to the practical conditions of lifelong learning. As Winterton describes, "in terms of its locus, VET [vocational and educational training] is mostly industry-led and centred on the workplace in the UK and Germany, whereas training is education-led and centred on school in Italy and France."[76] Naturally, works councils can only act on the company level[77] and partake in the design of lifelong learning only insofar as employers support or organise the training measures in a way that they can exert a dominant influence on the content and implementation of the measure.[78]

## 4.2 *Professional Limitations*

To understand the complex network of tools mentioned above and to use their respective participation rights, works council members must not only be professionalised and specially trained but also have sufficient time resources available for the topic of lifelong learning.

Works councils have a wide range of responsibilities, which in addition to helping to shape employees' lifelong learning also include reconciling work and family life, monitoring compliance with occupational health and safety regulations and many more. Particularly in the preventive phase, when there is no imminent threat of restructuring or layoffs, the issue of lifelong learning is therefore not at the top of

[73] Röder and Gebert (2017), p. 1294.

[74] Markowski (2022), p. 17.

[75] According to § 102 WCA, the works council must be consulted before every dismissal; a works council objection makes it easier for the dismissed employee to bring an action under the Protection against Dismissal Act (Kündigungsschutzgesetz).

[76] Winterton (2006), p. 66.

[77] See also Göpfert and Seier (2019), p. 590.

[78] Franzen (2001), p. 866 with reference to the jurisdiction of the Federal Labor Court (BAG).

the works council's priority list.[79] As a result, even the existing opportunities for co-determination are often not fully made use of.

A study on behalf of the trade union-affiliated Hans Böckler Foundation shows that works councils have insufficient strategic influence on vocational training.[80] As stated by the surveyed works councils, only 43% of companies provide employees with sufficient training to meet future professional requirements. Nevertheless, 38% of works councils stated that they had made proposals for further training in the last two years. Just under 40% had been involved in the design of training measures introduced by the employer.

As a solution, some authors propose the need for additional qualification of the works council committees.[81] This issue sheds light on a different subject area at the interface between lifelong learning and works councils: the training rights of works council members.[82] In Germany, all newly elected works council members are entitled to basic seminars on works constitution and labour law as well as occupational health and safety according to section 37§6 WCA. For specialised seminars, there must be a company-related cause. Such a company-related cause can be a conflict situation or an operational incident in the establishment for which the works council needs the knowledge imparted in the special seminar. However, the works council must be able to substantiate this special cause to the employer.[83]

It is therefore up to the works council members themselves to research and attend relevant training on lifelong learning. One challenge involves justifying the company-related cause to the employer. Timing plays a role here again: if the necessity can be easily justified due to planned restructuring and redundancies, it is often too late to ensure that works council members have sufficient expertise to be effectively involved in the planning of further training measures.

CTMs are at least a partial solution (see Sect. 3.3).[84] The training and provision of dedicated employees responsible for vocational training are answers to both the questions of capacity and expertise. The complexity of the topic can also be better managed by CTMs, especially as the issue does not have to be dealt with alongside the works council's other tasks but is given its own resources. Company-specific training from CTMs makes works councils more aware of the issue and more capa-

---

[79] Erol and Ahlers (2023), pp. 16, 18.

[80] Erol and Ahlers (2023), pp. 7–18.

[81] Markowski (2022), p. 15.

[82] For European works councils, the training rights are regulated in Art. 10(4) of Directive 2009/38/EC, which requires that training is necessary but does not guarantee a fixed amount of training: "In so far as this is necessary for the exercise of their representative duties in an international environment, the members of the special negotiating body and of the European Works Council shall be provided with training without loss of wages (Directive 2009/38/EC of the European Parliament and of the Council of 6 May 2009 on the establishment of a European Works Council or a procedure in Community-scale undertakings and Community-scale groups of undertakings for the purposes of informing and consulting employees).

[83] BUND Verlag Basiswissen Betriebsrat.

[84] Erol and Ahlers (2023), p. 18.

ble of getting involved in structuring further training. However, at a conference organised by the Federal Institute for Vocational Training (German: Bundesinstitut für Berufsbildung) to evaluate the project in December 2024,[85] experts emphasised that CTMs could only develop their full potential in close cooperation with existing works councils.

### 4.3 *Limits of Representation*

Works councils are elected through a majority vote of all eligible employees and are accordingly supposed to represent the interests of all employees in the establishment. Therefore, by co-designing suitable company training programmes, the works council should consider the demands of various employee groups in the area of lifelong learning and ideally guarantee and sustain everyone's employment. This can lead to the under-representations of some minority groups—e.g. temporary agency workers,[86] migrant workers,[87] or certain genders[88] (whereas a protective regulation exists for the latter in section 15§2 WCA). These are often the same groups that are at a heightened risk of job loss during the transformation or have special lifelong learning and training needs—which are not necessarily represented by the works council.

Based on Greifenstein's conceptualisation the "representation problem" regarding works councils in Germany can be characterised by three factors: (1) the low turnover of members and their frequent re-election, (2) the persistently low percentage of women in works councils, and (3) the increase in non-unionised members of works councils.[89] According to the author, the increasing diversity of the workforce and the ongoing economic transformation belong to the central problems that works councils must address to prevent alienation between representatives and the represented employees.

The issue of representation plays a role on two levels when it comes to lifelong learning: On the one hand, the training needs of underrepresented groups are less likely to be recognised by the works councils and appropriate measures proposed. On the other hand, the co-determination right of the works council to select the participants for a training measure poses a particular risk of discrimination, even if it is meant to promote equality.[90] Nonetheless, German works councils are required

---

[85] Bundesinstitut für Berufsbildung (2024).

[86] Barlen (2018), p. 95. In Germany, TAW can vote for the works council if their planned use in the establishment is for at least three months. However, they cannot be elected on the works council.

[87] Emmler and Brehmer (2019); Behrens et al. (2023), p. 464: The study shows a consistently low representation rate of migrant employees in the works council, with the highest representation rate in companies with a high unionisation rate. See also: Karakayali and Bouali (2021).

[88] Greene et al. (2021); for Germany: Roloff and Buchstaller (2020).

[89] Greifenstein (2014), pp. 101ff.

[90] See also Markowski (2022), p. 17.

to "promote the implementation of actual equality between women and men, in particular, as regards [...] training, further training and additional and vocational advancement".[91]

A study by the German Ministry of Education and Research from 2020 shows significant differences in participation in company training programmes among different groups of employees.[92] In 2020, 63% of employees without a history of migration participated in further training measures compared to 49% of first-generation migrants and 59% of second-generation migrants. Furthermore, more lifelong learning opportunities are utilised the higher the position of an employee in the company, the highest school diploma, and the highest vocational qualification. Thus, the participation rate is inversely proportional to the risks posed by the twin transformation and, consequently, the need for lifelong learning.[93] Finally, the study also found that employees with fixed-term contracts, whose risk of job loss is particularly high, participate in vocational training less frequently than permanent employees.

It therefore appears that a direct correlation between participation in company training programmes and representation by the works council cannot be diagnosed for all groups of employees. This makes sense, as works councils only participate in the design of company training in about 40% of cases.[94] Despite all this, a recent study also shows that, regardless of representation deficits, there is a positive correlation between the proportion of migrant employees in a company and the involvement of its works councils in CET.[95]

Two aspects should be emphasised, nonetheless. First, the better representation of groups with special training needs is likely to lead to works councils generally dedicating more attention to the topic of lifelong learning. Second, the overrepresentation of long-term and experienced employees in works councils[96] is ambivalent. On the one hand, it could promote the acquisition of the necessary expertise on the complex topic of lifelong learning. On the other hand, older employees who enjoy good job security and may be close to retirement might have less interest and awareness of the importance of company training.

[91] Under Sect. 80 §1 no. 2a WCA.

[92] Bundesministerium für Bildung und Forschung (2020), pp. 32ff.

[93] The same has been found for Slovenia by Franca et al. (2022), p. 14, and for Australia by Campbell and Price (2016), p. 322.

[94] Erol (2024), p. 434. However, they participated in the selection of employees to participate in a training measure in 51% of cases.

[95] Erol (2024), p. 437.

[96] Greifenstein (2014), p. 109.

## 5 Wanted: Far-sighted Strategies That Democratically Involve the Employees

As shown in Sect. 3, lifelong learning measures can roughly be classified as either preventive or reactive. There is a limited influence of reactive measures in general; preventive measures are more likely to prevent unemployment and to improve the employees' flexibility on the job market.[97] However, there aren't enough preventive measures that provide the works council with full co-determination rights. While the existing regulations in the SCB III were widely praised at their launch, their effectiveness is yet to be proven since they have only been applicable law since April 2024. Moreover, on a qualitative level, the works council's participation rights intensify as the measures move into the reactive phase. The more acute the risk of layoffs, the stronger the works council's participation rights. Of course, that makes proactive planning difficult.

According to the OECD, the German CET system is not yet effective and fair enough to cope with the structural changes mentioned above.[98] In its analysis, the OECD criticises, for example, the lack of a continuing education law and a regulation on paid training periods, thus the existence of a uniform legal framework in Germany.[99] Although the OECD report does not address the rights of the works councils specifically, it seems to us that only if the effectiveness of the works councils is fundamentally extended, a just transformation can happen.

Legislators are trying to find solutions in various ways: Be it through the establishment of company training mentors or through the adoption of new social legislation designed to dovetail co-determination and further training. However, more of this is needed, especially the expansion of co-determination rights is essential to create democratic participation of employees in the transformation. Especially giving works councils a general right to be involved in lifelong learning at the company level should be taken into consideration. Generally, the challenges posed by the many transformations and the resulting need for workplace education and training call for a democratic solution on a company level.

While the German regulations highlight the opportunities that exist for works councils, one must be aware of the fundamental, e.g. structural challenges, that works councils face when it comes to lifelong learning. A structural challenge arises from the fact that extensive co-determination rights only activate in crisis situations when redundancies are imminent.

Unfortunately, it is not only the power of works councils that is limited—the number of works councils in Germany is also constantly decreasing.[100] This is due

[97] BT-Drs. 20/6518, pp. 1ff.

[98] "Greater effectiveness and equity of the German CET system will only be achieved through fundamentally restructuring key aspects of the system and significantly reducing its complexity.", OECD (2021), p. 11.

[99] OECD (2021), pp. 16 and 20.

[100] Ellguth and Kohaut (2022), p. 332f.

to many factors like the increase of non-standard, "atypical" forms of employment[101] or the obstruction of works council elections.[102] In addition, the level of unionisation is steadily declining, although since 2023 there has been a small increase in some sectors.[103] This is not a problem that is specific to Germany, a declining level of union membership can even be observed in many European countries.[104]

Another challenge is to provide works councils with the capacity and knowledge to exercise their rights in the complex area of lifelong learning. The involvement of works councils can help to ensure that existing inequalities and discrimination in the selection of participants in lifelong learning programmes are reduced. Conversely, however, this also requires sufficient representativeness of the works councils.

In general, employee involvement in the design of lifelong learning in the workplace is extremely important—no one knows the individual learning needs as well as the employees themselves. In addition, the effectiveness of CET can be enhanced by integrating the employees in the process. In this sense, the German model and the mechanisms of co-determination presented here can serve as a role model to enable a minimum level of workplace co-determination of lifelong learning—despite the existing limitations.

However, future research will have to come up with different ways to develop company-specific solutions that encompass employee's participation, inclusion, and involvement apart from works councils. Moreover, it could investigate how different types of company ownership influence a businesses' ability to offer company-specific lifelong learning based on employee participation. Lastly, especially in sectors that are foreseeably shrinking or disappearing as a result of the twin transformation, it is important—particularly in order to avoid social disruptions caused by mass-layoffs—to investigate how employees can be involved in shaping lifelong learning at company level and thus take an active role in shaping their own professional future.

## References

Arrigo G, Casale G (2010) A comparative overview of terms and notions on employee participation. International Labour Office, Labour Administration and Inspection Programme. ILO, Geneva

Augustin M (2020) Influence of workers councils on employee engagement. University of Liverpool, 2020

Barlen V (2018) Analyse objektiver Prekaritätspotenziale der betrieblichen Mitbestimmung bei Leih- und Werkvertragsarbeit. In: Barlen V (ed) Zwischen zwei Arenen, 1st edn. Springer VS, Wiesbaden, pp 93–101

[101] Overview on the EU regulation on atypical work: Peers (2013).

[102] Thünken et al. (2020).

[103] Thünken et al. (2020).

[104] Hassel and Schroeder (2018), p. 48f.; The change in membership numbers of the DGB trade unions is available here: https://www.dgb.de/der-dgb/wer-wir-sind/#c8912.

Behrens M et al (2023) Repräsentation von Migrant*innen in Betriebsräten. WSI Mitteilungen 76(6):460–469

Bellmann L et al (2019) Works councils, training and employee satisfaction, SOEPpapers on Multidisciplinary Panel Data Research, No. 1020, Deutsches Institut für Wirtschaftsforschung, Berlin

BUND Verlag Basiswissen Betriebsrat. https://www.bund-verlag.de/betriebsrat/betriebsrat-sarbeit/basiswissen/betriebsrat-seminare#:~:text=Alle%20neugew%C3%A4hlten%20Betriebsratsmitglieder%20haben%20Anspruch,aus%2C%20es%20folgt%20ein%20Betriebsratsbeschluss. Accessed 17 Apr 2025

Bundesinstitut für Berufsbildung (2024) Dokumentation der Tagung "Weiterbildungsmentoring – Konzepte und Transfer". https://www.bibb.de/de/197803.php. Accessed 17 Apr 2025

Bundesministerium für Bildung und Forschung (2020) Weiterbildungsverhalten in Deutschland 2020, Ergebnisse des Adult Education Survey — AES-Trendbericht. https://www.bmbf.de/SharedDocs/Publikationen/de/bmbf/1/31690_AES-Trendbericht_2020.html. Accessed 17 Apr 2025

Bundesministerium für Bildung und Forschung, Interactive Chart. https://www.bmbf.de/SiteGlobals/Forms/Karte/interaktive-landkarte/interaktive-landkarte_formular.html?nn=1075772. Accessed 17 April 2025

Bundesministerium für Forschung, Technologie und Raumfahrt (2024) Bekanntmachung: Richtlinie zur Förderung von Projekten zur Steigerung und Stärkung der berufsbezogenen Weiterbildung durch Qualifizierung und Etablierung von Weiterbildungsmentorinnen und Weiterbildungsmentoren, Bundesanzeiger vom 14.11.2024. https://www.bmbf.de/SharedDocs/Bekanntmachungen/DE/2024/11/2024-11-14-bekanntmachung-weiterbildungsmentoren.html. Accessed 17 Apr 2025

Buschmann R (2024) Section 96. In: Däubler W, Klebe T, Wedde P (eds) BetrVG Betriebsverfassungsgesetz, 19th edn. Bund-Verlag, Frankfurt

Calmez A, Winkler M (2024) Weiterbildungsmentorinnen und -mentoren: Tätigkeiten und Kompetenzanforderungen. https://www.bibb.de/dokumente/ablage/2024-12-05%20Arbeitsergebnisse%20der%20wissens.pdf. Accessed 17 Apr 2025

Campbell I, Price R (2016) Precarious work and precarious workers: towards an improved conceptualization. Econ Labour Relat Rev 27(3):314–332

Cantner U et al (2014) Works councils, training activities and innovation: a study of German firms. Jena Economic Research Papers No. 2014-006. https://hdl.handle.net/10419/98440. Accessed 17 Apr 2025

Däubler W (2024) Sections 112, 112a. In: Däubler W, Klebe T, Wedde P (eds) BetrVG Betriebsverfassungsgesetz, 19th edn. Bund-Verlag, Frankfurt

Ellguth P, Kohaut P (2022) Tarifbindung und betriebliche Interessenvertretung: Ergebnisse aus dem IAB-Betriebspanel 2021. WSI Mitteilungen 75(4):328–336. https://doi.org/10.5771/0342-300X-2022-4-328

Emmler H, Brehmer W (2019) The composition of German Works Councils. Results from the WSI Works Council Survey. In: Behrens M, Dribbusch H (eds) Industrial relations in Germany. Dynamics and perspectives, WSI-Mitteilungen, Special Issue 2019, Baden Baden, pp 51–72. https://doi.org/10.5771/0342-300X-2023-6-460

Erol S (2024) Wie Betriebsräte die betriebliche Weiterbildung fördern, Handlungsoptionen und ihre Determinanten. WSI Mitteilungen 77(6):429–440

Erol S, Ahlers E (2023) Betriebliche Weiterbildung als Handlungsfeld der Betriebsräte in Zeiten der Transformation. WSI Policy Brief, No. 77, Hans-Böckler-Stiftung, Wirtschafts- und Sozialwissenschaftliches Institut (WSI), Düsseldorf

Fachliche Weisung der BA (2024) Qualifizierungsgeld, 1.4.2024

Franca V et al (2022) The multifaceted nature of precarious work: a mixed methods approach. Revija za socijalnu politiku 29(1):5–33. https://doi.org/10.3935/rsp.v29i1.1847

Franzen M (2001) Das Mitbestimmungsrecht des Betriebsrats bei der Einführung von Maßnahmen der betrieblichen Berufsbildung nach § 97 II BetrVG. NZA 2001

Göpfert B, Seier J (2019) Die “Transformations-Einigungsstelle”: Inhalt und Grenzen eines “Qualifizierungs-Sozialplans”. NZA 2019:588–594

Graf-Drasch V et al (2023) Driving Twin Transformation - the Interplay of Digital Transformation and Sustainability Transformation. May 11, 2023. https://publica.fraunhofer.de/handle/publica/457302

Greene A et al (2021) The gender representation gap: implications for workplace union effectiveness. Ind Relat J 52:40–63. https://doi.org/10.1111/irj.12316

Greifenstein R (2014) Repräsentationsprobleme, Politikfähigkeit und Sozialprofil der Betriebsräte. In: Bogumil J (ed) Arbeitsbeziehungen und Demokratie im Wandel, Festschrift für Leo Kißler, 1st edn. Nomos, Baden-Baden, pp 98–120. https://doi.org/10.5771/9783845249971_98

Hassel A, Schroeder W (2018) Gewerkschaftliche Mitgliederpolitik: Schlüssel für eine starke Sozialpartnerschaft. WSI Mitteilungen 71(6):485–496. https://doi.org/10.5771/0342-300X-2018-6-485

Homburg J (2024) Section 92. In: Däubler W, Klebe T, Wedde P (eds) BetrVG Betriebsverfassungsgesetz, 19th edn. Bund-Verlag, Frankfurt

Karakayali S, Bouali C (2021) Migrantische Aktive in der betrieblichen Mitbestimmung. Hans-Böckler-Stiftung: Working Paper Forschungsförderung Nr. 228, Düsseldorf

Klebe T (2024) Section 90. In: Däubler W, Klebe T, Wedde P (eds) BetrVG Betriebsverfassungsgesetz. Bund-Verlag, Frankfurt

Lammers A, Lukowski F, Weis K (2022) The relationship between works councils and firms’ further training provision in times of technological change. Br J Ind Relat 61(2):392–424

Markowski J (2022) Beiträge für die Beratungspraxis Mitbestimmung des Betriebsrats bei Qualifizierung Wiederbelebung durch betriebliche Transformation. ArbRB 2022:15–18

mendi.net (2024) Sie haben einfach gefehlt – Weiterbildungsmentor*innen als Impulsgeber für die betriebliche Qualifizierung. https://verdi-mendi.net/neue-broschuere-sie-haben-einfach-gefehlt-weiterbildungsmentorinnen-als-impulsgeber-fuer-die-betriebliche-qualifizierung/. Accessed 19 Dec 2024

Mohrenweiser J (2022) Works councils. In: Zimmermann K (ed) Handbook of labor, human resources and population economics. Springer, Cham, pp 1–40. https://doi.org/10.1007/978-3-319-57365-6_206-1

Nienhüser W (2020) Works councils. In: Wilkinson A, Donaghey J, Dundon T, Freeman R (eds) Handbook of research on employee voice. Edward Elgar Publishing, pp 260–276. https://doi.org/10.4337/9781788971188

OECD (2021) Continuing Education and Training in Germany, Getting Skills Right. OECD Publishing, Paris. https://doi.org/10.1787/1f552468-en

Oesingmann K (2015) Workplace representation in Europe: works councils and their economic effects on firms. CESifo DICE Report 13(4):59–64

Peers S (2013) Equal treatment of atypical workers: a new frontier for EU law? Yearb Eur Law 32(1):30–56. https://doi.org/10.1093/yel/yet002

Röder G, Gebert C (2017) Technologischer Wandel und Betriebsänderung – Bringen Industrie 4.0 und E-Mobilität den “Qualifizierungssozialplan”? NZA 2017:1289–1296

Rogers J, Streeck W (eds) (1995) Works councils: consultation, representation and cooperation in industrial relations. The University of Chicago Press, Chicago

Roloff S, Buchstaller C (2020) Die Vertretung des Minderheitengeschlechts im Betriebsrat. Arbeit und Recht 68(10):402–405

Ruhwedel K, Simon S (2023) Was bringt das Weiterbildungsgesetz? Working Paper für die Hans-Böckler-Stiftung. https://www.boeckler.de/fpdf/HBS-008735/p_fofoe_WP_310_2023.pdf. Accessed 17 Apr 2025

Ruhwedel K, Simon S (2024) Das Weiterbildungsgesetz – Darstellung, juristische Einordnung, Kritik. NZS 2024:241–252

Schütte R (2013) Transfergesellschaft und Einigungsstelle. NZA 5:249–253

Statistisches Bundesamt (2024). https://www.destatis.de/DE/Themen/Arbeit/Arbeitsmarkt/Qualitaet-Arbeit/Dimension-5/arbeitnehmervertretungen.html. Accessed 17 Apr 2025

Stegmaier J (2012) Effects of works councils on firm-provided further training in Germany. Br J Ind Relat 50(4):667–689. https://doi.org/10.1111/j.1467-8543.2012.00895.x

Thünken O, Morgenroth S, Hertwig M, Fischer A (2020) Kampf um Mitbestimmung. Antworten auf Union Busting und die Behinderung von Betriebsräten. Transcript, Bielefeld

Waas B (2014) Non-trade Union Workers' Representation in Germany. In: Blanpain R, Lyutov N (eds) Workers' Representation in Central and Eastern Europe: Challenges and Opportunities for the Works Councils' System. Alphen on the Rhine: Kluwer Law International BV, The Netherlands, pp 85–104

Winterton J (2006) Social dialogue and vocational training in Europe – are we witnessing the emergence of a European model? J Eur Ind Train 30(1):65–76

**Katharina Ruhwedel** is a doctoral candidate and researcher at the Hugo Sinzheimer Institute (HSI) in Frankfurt am Main, Germany. She is working on her doctoral thesis on employer resistance to works councils and co-determination. She was a research assistant in the research project 'Qualifying for Transformation' on continuing education law led by Daniel Ulber. She is also interested in legal and social theory.

**Jaqueline Stein** is a researcher at the Institute for Labour Law and Industrial Relations in the European Union (IAAEU) in Trier, Germany. Her research focuses on collective labour rights, anti-discrimination law, and the legal regulation of non-standard forms of labour.

# Elements of Lifelong Learning as a Labour Right?

# Lifelong Learning as a Workers' Right

## Lifelong Learning Within the Context of the Employment Relationship: The Worker's Perspective

**Agnieszka Zwolińska**

## 1 Introduction

Lifelong learning is perceived as an instrument to increase work productivity, as a factor stimulating the labour market, but also as a means of achieving social justice and promoting human self-development.[1]

The growing importance of lifelong learning policies is closely related to the dynamics of technological development. This is not a new phenomenon,[2] but in the era of technological development that societies are currently experiencing, new evidence can be found to support this thesis. An example of this, on the EU policy level, can be found in the comparison of Article 14 of the EU Charter of Fundamental Rights[3] with point 4 of the European Declaration on Digital Rights and Principles of the Digital Decade.[4] The Charter (the text adopted in 2000) establishes the right of everyone to education and access to vocational and continuing training. In turn, the Declaration (the text adopted in 2023), which is a response to the challenges of digital transformation, emphasizes, on the one hand, the right of everyone to educa-

[1] For instance, Council of the European Union (2002), p. 1, recital 1; European Commission (2017); European Commission (2020), p. 3; Council of the European Union (2022), p. 26, recital 1; ILO (2021); European Declaration on Digital Rights and Principles for the Digital Decade, OJ C 23, 23.1.2023, p. 1, in particular Chapter II, point 4 lit. b).

[2] Focacci and Perez (2022).

[3] OJ C 326, 26.10.2012, p. 391.

[4] OJ C 23, 23.1.2023, p. 1.

A. Zwolińska (✉)
The University of Warsaw, Faculty of Law and Administration, Labour Law and Social Policy Department, Warsaw, Poland
e-mail: a.zwolinska@wpia.uw.edu.pl


J. Murto, V. Franca (eds.), *Labour Law and Lifelong Learning*,
https://doi.org/10.1007/978-3-032-11035-0_10

tion, training, and lifelong learning, and, on the other hand, the goal of providing everyone with the opportunity to acquire basic as well as advanced digital skills. It follows that the extent and intensity of the digital transformation has highlighted the importance of lifelong learning at the EU policy level.[5] Thus, lifelong learning has gained in importance to ensure the effectiveness of fundamental rights and improve the quality of life, economic growth, and sustainability[6] in the new dual reality—meaning the real and digital world.

What is more, the technological change and its dynamics create an additional challenge for some workers—in particular, older workers and those with lower levels of education and income who are less sophisticated users of digital technology.[7] This difference in familiarity with digital technologies can in turn spill over into the labour market, benefiting those with more familiarity with digital technology.[8] Digitization can therefore also be seen as another source of inequality for people in the labour market and access to lifelong learning as an instrument for addressing these inequalities.[9]

In addition, another challenge accompanying technological change cannot be ignored, namely the psychosocial risks that go hand in hand with the experience of work-related stress. Work-related stress is a person's reaction to demands and pressures in their work, when work is not adapted to their knowledge and skills.[10] In this case, too, access to suitable learning opportunities could be an effective tool for coping with this challenge.

The aim of this chapter is to define lifelong learning in terms of workers' rights. The use of the word 'right' in this chapter is intended to emphasize a worker's capacity to make claims and the power to enforce them.[11] There are at least two reasons for adopting this understanding of the right of a worker in relation to lifelong learning. The first is based on the acceptance of the increase in the individual's freedom as a criterion for evaluation of social, economic, and political changes. Thus, changes resulting in an increase in the individual's freedom, in terms of and through lifelong learning, could be assessed as a sign of development.[12] The second argument comes from recognizing the importance of an individual's freedom for the effectiveness of the learning process.[13] Increasing an individual's freedom within

---

[5] For instance, the European Commission's initiative called on the Union of Skills to respond to a transforming world and a rapidly changing future; see European Commission (2025a).

[6] See points 2 and 3 of the preamble to the Declaration.

[7] Lee and Zarnic (2024), p. 30.

[8] Lee and Zarnic (2024), p. 30.

[9] See ILO (2021), part I points 3, 5 and 7; European Declaration on Digital Rights and Principles for the Digital Decade, Chap. II points 2 and 4.

[10] Leka and Jain (2010), p. 4.

[11] Osiatyński (2011), pp. 290–921.

[12] Referring here to the concept of Sen (2000). Also Bueno (2021), pp. 311–329. The author applying a freedom-based approach to labour law to demonstrate fundamental labour rights can and should be evaluated in terms of freedom.

[13] See, for instance, Council of the European Union (2022), Recital 11 in fine.

the learning process has a positive effect on their motivation to learn and the results of that learning.[14]

The main part of the chapter focuses on the identification and analysis of the legal institutions that can increase a worker's freedom with regard to lifelong learning. The objective of the chapter is to pinpoint a series of worker rights in relation to the employer, encompassing those designed to remove barriers to a worker's learning and those that offer incentives for a worker's learning. Individually and collectively, these rights can contribute to achieving the objective of lifelong learning within the context of the employment relationship. It begins by outlining the worker's right to be informed of learning needs and opportunities (Sect. 2). This is followed by the qualification of the worker's learning time from the perspective of the legal definition of working time (Sect. 3). Next, the legal framework of the principle of equality is analysed in the search for legal protection of workers' access to training and workers' entitlements related to participation in training (Sect. 4). Finally, the institution of the right to educational leave is presented (Sect. 5). The subject of the analysis are mainly EU and international labour law regulations.

The last part of the chapter reflects on the possible legal solutions were a human right to lifelong learning to be recognized.[15] Accordingly, the analysis of the worker's legal situation revolves around the question of how the human right to lifelong learning may, if recognized, affect the worker's rights, vis-à-vis, the employer.

## 2 The Employer's Obligation to Provide Information on Training Entitlement

An informed decision by a worker to undertake learning activities requires access to knowledge about the training available, as well as the benefits of completing it from the perspective of the current and future social, economic, technological, and labour market situation.[16] From the perspective of the worker, who has a legal obligation to his or her employer, it is also important that the worker has transparent information on how his or her decision to participate in learning activities will affect the performance of the employment relationship. Taking this into account, one way to facilitate lifelong learning for the worker is to ensure that he or she has access to relevant information.

The importance of access to adequate information on training entitlement has been recently recognized in Directive (EU) 2019/1152 of the European Parliament and of the Council of 20 June 2019 on transparent and predictable working

[14] Anders and Kuvaas (2014), pp. 221–222.

[15] UNESCO Institute for Lifelong Learning (2020).

[16] This element is widely recognized as being important in the life learning policies agenda. See for instance, European Commission (2020), p. 8; ILO (2021), in particular point 12 lit. e).

conditions in the European Union.[17] According to Article 4(2)(h), employers are obliged to inform workers about training entitlement provided by the employer, if any. Recital 17 explains that information on training entitlement should include information on the number of training days, if any, to which the worker is entitled during the year and information on the employer's general training policy.

It should be noted that information on training entitlement has been qualified as an essential aspect of the employment relationship. This is a significant change from the perspective of the importance of the worker's lifelong learning compared to the previous Directive 91/533/EEC.[18] The previous Directive did not qualify information on a worker's training entitlement as an essential aspect of the employment relationship. However, it should be also noted that neither the preamble of Directive 2019/1152 nor its Article 4 impose an obligation on the employer to grant training entitlement to workers, but only an obligation to inform them of whether such entitlements are provided for by the employer.

It is also noteworthy that the provision of the Directive under scrutiny is applicable irrespective of the employer's size or the characteristics of the worker. This suggests that the analysed provision may not be effective in removing barriers to access to training for workers in small- and medium-sized enterprises or individuals in atypical work (e.g. temporary agency workers, digital platform workers). This comment seems justified, especially since the relevant EU documents note that small- and medium-sized enterprises do not provide or fund training for their staff and that atypical workers have less or no access to training entitlements.[19] It is worth noting that this issue was already identified in Directive 2008/104/EC of the European Parliament and of the Council of 19 November 2008 on temporary agency work.[20] The Directive emphasizes the importance of improving temporary agency workers' access to training within temporary work agencies and through user undertakings (Article 6(5)). It obliges Member States to improve access to such training for temporary agency workers. From this perspective, Directive 2019/1152 does not seem to consider the specific situation of temporary agency workers. Consequently, it perpetuates rather than removes barriers to training access for temporary agency workers. This is because Article 4(2)(h) of Directive 2019/1152 does not impose an obligation on employers who are user undertakings to inform temporary agency workers of their training entitlements nor does it impose an obligation on temporary work agencies to inform temporary agency workers of training entitlements available for them in user undertakings.

Another group of atypical workers who may face a similar problem to that experienced by temporary agency workers are platform workers, who are employed by intermediaries. An analysis of Article 4(2)(h) of Directive 2019/1152 and Directive

[17] OJ L 186, 11.7.2019, p. 105.

[18] Council Directive of 14 October 1991 on an employer's obligation to inform employees of the conditions applicable to the contract or employment relationship (91/533/EEC) - OJ L 288, 18.10.1991, p. 32.

[19] Council of the European Union (2022), Recitals 9–11.

[20] OJ L 327, 5.12.2008, p. 9.

(EU) 2024/2831 of the European Parliament and of the Council of 23 October 2024 on improving working conditions in platform work[21] leads to the conclusion that there are no legal provisions requiring a digital labour platform or an intermediary to inform the platform worker employed by the intermediary about training entitlements provided by the digital labour platform.

## 3 Working Time and a Worker's Learning Time

Referring here to the EU definition of 'working time',[22] 'working time' means any period during which the worker is working, at the employer's disposal, and carrying out his or her activities or duties, in accordance with national laws and/or practice. It is worth noting that Directive 2003/88/EC also defines the term 'rest period' as any period which is not working time. It means that EU law adopts a binary concept of a worker's time divided into working time and rest time.[23] Consequently, there is no intermediate category between working time and rest period.[24] This is relevant information from the perspective of classifying the time of the worker's learning activities. Given the EU law concepts of working time and rest period, the condition for a worker to benefit from their rest time is for them to be away from the place of work.[25] In the recent ECJ jurisprudence, another criterion is additionally applied—the extent of the restrictions imposed on the worker which, objectively assessed, have a significant impact on his or her ability to freely manage their time (attend to their own affairs).[26]

Applying these general remarks on the concept of 'working time' to the classification of a period of worker's learning, the following questions arise. First, there is the question of whether the time of such learning constitutes working time. Second, taking into account the possibility of attending learning activities outside the workplace, does the location of the training (e.g. the workplace, another location

---

[21] OJ L 2831 z 2024, 11.11.2024.

[22] Article 2(1) of Directive 2003/88/EC of the European Parliament and of the Council of 4 November 2003 concerning certain aspects of the organization of working time (OJ L 299 of 2003, p. 9).

[23] See judgment of 3 October 2000, C-303/98, *Simap*, ECLI:EU:C:2000:528, paras 47–50; judgment of 9 September 2003, C-151/02, *Jaeger*, para 48; opinion of the Advocate General of 12 July 2005 in Case C-14/04, *Dellas and others*, ECLI: EU:C:2005:448, para 61 and judgment in that case, para 42; order of 11 January 2007, C-437/05, *Vorel*, ECLI: EU:C:2007:23, para 25; judgment of 21 February 2018, C-518/15, *Matzak*, para 55; judgment of 9 March 2001, C-344/19, *D.J.*, para 29.

[24] It is worth noting that in the literature the need has been pointed out for an intermediate category between working time and rest period at the EU level, in order to increase the flexibility of EU law and to take into account current labour market conditions; see Mitrus (2019), pp. 393–397.

[25] Judgment of 9 September 2003, C-151/02, *Jaeger*, para 95.

[26] See judgment of 21 February 2018, C-518/15, *Matzak*, paras 63–66; judgment of 9 March 2021, C-344/19, *D.J.*, paras 36–40 and 45–46.

designated by the employer, or the worker's home in the case of online training) constitute a criterion for classifying the training period as working time.

Inspiration for answers to these questions may come from the ECJ's judgment in the case of *BX v. Unitatea Administrativ Teritorială D.*[27] The case concerned whether time spent on vocational training should be classified as 'working time'. Nonetheless, the criteria presented in this case can be applied to classify the time of other lifelong learning activities, and not just vocational training. The ECJ stated that Article 2(1) of Directive 2003/88/EC must be interpreted as meaning that the period during which a worker attends vocational training required by his or her employer, which takes place away from his or her usual place of work, during which he or she does not perform his or her normal duties, constitutes 'working time' within the meaning of that provision. The ECJ emphasized that when a worker receives instructions from their employer to attend vocational training so as to be able to carry out his or her duties and, moreover, where that employer has itself signed the vocational training contract with the undertaking called upon to provide that training, it must be held that, during the periods of vocational training, that worker is at his or her employer's disposal within the meaning of Article 2(1) of Directive 2003/88/EC.[28] Recognizing the training period as working time means that this period is included when calculating the maximum average weekly working time (Article 6 of Directive 2003/88/EC). Accordingly, it does not constitute a rest period and therefore cannot deprive the worker of rights to minimum daily and weekly rest (Articles 3 and 5 of Directive 2003/88/EC). Thus, in this case, the limits of the worker's training obligation have been set due to the need to protect the worker's health and safety. More specifically, these limits have been defined in view of the fundamental rights of the worker to a maximum working time and to daily and weekly rest periods established in Article 31(2) of the Charter and clarified in Directive 2003/88/EC. 31(2) of the Charter and specified in Directive 2003/88/EC.

Taking into account the comments made so far on the concept of 'working time' and the ruling of the Court of Justice presented above, the following conclusion is justified that the extent of the worker's autonomy in deciding to participate in the learning activities is a relevant criterion for the legal classification of learning time as working time. Training undertaken by a worker at their own initiative, as opposed to that undertaken at the initiative of the employer, shall not constitute working time. In the absence of specific regulations on the classification of such learning time, it shall therefore constitute rest time, in the meaning of EU law, from the perspective of the employment relationship.

Referring to the aforementioned relationship between the degree of learner autonomy and learner motivation and training effectiveness, the above findings do not encourage workers to take learning initiatives themselves. What is more, time constraints are mentioned as an important factor preventing adults from seeking

[27] C-909/19, EU:C:2021 :893.

[28] C-909/19, p. 42.

training.[29] One solution could be to introduce special regulations that promote learning activities among workers. This aim can be achieved by granting workers the right to paid training leave. The objectives of this institution are presented in more detail in Sect. 5.

## 4 The Equality Principle and a Worker's Lifelong Learning

When seeking to identify workers' rights that could provide legal protection in relation to their access to lifelong learning and during and after such learning, it is important not to overlook the legal protection afforded by the principle of equal treatment. This section analyses the principle of equal treatment in terms of its potential to protect workers' access to and participation in lifelong learning.

### *4.1 Qualifications as a Criterion for the Differential Treatment of Workers*

At the outset, it should be clarified that equal treatment means a situation in which persons in similar situations are treated in the same way and persons in different situations are treated differently (formal understanding of equal treatment).[30] At the same time, it should be emphasized that the criterion of possession of certain qualifications constitutes an objective criterion for differential treatment in the context of access to employment and for differential employment conditions.[31] Thus, the key when applying the principle of equal treatment is to understand the concept of 'qualifications'.

If the EU equal treatment legislation is taken as a point of reference, the concept of qualifications is not defined therein. Furthermore, as an analysis of ECJ case law shows, it can be understood more broadly than the requirements of the post to be

---

[29] Council of the European Union (2022), Recital 10.

[30] See, for instance, the ECJ judgments: of 14 September 2010, C-550/07 *P Akzo Nobel Chemicals and Akcros Chemicals v Commission* EU:C:2010:512, paras 54 and 55; 22 May 2014, C-356/12 *Glatzel*, EU:C:2014:350, para 43; of 21 December 2016, *Vervloet and Others*, C-76/15, EU:C:2016:975, para 74; of March 2017, C-406/16, *Milkova*, para 55.

[31] The objectivity of a qualifications criterion is also recognized with regard to the positive action. Analysis of the case-law of the Court of Justice justified the statement that, as a rule, a measure aimed at promoting access to employment of a group that is underrepresented is compatible with EU law, provided that a candidate from the underrepresented group has the same qualifications as a candidate from the dominant group—See, for instance, the ECJ judgments: of 11 November 1997, C-409/95, *Marschall*, EU:C:1997:533, paras 30–33; of 28 March 2000, C-158/97, *Badeck and Others*, EU:C:2000:163, paras 30–33; of 6 July 2000, C-407/98 *Abrahamsson*, EU:C:2000:367, paras 49–53. This idea is also reflected in Article 6(2) of Directive (EU) 2022/2381 on improving the gender balance among directors of listed companies and relevant measures.

filled.[32] The absence of a definition for the term 'qualifications' in EU equal treatment legislation means it can be interpreted in various ways, potentially more restrictively than in lifelong learning policies. Inconsistent terminology may hinder the legal protection afforded to workers by equal treatment legislation in relation to access to lifelong learning and lifelong learning activities undertaken during their employment.

The above observation regarding qualifications as an objective criterion for differential treatment of workers seems relevant when considering the relation between the equality principle and workers' lifelong learning. This is because it implies that the protective role of the principle of equal treatment of workers will therefore operate at the stage prior to the acquisition of qualifications—i.e. at the stage of access to training or even access to employment (whereas, in the context of the definition of lifelong learning, working can also be a learning process).[33]

## *4.2 The Scope of the Principle of Equality: Vocational Training and Working Conditions Categories*

Referring again to EU law, the principle of equal treatment covers conditions of access to employment and also conditions for access to self-employment and occupation. For access to vocational training, it has been clarified that it covers access to all types and all levels of vocational guidance, vocational training, advanced vocational training, and retraining, including practical work experience. It also covers employment and working conditions.[34] It is interesting to note that, referring to ECJ case law, the categories of access to employment and working conditions are not disjoint categories, in the sense that a given condition can be covered by both categories at the same time.[35]

[32] See, for instance, the ECJ judgment of 28 March 2000, C-158/97 *Georg Badeck and Others*, para 9, where according to national law, in the process of assessing candidates' qualifications, capabilities and experience were to be taken into account that had been acquired by family work in so far as they are of importance for the suitability, performance, and capability of applicants.

[33] Referring here to the definition of lifelong learning provided in Art. 2 Regulation (EU) 2021/817 of the European Parliament and of the Council of 20 May 2021 establishing Erasmus+: the Union Programme for education and training, youth and sport and repealing Regulation (EU) No 1288/2013; also Lifelong Learning Platform (2022), p. 52.

[34] See Article 3 (1) lit. a - c) of Directive 2000/43/EC implementing the principle of equal treatment between persons irrespective of racial or ethnic origin; Article 3(1) lit. a-c) of Directive 2000/78/EC establishing a general framework for equal treatment in employment and occupation (covering the discrimination on the grounds on religion or belief, disability, age and sexual orientation); Article 14 (1) lit. a) - c) Directive 2006/54/EC on the implementation of the principle of equal opportunities and equal treatment of men and women in matters of employment and occupation (recast).

[35] See ECJ judgment of 13 July 1995, C-116/94, *Meyers*, EU:C:1995:247, para. 25. The case concerned access to family credit, an income-related benefit granted to supplement the income of

It is also worth mentioning that, within the framework of the principle of equal treatment, 'working conditions' are understood broadly. Their meaning is not limited to conditions set out in the employment contract or applied by the employer in respect of the worker's employment. They include, inter alia, a family credit that constitutes a part of the national social security system and is awarded to low-paid workers,[36] making it available to employees, by the employer, of nursery places at their place of work, or outside it.[37] An understanding of the concept of 'working conditions' justifies the conclusion that this category is so broad that it may also include the entitlements granted to workers by the employer to take up and participate in learning activities that do not fall within the category of vocational training, or entitlements that facilitate participation in such learning activities (e.g. leave from work in order to participate in learning activities). As a result, access to such learning activities and related entitlements can be assessed from the perspective of compliance with the EU principle of equal treatment.

## 4.3 *Worker's Learning Activities as Unlawful Criterion of Differential Treatment*

When considering the EU principle of equal treatment in the context of workers' participation in lifelong learning, it is necessary to stress the limitations of the legal protection arising from a limited list of discriminatory grounds.[38] However, at the level of national laws, the catalogue of discriminatory criteria may be open. Moreover, it cannot be ruled out that the circumstance of taking up training unrelated to the requirements of a worker's post may be considered an unlawful criterion of differential treatment. An example of such way of thinking on the principle of equal treatment is the ruling of the Supreme Court of the Republic of Poland. It should be made clear that Polish labour law adopts an open catalogue of discriminatory criteria.[39] Thus, the labour court may, in the circumstances of a particular case, consider as discriminatory a criterion that is not explicitly mentioned by the legislator as a discriminatory criterion. It is noteworthy that under Polish law, which was applicable to this dispute, the worker, as a trainee legal adviser, benefited from

low-paid workers responsible for a child, and one of the conditions for receiving it was having low-paid work.

[36] See ECJ judgment of 13 July 1995, C-116/94, *Meyers*, EU:C:1995:247, para 24. In this case, the ECJ interpreted Article 5 of Council Directive 76/207/EEC of 9 February 1976 on the implementation of the principle of equal treatment for men and women as regards access to employment, vocational training and promotion, and working conditions, repealed by Directive 2006/54.

[37] See, ECJ judgment of 19 March 2002, C-476/99, *H. Lommers*, EU:C:2002:183, para 26.

[38] See, the ECJ judgment of 18 December 2014, C-354/13, *Kaltoft*, EU:C:2014:2463, paras 31–40.

[39] Article 32 of the Constitution of the Republic of Poland of 2 April 1997, Journal of Laws 1997 No 78, item 483; Articles $11^3$ and $18^{3a}$ (1) of Act of 26 June 1974 Labour Code, consolidated version Journal of Laws 2025, item 277.

statutory time off from work in order to attend legal training courses. As a result, her actual working hours were lower than those of other workers. In this case, the worker raised an allegation of discrimination, pointing out that she had been overlooked for promotions because she was doing her legal adviser training. The Supreme Court held that pursuing a legal adviser's apprenticeship, with the employer's consent, which was not required for the position held by the worker (the legal adviser's qualifications were too high in comparison to the requirements needed for the job held by the worker) could constitute a discriminatory criterion.[40]

## 4.4 *Lifelong Learning as a Positive Action Measure*

A formal understanding of the principle of equal treatment has been presented at the beginning of this section. When looking for links between the principle of equal treatment and workers' lifelong learning, it is necessary to extend the consideration of the concept of substantive equality. Referring to the concept put forward by Fredman, the objectives of substantive equality are: (i) remedy disadvantage, (ii) redress stigma, stereotyping, violence against members of protected groups, (iii) enhance participation of under-represented groups (politically, socially), and (iv) address systematic disadvantage.[41] In line with the objective of remedy disadvantage are positive action measures. Positive action is a permissible derogation of the formally understood principle of equal treatment. As part of positive action, a worker belonging to a disadvantaged group may be entitled to better treatment compared to those not belonging to the disadvantaged group, for instance in terms of access to training or conditions of participation in that training. Thus, given the objectives and nature of positive action measures, providing an underrepresented group with preferential access to lifelong learning may constitute a positive action measure.

Referring to EU law, positive action measures are recognized by the EU legislator. There are specific measures to prevent or compensate for disadvantages linked to the grounds of discrimination recognized in EU law, namely religion or belief, disability, age, sexual orientation, race or ethnic origin, and gender.[42] EU law

[40] The judgment of the Polish Supreme Court of 14 January 2013 r., Case No. I PK 164/12, https://www.sn.pl/sites/orzecznictwo/orzeczenia2/i%20pk%20164-12-1.pdf. Accessed 30 March 2025.

[41] Fredman (2016), p. 392.

[42] See in particular Article 4(1) of Convention on the Elimination of All Forms of Discrimination against Women New York of 18 December 1979; Article 157(4) of the Treaty on the Functioning of the European Union (consolidated version), OJ C 326, 26.10.2012, p. 47; Article 5 of Council Directive 2000/43/EC of 29 June 2000 implementing the principle of equal treatment between persons irrespective of racial and ethnic origin, OJ L 180, 19.7.200, p. 22; Article 7 Council Directive 2000/78/EC of 27 November 2000 establishing a general framework for equal treatment in employment and occupation, OJ L 303, 2.12.2000, p. 16; Article 3 of Directive 2006/54/EC of the European Parliament and of the Council of 5 July 2006 on the implementation of the principle

provides the possibility for Member States to take positive action measures.[43] However, positive action measures are not an obligation for Member States, even within the limits of the EU principle of equal treatment linked to a closed list of discriminatory criteria.

The EU definitively promotes positive action measures. This is confirmed by the European Pillar of Social Rights (EPSR). Equal opportunities between women and men are mentioned in the second principle of the EPSR. According to this principle, equal opportunities must be ensured and fostered in all areas, including participation in the labour market, terms and conditions of employment, and career progression. In turn, equal opportunities of underrepresented groups distinguished by gender, racial or ethnic origin, religion or belief, disability, age, or sexual orientation are mentioned within the third principle of the EPRS. According to this principle, equal opportunities also apply to employment and education.

The importance of reducing inequalities in access to learning for disadvantaged groups is emphasized in actions aimed at strengthening adult learning. One example of this approach is the Council Recommendation on individual learning accounts. The Recommendation explicitly states that Member States may establish additional training entitlements for those most in need, depending on the national context and the changing labour market. According to the Recommendation, individuals who experience particular barriers to accessing adult learning include atypical workers, the unemployed[44] or those with low economic activity, and those adults with low qualifications, but also workers employed by small- or medium-sized companies.[45]

## 5 A Worker's Right to Educational Leave

The concept of a worker's right to leave for learning purposes is not a new one. Its principles have been formulated in the ILO Convention on Paid Educational Leave No. 140 (1974).

The objectives of educational leave as defined in the Convention go beyond the purely economic objectives of the worker's learning, reflecting a holistic approach

of equal opportunities and equal treatment of men and women in matters of employment and occupation (recast), OJ L 204, 26.7.2006, p. 23.

[43] Article 157(4) of the Treaty on the Functioning of the European Union; Article 5 of the Council Directive 2000/43/EC; Article 7 of the Council Directive 2000/78/EC of 27; Article 3 of the Directive 2006/54/EC.

[44] According to EUROSTAT adult learning statistics—in the EU 14.1% of unemployed adults aged 25–64 had a recent learning experience in 2023, when in 2022 47% of adults aged 25–64 had participated in education and training in the last 12 months and 64.2% of adults had participated in informal learning in the EU - https://ec.europa.eu/eurostat/statistics-explained/index.php?title=Adult_learning_statistics#In_the_EU.2C_14.1_.25_of_unemployed_adults_aged_25_to_64_had_a_recent_learning_experience_in_2023. Accessed 24 April 2025.

[45] Recitals 15 and 9–11.

to lifelong learning.[46] The Convention specifies educational purposes as: (a) training, (b) general, social and civic education, and (c) trade union education.[47] In turn, the preamble emphasizes that education leave should meet new aspirations, needs, and objectives of social, economic, technological, and cultural characters, and the real needs of individual workers in a modern society. This broad approach to the objectives of a worker's educational leave is also reflected in Article 3 of the ILO Convention.

The Convention defines 'paid educational leave' as leave granted to a worker for educational purposes for a specified period during working hours, with adequate financial entitlements.[48] In turn, ILO Recommendation on Paid Educational Leave No. 148 (1974) emphasizes that workers should be free to decide which education or training programmes they wish to participate in (Part V.14).

It is worth noting, first, that the leave is to be granted for a specific period of time, so there is a need to indicate its beginning and end. Second, the time of the leave is to fall within the worker's working hours. The taking of leave therefore does not cause termination of the employment relationship. The Convention does not explain how the leave will be treated within the context of the employment relationship. For example, will it be treated as time equivalent to working time, or perhaps as a period when the employment relationship is suspended? This qualification is relevant from the worker's perspective, given that some of their entitlements may depend on the amount of work performed (e.g. measured by working time). Article 11 of the Convention and Part V.21 of ILO Recommendation on Paid Educational Leave No. 148 (1974) allows the conclusion to be drawn that the period of educational leave should constitute a period of employment for the purposes of claims for social benefits and rights arising from the employment relationship.

In creating a framework for a worker's entitlement to paid educational leave, the Convention does not provide for an obligation for the employer to grant such leave to workers. This conclusion is also supported by ILO Recommendation No. 148. Referring to Part III.8 e) of the Recommendation, the public authorities, employers' and workers' organizations, and institutions or bodies providing education and training have been obliged to adopt measures that encourage (only) employers to grant paid educational leave to workers.[49]

While recognizing a worker's right to paid educational leave, the Convention does not specify the source of financing the leave. In particular, it does not state that the employer should bear the cost of that leave, which, in turn, leads to the conclusion that the condition of 'paid' leave can be understood more broadly than the worker's right vis-à-vis the employer to be paid for the period of leave. From the employer's perspective, the period of leave may therefore be an unpaid period, as long as the worker receives his or her livelihood for the period of leave from another

[46] UNESCO Institute for Lifelong Learning (2020).

[47] Article 2.

[48] Article 1.

[49] Świątkowski (2008), p. 546.

source (meaning outside the employment relationship). This conclusion is in line with Part V.20 of ILO Recommendation No. 148. It indicates that workers during paid educational leave should: maintain their earnings levels through continued payment of wages and other benefits or through appropriate compensation for this, in accordance with national laws or regulations, collective agreements, arbitration awards, or otherwise in accordance with national practice. In addition, financial entitlements should take into account any significant additional costs of education or training.

It is also worth noting that the Convention allows the entitlement to paid educational leave to vary according to: the characteristics of the worker (in the case of workers in small undertakings, rural workers, workers residing in isolated areas, shift workers, workers with family responsibilities who find it difficult to fit into general arrangements)[50] or the characteristics of the employing entity (in particular in the case of small and seasonal undertakings that find it difficult to fit into general arrangements),[51] but also the purpose of the training.[52] Thus, the right to educational leave is not necessarily a universal concept, in the sense that it is enjoyed by every worker.

## 6 Human Right to Lifelong Learning and a Worker's Legal Situation: The Conceptual Approach

In this section, the possible influence of lifelong learning policies on the construction of workers' rights will be analysed from the perspective of a holistic approach to lifelong learning. Briefly summarizing the holistic view emphasizes that learning is lifelong and encompasses the entire life span, from birth to death (anytime), and exists within and outside the education system (everywhere); it is undertaken by people of all ages (everyone), takes place through a range of modalities, and involves all areas of knowledge (everything). According to this policy, lifelong learning is seen as an individual human right and a social right.[53] This leads to the conclusion that in the holistic view of lifelong learning its goals go beyond the context of employment and are not solely subordinated to labour market needs.

If lifelong learning were to be recognized as a human right, the question arises as to what impact this may have on the worker's legal situation within the employment relationship? When the worker is the one who is free to choose the learning activity, the obvious conclusion is that their choice of learning activity may not always be optimal from the perspective of the needs of the employer. On the other hand, it should be noted that for the employer an alternative to investing in or enabling the

[50] Article 9 lit. a).

[51] Article 9 lit. b).

[52] Article 10.

[53] UNESCO Institute for Lifelong Learning (2020).

worker's learning activity is to replace a person who does not have the relevant qualifications, competences, or skills with someone who already has them. To illustrate here the scale of the problem, it is worth noting the recent changes in labour—market patterns. Employers now have a broader range of options for getting work done, e.g. automatization, offshoring, and crowdsourcing. Thus, the same logic may apply in the case of a worker who wants to exercise his or her right to lifelong learning within the employment relationship. There is a risk that the employer replaces him or her with something or someone who does not want to exercise his or her right to learn during employment. Taking all of the above into consideration, it can be concluded that the operation of market mechanisms does not encourage the employer to enable the worker to undertake learning activity of their choice. Thus, some kind of external intervention into the construction of the employment relationship would be needed in order to make the human right to lifelong learning a reality within the context of the employment relationship. The goal of any such intervention should be twofold: first, to make learning activities more appealing to those who are already employed, and to their employer. On the other hand, it should protect workers who exercise their right to lifelong learning from any detrimental treatment due to exercising this right within the employment relationship.

Ensuring the effectiveness of a worker's right to lifelong learning may involve resolving, by means of legal instruments, potential conflicts between the learning activities undertaken by the worker and his or her obligations to the employer in the context of the employment relationship. In this regard, an obligation on the employer to adjust the organization of working time or the place where work is carried out (e.g. an entitlement to remote working) to the time and place of the worker's learning activity may be introduced. This would imply an obligation for the employer to take the worker's learning activity into account when organizing the worker's working time, provided, of course, that the employer organizes the worker's working time.[54] In such a situation, it cannot be excluded that the worker's learning activity would take place during his or her rest time, which in turn would not be an optimal solution from the perspective of the efficiency of the learning process and the worker's right to rest. Another possible entitlement could be to establish an obligation for the employer to grant the worker educational leave. This solution modifies the work obligation towards the employer and goes beyond the legal framework for paid educational leave presented above as it is based on the employer's obligation to grant leave at the worker's request.

[54] For example, see the categories of workers listed in Article 17(1) of Directive 2003/88.

## 7 Concluding Remarks

Increasing adult participation in learning requires consideration of the legal and factual conditions that arise from an employment relationship. Given that the main obligation of a worker is to perform work for the employer under the direction of the employer in return for remuneration,[55] it is reasonable to conclude that the main purpose of an employment relationship differs from learning new skills, qualifications, or gaining new experiences. However, the employment and the organizational structure within which it takes place is an important environment for changing the way individuals think about lifelong learning.

When lifelong learning is reduced to an economic objective (increase in labour productivity), this objective does not constitute a justification for establishing the worker's right to lifelong learning effective against the employer. In such a case, it is noticeable that legal protection of the worker is established by limiting the employer's exercise of its managerial powers with respect to learning activities, e.g. by considering training time under instruction of the employer as working time, or by establishing a prohibition of discrimination in access to employment, working conditions, and access to vocational training.

The principle of equal treatment in subjective dimension illustrates that privileged access to learning activities may constitute one of the positive action measures, taking into account, on the one hand, the actual differences in the competences and skills in the European Union associated with workers' groups distinguished by discriminatory criteria (e.g. gender disparities).[56] On the other hand, importance is attributed to equal opportunity. The application at the national level of lifelong learning measures in combating inequalities constitutes an interesting subject for further legal comparative research.

When lifelong learning is viewed from a humanistic perspective, this perspective provides a justification for the establishment of an individual human right to lifelong learning. In turn, the recognition of the individual human right to lifelong learning would justify the introduction of legal instruments to ensure the realization of this right within the employment relationship. In this context, an interesting area for further comparative legal research is the legal regulations of the worker's right to educational leave—its legal construction as a worker's right within the employment relationship and as a human right outside the content of the employment

[55] Judgments of the ECJ: of 3 July 1986, *Deborah Lawrie-Blum v Land Baden-Württemberg*, C-66/85, ECLI:EU:C:1986:284, para 17; 14 October 2010, *Union Syndicale Solidaires Isère v Premier ministre and Others*, C-428/09, ECLI:EU:C:2010:612; para 28; 4 December 2014, *FNV Kunsten Informatie en Media v Staat der Nederlanden*, C-413/13, ECLI:EU:C:2014:2411, para 34; 9 July 2015, *Ender Balkaya v Kiesel Abbruch- und Recycling Technik GmbH*, C-229/14, ECLI:EU:C:2015:455; para 34; and 17 November 2016, *Betriebsrat der Ruhrlandklinik gGmbH v Ruhrlandklinik gGmbH*, C-216/15, ECLI:EU:C:2016:883, para 27.

[56] See European Commission (2025b), pp. 3–6, and the situation of women mentioned there, who remain under-represented in STEM fields such as science, technology, engineering, and mathematics.

relationship. Another interesting area is the existence of the prohibition of discrimination against workers on the grounds of their learning activities.

## References


Anders D, Kuvaas B (2014) Self-determination theory and workplace training and development. In: Gagné M (ed) The Oxford handbook of work engagement, motivation, and self-determination theory, online edition. Oxford Library of Psychology, Oxford Academic, pp 221–222. https://doi.org/10.1093/oxfordhb/9780199794911.013.014

Bueno N (2021) Freedom at, through and from work: rethinking labour rights. Int Labour Rev 160(2):311–329. https://doi.org/10.1111/ilr.12192

Council of the European Union (2002) Council Resolution of 27 June 2002 on lifelong learning. OJ C 163, 9.7.2002

Council of the European Union (2022) Council Recommendation of 16 June 2022 on individual learning accounts. OJ C 243, 27.6.2022

European Commission (2017) Investment in Human Capital – Assessing the Efficiency of Public Spending on Education, Note for the Eurogroup on 6 November 2017

European Commission (2020) Communication from the Commission. European Skills Agenda for sustainable competitiveness, social fairness and resilience. COM(2020) 274 final. https://eur-lex.europa.eu/legal-content/EN/TXT/?uri=celex:52020DC0274

European Commission (2025a) Communication from the Commission. Commission Work Programme, Moving forward together: A Bolder, Simpler, Faster Union. COM(2025) 45 final. https://commission.europa.eu/document/download/f80922dd-932d-4c4a-a18c-d800837fbb23_en?filename=COM_2025_45_1_EN.pdf. Accessed 22 Apr 2025

European Commission (2025b) Communication from the Commission. The Union of Skills. COM(2025) 90 final. https://employment-social-affairs.ec.europa.eu/document/download/915b147d-c5af-44bb-9820-c252d872fd31_en?filename=Communication%20-%20Union%20of%20Skills.pdf

Focacci CN, Perez C (2022) The importance of education and training policies in supporting technological revolutions: a comparative and historical analysis of UK, US, Germany and Sweden (1830-1970). Technology in Society. https://doi.org/10.1016/j.techsoc.2022.102000

Fredman S (2016) Past and futures: EU equality law. In: Bogg A, Costello C, Davis ACL (eds) Research handbook on EU labour law. Edward Elgar Publishing, Cheltenham, pp 391–421

ILO (2021) International Labour Conference – 109th Session, 2021, Resolution XVII concerning skills and lifelong learning; European Declaration on Digital Rights and Principles for the Digital Decade. OJ C 23, 23.1.2023

Lee J, Zarnic Z (2024) The impact of digital technologies on well-being: main insights from the literature. OECD Papers on Well-being and Inequalities. Working paper No. 29, OECD, Paris

Leka S, Jain A (2010) Health impact of psychosocial hazards at work: an overview, WHO. https://iris.who.int/handle/10665/44428

Lifelong Learning Platform (2022) LLL Glossary, review of lifelong learning terminology. https://cradall.org/sites/default/files/lllglossary.pdf

Mitrus L (2019) Potential implications of the Matzak judgment (quality of rest time, right to disconnect). Eur Labour Law J 10(4):386–397. https://doi.org/10.1177/2031952519886146

Osiatyński W (2011) Prawa człowieka i ich granice. Znak, Kraków

Sen A (2000) Development as freedom, 1st edn. Anchor Books, New York

Świątkowski AM (2008) Międzynarodowe prawo pracy. Tom 1 Międzynarodowe publiczne prawo pracy – standardy międzynarodowe, vol 2. C.H. Beck, Munich

UNESCO Institute for Lifelong Learning (2020) Embracing a culture of lifelong learning – contribution to the futures of education initiative. https://unesdoc.unesco.org/ark:/48223/pf0000374112. Accessed 28 Mar 2025

**Agnieszka Zwolińska** is assistant professor at the Department of Labour Law and Social Policy at the Faculty of Law and Administration of the University of Warsaw, as well as assistant specialist for jurisprudence at the Labour Law and Social Security Chamber of the Supreme Court of the Republic of Poland. She was previously attorney-at-law specializing at labour law and industrial relations. She was awarded distinction for her doctoral thesis on 'Employee Obligation to Work' at the Faculty of Law and Administration of the University of Warsaw. Author of a monograph 'Obowiązek wykonywania pracy przez pracownika' (2022), a commentary on the Labour Code together with Małgorzata Gersdorf, Krzysztof Rączka, Michał Raczkowski and Wojciech Ostaszewski (2024), as well as numerous chapters in monographs and articles.

# Lifelong Learning as a Contractual Issue: Is it an Employer's Obligation or an Empty Right?

**Peter Sipka**

## 1 Introduction

Contracts, especially employment contracts, serve as the basis of a protective legal framework that ensures fair and predictable working conditions: they settle clear rights and obligations for the parties, with which they prevent disputes and mitigate risks.[1] This characteristic helps to safeguard performance expectations,[2] from the employer's side, allocate risks for both parties,[3] and prevent legal abuses.[4] Additionally, the fundamental doctrines of good faith and fair dealing support the security and ensure that neither party exploits ambiguities to their advantage.[5]

Contract law, from the perspective of labour law, is unique because there is a strong public intervention by the state, which means that the parties are not only bound by the contract but by other different legal sources as well. The state intervenes significantly in the freedom to conclude contracts and sets specific limits for the parties in order to enforce various protective functions (e.g. working time, occupational health and safety, etc.).

Additionally, in the world of work, it is mainly long-term contracts that, unlike short-term agreements that operate in relatively static environments, require

[1] MacNeil (1978), p. 862.

[2] Hogg (2011), p. 334.

[3] MacNeil (1978), p. 865.

[4] Gordley (2001), p. 9.

[5] Hogg (2011), p. 257.

P. Sipka (✉)
University of Debrecen, Department of Agricultural and Labour Law, Debrecen, Hungary
e-mail: sipka.peter@law.unideb.hu



J. Murto, V. Franca (eds.), *Labour Law and Lifelong Learning*,
https://doi.org/10.1007/978-3-032-11035-0_11

mechanisms that allow for flexibility and adaptation to unforeseen circumstances.[6] Thus, it is accepted in the legal literature that employment contracts are generally long-term relationships,[7] which results in the inability to list all the obligations of the parties since the changing circumstances modify the way of performance. The solution to this problem can be various, but there are two general phenomena: the importance of the promise and the appearance of the implied terms.[8]

This chapter explores lifelong learning from a contractual perspective, and the analysis is focused on the employment contract and how it can be perceived in relation to lifelong learning. It observes the evolving nature of employment obligations and regulatory responses to lifelong learning to clarify whether such training should be seen as a contractual right and /or obligation condition. In order to outline the employment contract in the context of lifelong learning, in this chapter some observation concerning legislative intervention, unilateral employer policies, or voluntary agreements are made.

As regards lifelong learning, the question is whether the employment contract itself implies the right to lifelong learning, i.e. whether it can be included in the existing system of rights and obligations. The aim of this chapter is to examine lifelong learning from the employer's perspective, namely the financial and strategic implications of workforce training. It also evaluates the extent to which employees should be required to participate in training programmes and whether such participation should be contractually mandated. The economic dimensions of lifelong learning are critically assessed, investigating the balance between market-driven solutions and state intervention.

In this chapter, it is examined whether the right to lifelong learning can be guaranteed by the employment contract alone or whether state intervention is necessary in its absence.

The chapter begins by examining the contractual nature of lifelong learning. It outlines how training obligations have been framed within employment contracts and whether they can be expanded to include continuous professional development. In particular, this section examines the extent to which the binding nature of employment contracts, which are essentially long-term (sometimes even decades), is compatible with the changing requirements arise from the challenge of lifelong learning.

The chapter then examines the role of non-written elements in the employment contract, with particular reference to specific principles in labour law such as implied terms, duty of loyalty and the role of the promise. As a result, it will be shown whether there are other obligations on the parties in addition to those not explicitly laid down in the contract and, if so, whether this has an impact on lifelong learning.

---

[6] Breining-Kaufmann (2007), p. 9.

[7] Kiss (2020), p. 186 and MacNeil (1978), p. 900.

[8] The implied terms are originally rooted in the common law system but became accepted broadly in Europe as well; see Kirchner et al. (2010), p. 30.

The regulatory methods that employers can use to influence employee training outside the employment contract will be discussed later. In this context, the distinction between lifelong learning and training arising from the employment relationship will be discussed.

Finally, the chapter concludes with a summary of the research findings and possible solutions.

## 2 Lifelong Learning from a Contractual Perspective

This section examines the importance of training, its place in the employment contract and its position in the system of rights and obligations.

### *2.1 The Importance of Training in the Contract*

The employer is undoubtedly the dominant party in the employment relationship, as they have a fundamental role in setting up the general terms of the relationship, including regulating lifelong learning.[9] Once the contractual terms are settled and the contract is signed, dogmatically, every modification results in an amendment of the contract. This means that on a contractual basis, every amendment needs mutual consent from the parties. However, what happens if a party has no intention to amend the contract? The problem is further complicated by the fact that the employer has the right to influence the content of the legal relationship by means of internal regulations, which allows it to unilaterally alter and shape the content of the legal relationship in certain respects.

Apart from some special areas, it is not necessary for the employer to take any obligation to train/retrain the employees at their own expense beyond the occupational training.[10] Thus, to achieve a general level of fulfilment of these rights, an obligatory regulation must be put somewhere in the regulation of the employment (at the contractual level or higher levels). However, it must also be mentioned that foundational principles, such as good faith, mutual trust and confidence,[11] play a vital role in the regulation system since those basic interpretation methods help to fill the gaps which result from the incompleteness of the contracts.[12] In this chapter, the contractual level will be examined.

At the first level, the base of the relationship is the employment contract itself, where clear rights and obligations, or at least the essential elements, are stated.

---

[9] As Collins called this situation: take it or leave it. Collins (2010), p. 7.

[10] Davies (2009), p. 30.

[11] Brodie (1998), p. 79.

[12] Collins (2007), p. 8.

Traditionally, the obligation of constant training was not among the core elements of the contract. However, during the development of labour law, work-related training has clearly become mandatory, primarily due to the increasing importance of safety at work. This could be considered as a first step on the path towards lifelong learning. From the second half of the twentieth century onwards, an increasing number of EU and ILO documents have been published and safety at work has been given a prominent place.[13] It should be noted, however, that the obligation to provide a safe workplace primarily stems from economic reasons. The creation of a stable workforce necessitates a safe workplace, highlighting the practicality and necessity of such obligations.[14]

Today, there is no question that various types of lifelong training is essential for employers to meet their health and safety obligations, as any technological developments in the workplace must be accompanied by training to ensure that workers acquire the knowledge they need to use them.[15] This obligation on the employer's part is reflected in the fact that regular training can guarantee that the worker can carry out his work with the necessary competence and, thus, safety. Therefore, a part of lifelong learning is closely linked to the employment relationship, which clearly falls within the scope of the employer's obligations already in the current legal context.

Retention is a significant objective in the current labour market conditions, and most employers consider it a priority.[16] Of course, there may be cases where providing training and supporting the progress of the employee is a means of retaining the employee. However, if the employee gains knowledge during the training, which will enable them to find a job in other areas of the labour market, then supporting this is essentially a way for the employer to facilitate the departure of its employee. The process undoubtedly has considerable benefits at the level of society as a whole. Still, in the context of scarce employee resources, the employer's motivation is naturally driven by its economic interests.

## *2.2 The Structure of Rights and Obligations Regarding Training*

From the employer's perspective, training can be interpreted at two levels: first, it is an essential tool for ensuring safety at work, which is why it is mandatory to provide such training. This compulsory training is essential to achieve worker safety at work

[13] Davies (2009), p. 65. This development is further examined in this volume in Kain F, Legal Foundations of Lifelong Learning and Labour Law in Europe, Sect. 3.2.

[14] Gerner-Beuerle et al. (2013), p. 78.

[15] Davies (2009), p. 31.

[16] Leka, Cox and Zwetsloot (2008), p. 99.

and, therefore, cannot be interpreted as a right but rather as an obligation arising from employment.

On the other hand, training may not only be an obligation but also a right: by providing training, the employer can, for example, prepare the employees for technical improvements or simply by meeting the employee's career goals, which can improve job retention. Those two forms of training should, of course, be clearly distinguished: the employer is obliged to provide training under current legislation and may have the right to provide it at its own business discretion.

In the latter context, it is the employer's right to determine the nature, scope and extent of training provided to their employees. This is particularly evident in industries where technological advancements and regulatory compliance necessitate continuous skill development. During this decision procedure, employers have the right to impose contractual obligations related to training, which are connected to the employee's current positions or work performance.[17]

While employers enjoy certain rights, they are also bound by obligations arising from labour laws, contractual duties and ethical responsibilities. As detailed in Chapter 3 by Kain, the EU emphasises the employer's duty to foster employee training as part of labour law–related obligations. EU labour policies must recognise lifelong learning as an employer's obligation, particularly in cases where automation and digital transformation threaten job security.[18]

In summary, the nature of training is dual. Some parts arise from the employer's apparent obligation, according to which they are entitled to share all information and resources required to perform the job safely. Another part of this phenomenon can be handled as a right: if it helps the employer's business interests, they may provide further education for the employees.

## 3 Lifelong Learning as a Contractual Obligation

Analysing lifelong learning from a contractual point of view, it can be stated that the content of the legal relationship is essentially determined by the contract itself and other rules governing the employment relationship.[19] Nevertheless, it is an undisputed fact that the employer has a significantly more significant influence in determining the content of the contract, i.e. the employee is the weaker party in the negotiation of the contractual terms.[20] This also follows from the fact that when the employment relationship is established, the employee typically receives a draft employment contract prepared by the employer, in which most of the provisions are drafted by the employer. This naturally reduces the employee's potential for assert-

[17] Noe (2020), p. 392.

[18] Eurofound (2020).

[19] Deakin (2006), p. 104.

[20] Glowacka (2021), p. 116.

ing their interests, while at the same time contributing to the signing of a contract with more favourable content for the employer.

Thus, the rights and obligations of the parties vis-à-vis each other are primarily contractual. The employment contract mainly determines the content of the legal relationship between the parties. However, the rights and obligations not contained in the contract are not enforceable as such since the party that concluded the contract did not undertake to do so. These parts of the employment relationship are mainly regulated in different documents, e.g. collective agreements, national law, EU law, etc.

As a general rule, based only on an employment contract, the employer is not naturally obliged to provide specific support for lifelong learning arising from the employment contract; i.e. this obligation occurs for the employer only if it is regulated by a Member-State using normative instruments.

However, it is an interesting question whether, in the absence of a specific norm, this can be derived from other obligations: for example, can the principle of the employer's responsibility to employ be extended to include support for the employee's professional development, i.e. is the employer legally obliged to contribute to the employee's further training and to cooperate in this? In the traditional sense, the employer's employment obligation generally involves providing the work, giving the appropriate guidance and providing the material conditions (or paying wages in return for the work), so it does not necessarily imply active support for the employee's career development. These obligations may come from different legal sources and may be interpreted in a broader sense. In that case, the employer's responsibility can be derived from the duty of care and employment, including the responsibility for the development of employability. Thus, the employer's obligation appears on two levels: first, the responsibility to provide training, supporting the employee's developments within the company and attempting to avoid dismissals.

### 3.1 The Lifelong Learning Between the Lines of the Employment Contract: The Role of Implied Terms

Based on the legal literature, there are more ways to find a solution that ensures lifelong learning without normative intervention.

One solution could be the theory of implied terms, which is prominent mainly in the UK legal literature.[21] According to this, not only the literal wording of the contract binds the employer, but any conduct that threatens to erode the employee's rights, which may result in the employee being disadvantaged, are also included.[22] Several approaches could support the idea: the use of implied terms by combining them with statutory protections can ensure that employment law can adequately

[21] Collins (2007), p. 7.

[22] Kiss (2020), p. 224.

respond to the labour market challenges.[23] Moreover, the potential for implied terms in employment contracts could be a safeguard for employees' human rights, which arises from the role of mutual trust and confidence and its limitations in ensuring human rights protection.[24]

One of the primary benefits of implied terms is their role in filling gaps within contracts to ensure that they remain enforceable and practical even when parties have not explicitly addressed every possible scenario.[25] Undoubtedly, the problem of incorporating lifelong learning into the contract could easily be solved by using implied terms. However, at the same time, it should be remembered that despite the advantages, the use of implied terms also presents significant drawbacks, particularly concerning legal certainty and predictability. The potential for judicial intervention in contract interpretation raises concerns about whether implied terms align with the original intent of the parties or instead reflect broader policy goals. In connection to this, the concept of "contemporaneity" examines how employment can exist beyond the terms of a specific contract, particularly in pre-work and post-work phases.[26]

In sum, the theory of implied terms may serve to fill the gaps where explicit contractual provisions are absent, and they often represent fundamental principles or expectations shared by both employer and employee. Also, based on Collins's and Golding's paper about procedural fairness[27]—an evolving concept that ensures fair treatment during disciplinary processes—lifelong learning can also be implied into contracts to reflect modern employment standards and meet the growing demand for continuous professional development in a changing economy. Lifelong learning could be seen as a duty for employers, just as procedural fairness is considered vital for maintaining trust and confidence in the employment relationship.

Based on the discussions in the above-mentioned studies, it would be a possible solution to handle lifelong learning as an implied term in employment contracts, especially considering the growing importance of continuous professional development in today's economy. Implied terms may play a critical role in ensuring fairness and filling gaps where statutory protections are lacking. Given the increasing demand for upskilling in the modern workforce, lifelong learning might naturally be included under this evolving doctrine. It should be pointed out, however, that this principle is not necessarily applied to such an extent in the continental legal systems, which would require either legislative action or judicial decisions to reinforce the principle. Nevertheless, it may be an appropriate tool to address the problem of lifelong learning, as the application of this principle would make the employer's obligation derivable from the employment contract.

---

[23] Collins (2007), p. 11.

[24] Atkinson (2019).

[25] Vogenauer and Weatherill (2006), pp. 105–148.

[26] Honeyball and Pearce (2006).

[27] Collins and Golding (2024).

### 3.2 The Issue of the Employee's Duty of Loyalty

It is essential to mention the employee's duty of loyalty, which is to be considered a contractual obligation. The conclusion of a contract is a matter of mutual trust between the parties: on the one hand, it creates a very broad duty of care on the employer's side and a duty of loyalty on the employee's side.[28] This obligation may arise not only during the employment relationship but also before or after its termination. On the one hand, the employee must keep all confidential information after termination of employment, and sometimes they may have non-competition agreements to distance themselves from competing firms.[29] Of course, this obligation on the part of the parties exists in the performance of the employment contract, one important manifestation of which is that the employer must also respect the human rights of employees to a large extent. This, according to Atkinson, can be derived from the principle of mutual trust and respect, which is naturally linked to the principles of good faith and fair dealing.[30]

Overall, however, we can see that the special relationship system of labour law has a significant impact both on the relationship between the parties and on labour market processes: the principle of mutual trust goes beyond general financial interests and creates points of reference beyond them.[31]

### 3.3 The Role of Promise

Promises are essential in contract law, shaping the fundamental principles governing the enforceability and formation of agreements. However, it is debated whether contract law primarily exists to enforce moral obligations or to facilitate economic transactions.[32] The idea of offer and acceptance underscores the necessity of a promise for an offer to be legally effective: it serves as a declaration of commitment that provides the offeree the power to accept and form a binding agreement.[33] Unlike moral obligations, contractual promises acquire legal significance through their manifestation in a legally recognised form.[34] This distinction is crucial in differentiating binding contracts from informal assurances that lack the requisite legal elements for enforceability.

---

[28] Cabrelli (2005).

[29] Honeyball and Pearce (2006), p. 44.

[30] Atkinson (2019), p. 524.

[31] Deakin (2013), p. 6.

[32] Craswell (2001), p. 19.

[33] Benson (2001), p. 26.

[34] Eisenberg (2001), p. 206.

The promissory theory of contract, as articulated by Fried,[35] asserts that contractual obligations derive their binding force from the moral duty to keep promises. However, critics argue that contract law serves broader economic and social functions beyond mere promise enforcement.[36] For instance, contract remedies often focus on compensating for expectation losses rather than ensuring the literal performance of a promise.[37] This approach highlights contract law's role in risk allocation and economic efficiency rather than strict adherence to promissory morality. In long-term contractual relationships (like employment relationships mainly), promises provide stability while allowing flexibility for future contingencies. MacNeil argues that relational contract theory acknowledges the evolving nature of promises, emphasising cooperation and adaptability over rigid enforcement.[38] Many long-term contracts incorporate implied terms and re-negotiation clauses to accommodate changing circumstances, reflecting the dynamic nature of contractual commitments.[39]

In the case of lifelong learning, an explicit promise cannot be observed from the employer's side. However, there are some elements of training and learning methods which could lead to the continuous training of the employee. At the same time, the question arises as to whether the promise of long-term employment implies that the employer will constantly strive to ensure that the employee is adequately qualified, i.e. able to do the job. If the answer to this question is yes, it is feasible to interpret lifelong learning within the contract. However, it can only cover those forms of training that are provided in the context of the employment contract, i.e. either to support the performance of the duties of the position or to provide in-service training within the organisation.

On the other hand, if lifelong learning is interpreted as a comprehensive phenomenon covering any learning process, the employer's promise can no longer be shown to be a promise. The promise of employment can only be interpreted within the context of a specific contract, i.e. the employer can have neither the obligation nor the objective (arising from the contract) to improve the general employability of the employee. This may, of course, constitute a broad social interest. However, it must then be interpreted not as an obligation on the employer but as a general social interest, which must be secured by legislation while compensating the employer.

[35] Fried (1981), p. 1.

[36] Craswell (2001), p. 19.

[37] Eisenberg 2001, p. 223.

[38] MacNeil (1978), p. 854.

[39] MacNeil (1978), p. 865.

### 3.4 *The Legal Nature of Corporate Self-regulation in the Light of the Contract*

If the principles above cannot lead to the appointed goal, it is possible to examine whether there is a source of law that can compensate for the absence of contractual terms. At this point, it is essential to refer to the theory of Bob Hepple, who argues that one of the main features of future labour law will be a layered legal regime based on the interaction of different legal techniques, in which, in addition to traditional legal sources, corporate self-regulation (which essentially takes the form of employer internal policies) will play an increasingly important role.[40]

This theory is also supported by Gyulavári and Kun, who examine the growing role of employer-issued regulations in labour law, particularly in the private sector.[41] They discuss how employers increasingly adopt internal regulations to manage employment relationships, which raises critical questions about the legal status and impact of these rules. They argue that the operation of multinational organisations, mainly when they operate beyond the national regulations, can reflect a shift in the role of the state in labour law, from direct intervention to more indirect, often "soft law" approaches, encouraging corporate self-regulation as a supplement to state law. This shift is also tied to broader global trends, such as corporate social responsibility (CSR) and the changing expectations of businesses in response to globalisation, but it is always based on the employer's sole decision.[42]

However, they also underline the legal ambiguity surrounding employer regulations, mainly whether they can be considered binding legal norms or merely voluntary guidelines.

Although the legal interpretation of employee codes of conduct may vary from one jurisdiction to another, it is accepted that, in principle, the employer can extend its contractual obligations through these codes, which, even in the absence of a legal provision, can provide a legal basis for implementing lifelong learning within the company.

Although the legal interpretation of employee codes of conduct may vary from one jurisdiction to another, it is accepted that, in principle, the employer can extend its contractual obligations through these codes, which, even in the absence of a legal provision, can provide a legal basis for the implementation of lifelong learning within the company.[43] Going even further, it can be seen that within the framework of a collective partnership, lifelong learning can be made more secure, and it can, therefore, be assumed that the presence of trade unions and collective agreements has a beneficial effect on the enforcement of lifelong learning.[44]

---

[40] Hepple (2003).

[41] Gyulavári and Kun (2012), pp. 157–170.

[42] Murto and Korpisaari (2024).

[43] Clough (1997), p. 262.

[44] Holford (2023), p. 22; - See in this volume Murto J, Lifelong Learning and Labour Law – Mapping the new Phenomenon in the Systematics of Labour Law, section 4.2 and Johansson C,

## 4 The Limits of the Employer's Obligation

When examining the employer's obligation, we must distinguish between forms of training that the employee undertakes because it provides them with the knowledge that is an integral part of their job and those that they undertake entirely independently of their job, even as a hobby. In this context, an additional distinction should be made between the training provided and financed by the Member States or even the EU in the context of labour market regulations and the training provided by the employer to the employee to perform the job. The first category is a regulatory instrument to improve employability,[45] while the latter is a contractual obligation.

Even if it is accepted that the legal relationship between the employer and the employee is such that the employer must support the continuing training of employees based on the contract itself, this can only be recognised in the sense of the employment relationship.[46]

If we accept that the employee has a right to be trained and that this right derives from the employment contract, then the employer is obviously the only one who is obliged to do so. In this case, the employer's employment obligation created a sufficient legal basis, which would still cover the continuing training. However, it can be seen that the European Union's idea of continuity follows an entirely different logic when it comes to training:[47] it is not limited to purely vocational training but covers any type of learning. It follows from this that it is unnecessary and impossible to interpret the employee's right to further training within the framework of a contractual relationship since the employer's duty of care and employment obligation clearly cannot extend to the point where the employee's right to further training would give rise to a right to claim support for training which is entirely independent of the performance of the contract. In this sense, it is justified to distinguish, from the point of view of employment law, between the two types of training. One, from the employer's point of view, constitutes an economic advantage, that is to say, training which, once completed, enables the employee to work more effectively, more quickly, at a higher level or only generally to perform more complex tasks and to acquire knowledge, and second, a training which is entirely independent of the position which the employee holds with the employer. The latter is not necessarily related to the actual employment relationship and is typically not to be understood in the employer–employee context but in the labour market context.[48] It is undoubtedly that the idea of lifelong learning is primarily intended to help workers become more valuable players in the labour market, not necessarily by deepening the knowl-

Regulating lifelong-learning in collective agreements, section ?? as well as Franca, V. – De Becker, A. Social Dialogue and Lifelong learning: the difficult interplay at EU-level and national level.

[45] Korver and Oeij (2008), p. 147.

[46] It should be mentioned that some authors argue that modern employment relations impose an obligation on the employer to provide general, broad-based training; see Stone (2006), p. 161.

[47] Hyman and Gumbrell-McCormick (2024), p. 64.

[48] Bercusson (2009), p. 651.

edge they have acquired in their particular profession, but, on the contrary, often by gaining knowledge that can be used to take up other jobs in other types of workplace. However, this objective can in no way be regarded as an employer's objective since the employer's primary interest is to ensure that it has the necessary labour force and where it wishes to support the training of an employee, whether using a study contract or other agreement, it will in most cases do so to enable the employee to put that knowledge to good use.

It follows from the above that the employer's right to training in the broad sense cannot give rise to an obligation to provide this right in the employment contract since the employer is only obliged to provide appropriate training for the position in question (again, for reasons of health and safety at work), which cannot be extended to training that is independent of the employment relationship and does not serve the purposes of the employment contract.

## 4.1 Lifelong Learning as a Type of Study Contract

The idea of lifelong learning goes far beyond the framework of the general and familiar learning contract, and in many cases, it is intended to have a substantially opposite effect. In many cases, the skills and competencies that the person concerned is acquiring are not being acquired to remain in the workplace but to find a better job in the labour market after their current employment relationship has ended. If we look at this aspect, we can even conclude that employers are primarily interested in developing the skills that enable employees to work more effectively for their employer.[49] Therefore, investing in other skills is not in their interest, as it undermines their labour market position, making it easier and quicker for them to find a new job, thus reducing their commitment (which is one of the aims of introducing lifelong learning).[50]

A study contract, on the other hand, is precisely a tool to ensure the employer's need for skilled labour, i.e. the employer intends to meet its own labour needs in the future and, in this respect, contributes to the employee's training at the employer's expense, keeping them away from the workplace, as a result of which they will be a better professional in the work organisation, i.e. at the end of the day, the economic benefit will also be passed on to the employer.

In contrast, the principle of Lifelong Learning at the EU level aims at creating a higher level of employment, which, on the one hand, is naturally (and systemically) in the interests of employers, but at the same time, is possible in a limited way within the employment relationship due to the different purpose of the currently recognised legal institutions. As already explained, the employment contract alone does not impose any obligation on employers to promote lifelong learning for

---

[49] Kirpal (2011), p. 43.

[50] Kirpal (2011), p. 39.

employees, which does not mean, of course, that some employers cannot themselves be the driving force behind this process in the context of social responsibility or efficiency or green transformation, since many employers choose to develop, train and offer flexible employment in their business/market interests. However, in all cases, this is business-driven, i.e. the obligation cannot be generalised.

Therefore, it is clear that if Member States wish to ensure lifelong learning, it must be incorporated into their labour law regulations using public law or ensured that collective agreements regulate the right.

In the absence of this, even if the employer were to provide the employee with the opportunity to participate in studies, for example, using a working time discount or flexible working or in some other way, under current concepts, this would have to be done during working hours, if possible, and therefore needs to be compensated in some way. A good example is Austria, where, on the one hand, the employer and the employee can agree on so-called educational leave for the duration of the training,[51] during which the state covers the lost wages in the form of labour market allowances.[52] Under this regulation, the parties can also agree on a temporary reduction in working time, during which the employee can take training.[53]

Training to increase employability, therefore, does not necessarily have to be linked to a specific employment relationship but can be undertaken independently or even in parallel with it. In this case, the agreement on the training (or the working time allowance for the duration of the training) does not necessarily belong to the employment contract but is separate from it. This raises the question of who should cover the costs of the training. On the one hand, there is the possibility that the legislator could pass this on to the employer sector in its entirety, which would create a considerable burden for the financially most vulnerable small and medium-sized enterprises, which would even call into question the success of the legal instrument. On the other hand, it also does not seem a good solution if it is entirely taken over by the state as a limitless opportunity employee since, in this case, the learning opportunity could quickly become worthless and be used in an insufficiently justified way.[54] Consequently, it is advisable to involve the employee in bearing the burden, even if it is shared between the State and the employer so that the parties can share the burden. This arrangement is otherwise in line with the system set out in the Recommendation on individual training accounts, which also states that the parties must jointly create the conditions for the training.

---

[51] Arbeitsvertragsrechts-Anpassungsgesetz (BGBl. Nr. 459/1993 1 BGBl. I Nr. 174/2021), 11.§11

[52] Arbeitslosenversicherungsgesetz 1977 (BGBl. Nr. 609/1977 zuletzt geändert durch BGBl. I Nr. 53/2016), 26.§ 26.

[53] Arbeitsvertragsrechts-Anpassungsgesetz (BGBl. Nr. 459/1993 zuletzt geändert durch BGBl. I Nr. 67/2013), §11a.

[54] For example, on the basis of this experience, in 2024 Finland changed the rules on support for lifelong learning, citing the fact that the previous system was too costly and employment growth was lagging behind. See Eurydice (2024) https://eurydice.eacea.ec.europa.eu/national-education-systems/finland/national-reforms-vocational-education-and-training.

### 4.2 *Relevant Examples of the Regulation of Lifelong Learning in EU Member States*

It must be mentioned that the implementation of specific EU legislation may also result in progress in regulating lifelong learning. A good example could be the directive on transparent and predictable working conditions, which mentions and ensures the requirement of mandatory training. This implementation resulted in various solutions in some member states.

**In Slovenia**, employers are legally obligated to provide health and safety training and all requirements for work performance, such as acquiring or renewing licenses. Employers must finance such training, and the time spent in training is recognised as working hours. However, beyond these clear obligations, implementation largely depends on employer discretion. Collective agreements generally contain broad provisions on training but are often weakly enforced. While some employers provide robust training programmes, others do not, making actual implementation inconsistent.[55]

**Belgium** enacted legislation to implement the directive partially, primarily affecting contractual training provisions. A new clause (9 §) was added to Article 22bis of the Employment Contracts Act, preventing employers from reclaiming training costs in cases of mandatory training when an employee leaves. However, this only applies to specific contractual cases with salary thresholds and explicit contractual agreements. One prominent example of compulsory training in Belgium is the requirement for workers in the transport sector to obtain an ADR certificate. Additionally, an ongoing debate in the Netherlands about the scope of mandatory training under the directive has influenced Belgian discussions, with legal proceedings pending at the Dutch Supreme Court (Hoge Raad) on the matter.

**In Finland**, the Employment Contracts Act was amended to align with the directive. Employers must inform employees about their training rights (Chapter 2, Section 4). The law mandates that compulsory training be provided free of charge and counted as working hours whenever possible (Chapter 2, Section 19). Additionally, the employer is required to facilitate training to support employees when workplace operations or methods change (Chapter 2, Section 1). Finland also enforces training requirements when employees receive notice of termination, ensuring they receive coaching or reskilling support (Chapter 7, Section 4 and Section 13).

**Sweden** integrated the directive into the Employment Protection Act (6 c §, point 9), requiring employers to provide employees with information regarding training rights. However, statutory mandatory training is primarily confined to workplace health and safety, focusing on risk assessment rather than continuous professional development. Collective agreements do not generally mandate training, and additional training obligations derived from employment contracts are considered situational, such as training for job relocation.

[55] Franca (2023).

**In Hungary**, the right to lifelong learning is currently not declared in the Labour Code, but there are several provisions on training. On the one hand, the law provides that the employee may be exempted from their obligation to be available for work and to perform their work duties for the time necessary to complete their general education and, in the case of training or further training agreed by the parties, for the time required to complete the training (Section 55.) This means that the employer's permission is not required for general education (since, in this case, the employee is exempted by law). Still, in other cases, an agreement is necessary. In practice, this, in any case, raises the problem that even if the parties agree that the employee may attend training during their working time, it is not a requirement that they receive an allowance from the employer for this period, i.e. they are essentially without earnings.

While Slovenia, Belgium, Finland, Sweden and Hungary have all taken steps to address employee training in their national legislation, their approaches diverge significantly in scope, enforceability and practical impact.

Finland stands out with its comprehensive legislative framework: the Employment Contracts Act not only enshrines the right to free compulsory training but also integrates training support in contexts of operational change and termination. Similarly, Slovenia legally obliges employers to fund and recognise some training as working time, though the lack of strong enforcement mechanisms and variability in employer practice results in inconsistent application.

In contrast, Belgium's implementation is more limited in scope. While legislation was amended to protect employees from repayment obligations in specific contractual contexts, its reach is restricted to training arrangements meeting salary and contractual thresholds. The Belgian model thus appears more protective in select individual cases, but does not generalise training access or provision as a systemic right.

Sweden shares Belgium's narrower interpretation. Its legislative response is confined mainly to informing workers of training rights, with actual obligations centred on workplace health and safety. The absence of strong collective or contractual enforcement mechanisms makes training access largely contingent on situational needs rather than structural guarantees.

Hungary presents a distinctive case, as the Labour Code does not affirm a right to lifelong learning. While employees may be exempted from work for general education or agreed training, there is no requirement for remuneration, resulting in de facto barriers to access, particularly for lower income workers. This illustrates a formal permissiveness coupled with substantive inaccessibility.

### *4.3 The Need for Lifelong Learning from the Employer's Perspective*

From the employer's point of view, training should be understood primarily in relation to the performance of the particular job. There is no doubt that the employer must provide continuous training and development for the employee, but this does not in itself mean that it should also play a role in developing the employee's other skills (not used in the employment relationship).[56] So, it is indisputable that employers can decide at any time to support the training of their employees based on their own perceived or real interests (often under the aegis of social responsibility) and within the framework of the current labour market regulations.[57] Accordingly, employers may create the framework for the training within the legal framework that governs them and incorporate it into their corporate processes. If the form, content and depth of the training depends solely on the employer's commercial interests,[58] it will be purely market-based. It may violate general labour law principles (e.g. the requirement of equal treatment).[59] Additionally, employers usually provide active (financial) assistance for training that represents real added value for them (e.g. it is usually not supported for the employees to train themselves for a completely different profession). Consequently, to guarantee the role of lifelong learning within the employment relationship, it is not necessarily possible to do so by means of employment-contract regulation, but by applying sectoral rules, but by applying sectoral rules (e.g. labour market programmes), which are placed above individual labour law rules (at least in the framework of collective legal instruments or public law legislation).[60]

## 5 Conclusion: The Importance of Legislation

This chapter has highlighted the legal and economic complexities surrounding lifelong learning within the employment relationship. While it is widely accepted that continuous training is essential for workforce adaptability and economic competitiveness, its integration into employment contracts remains legally ambiguous. The analysis reveals that lifelong learning cannot be regarded as a strict contractual obligation unless supported by explicit legal frameworks or collective agreements.

A key challenge is the distinction between employer-mandated training and broader educational opportunities. While employers must ensure workplace safety and competency, extending this duty to general skills development raises questions

---

[56] Kirpal (2011), p. 45.

[57] Supiot (2000) p. 337.

[58] Kirpal (2011), p. 44.

[59] Schmid (2006), p. 49.

[60] Bercusson (2002), p. 10.

about cost allocation and business sustainability. This chapter's results show that without legislative intervention, employers are unlikely to voluntarily assume financial responsibility for lifelong learning, mainly when the benefits of training may not remain within their organisations.

From a policy perspective, the European Union's initiatives on lifelong learning indicate a broader commitment to workforce development, but these measures often rely on national implementation. Thus, Member States play a crucial role in determining whether lifelong learning is treated as an enforceable right or an economic incentive.

Ultimately, the chapter concludes that a balanced approach is necessary. While contractual mechanisms such as employer policies, implied terms and collective agreements can promote lifelong learning, state intervention is required to establish minimum legal standards. A cooperative model involving employers, employees, trade unions and governmental bodies may provide the most effective solution, ensuring that lifelong learning is both a protected right and a shared responsibility. In view of the above, the answer to the research question is that lifelong learning is certainly not enforceable without actual legislation or state intervention since the employment contract alone does not impose such an obligation on the employer.

By acknowledging the economic realities of business operations while upholding the importance of continuous education, policymakers can create sustainable frameworks that benefit both employers and employees, fostering a resilient and adaptable workforce in an evolving labour market.

The next step in this area is therefore to have a normative regulation in all Member States that guarantees the right to lifelong learning. This must be based on the principle of sharing the burden and the risks, with both the state, the employer and the employee. Different legal systems will inevitably lead to different legal solutions, so further research may be needed in the future to determine which solution best serves the objective to be achieved. In this connection, the possibility of a single EU regulation could be raised in the future.

## References

Atkinson J (2019) Implied terms and human rights in the contract of employment. Ind Law J 48(4):515–548

Benson P (ed.) (2001) The Theory of Contract Law, New Essays. Cambridge

Bercusson B (ed) (2002) European labour law and the EU Charter of Fundamental Rights (summary version). European Trade Union Institute (ETUI), Brussels

Bercusson B (2009) European labour law. CUP, Cambridge

Breining-Kaufmann C (2007) Globalisation and labour rights. Hart Publishing, Oxford

Brodie D (1998) Beyond exchange: the new contract of employment. Ind Law J 27(2):79–102

Clough B (1997) Union partnerships for lifelong learning. Local Econ London South Bank University 12(3):262–267

Collins H (2007) Legal responses to the standard form contract of employment. Ind Law J 36(1):2–18

Collins H (2010) Employment law, 2nd edn. OUP, Oxford

Collins P, Golding G (2024) An implied term of procedural fairness during disciplinary processes: into contracts of employment and beyond? Ind Law J 53(2):125–156
Craswell R (2001) Two economic theories of enforcing promises. In: Benson P (ed) The theory of contract law: new essays. CUP, Cambridge, pp 19–44
David, C (2005) The Implied Duty of Mutual Trust and Confidence: An Emerging Overarching Principle? Industrial Law Journal 34(4) 284–307. https://doi.org/10.1093/indlaw/dwi022
Davies ACL (2009) Perspectives on labour law. CUP, Cambridge
Deakin S (2006) The comparative evolution of employment. In: Davidov G, Langille B (eds) Boundaries and frontiers of labour law. Hart Publishing, Oxford
Deakin S (2013) Addressing labour market segmentation: the role of labour law. Centre for Business Research, University of Cambridge Working Paper No. 446
Eisenberg M (2001) The theory of contracts. In: Benson P (ed) The theory of contract law: new essays. CUP, Cambridge, pp 206–264
Eurofound (2020) Lifelong learning and employer responsibilities. https://www.eurofound.europa.eu/en/skills-learning-and-employability
Franca V (2023) Pravni vidiki izobraževanja in usposabljanja delavcev : dejansko stanje in pogled naprej. In: Lepičnik-Vodopivec J, Mezgec M (eds) Vseživljenjsko učenje odraslih za trajnostni razvoj in digitalni preboj. Brezplačna elektronska izd. Založba Univerze na Primorskem, pp 73–86
Fried C (1981) Contract as promise: a theory of contractual obligation. Cambridge
Gerner-Beuerle C, Paech P, Schuster E-P (2013) Study on directors' duties and liability. LSE Enterprise, London
Glowacka M (2021) A little less autonomy? The future of working time flexibility and its limits. Eur Labour Law J 12(2):113–133
Gordley J (ed) (2001) The enforcability of promises in European contract law. CUP, Cambridge
Gyulavári T, Kun A (2012) Employer legislation? The role of employer regulations in employment law. Munkajog
Hepple B (2003) Four approaches to the modernisation of individual employment rights. In: Blainpain R, Weiss M (eds) Changing industrial relations and modernisation of labour law. Liber Amicorum in Honour of Professor Marco Biaggi. Kluwer Law International, The Hague, pp 181–190
Hogg M (2011) Promises and contract law. CUP, Cambridge
Holford J (2023) Lifelong learning, the European Union, and the social inclusion of young adults: rethinking policy. In: Holford J, Boyadjieva P, Clancy S, Hefler G, Studená I (eds) Lifelong learning, young adults and the challenges of disadvantage in Europe, Palgrave studies in adult education and lifelong learning. Palgrave Macmillan, Cham
Honeyball S, Pearce D (2006) Contract, employment and the contract of employment. Ind Law J 35(1):30–55
Hyman R, Gumbrell-McCormick R (2024) Towards a European system of industrial relations? The ETUC in the twenty-first century. ETUI, Brussels
Jain, Aditya & Leka, Stavroula & Zwetsloot, Gerard. (2011). Corporate Social Responsibility and Psychosocial Risk Management, in: Leka, S. & Cox, Thomas & Zwetsloot, Gerard. (2008). The European framework for psychosocial risk management (PRIMA-EF). The European Framework for Psychosocial Risk Management: PRIMA-EF. 1–16.
Kirchner J, Kremp P, Magotsch M (eds) (2010) Key aspects of german employment and labour law. Springer
Kirpal S (2011) Labour-market flexibility and individual careers, a comparative study. Springer-Verlag, Heidelberg
Kiss G (2020) Employment flexibility and the protection of the status of employees (a possible approach to the examination of the content of the employment relationship). Wolters Kluwer Hungary, Budapest

Korver T, Oeij P (2008) Employability through covenants: taking external effects seriously. In: Rogowski R (ed) The European social model and transitional labour markets, law and policy. Ashgate Publishing Limited, Farnham

MacNeil I (1978) Contracts: adjustment of long-term economic relations under classical, neoclassical, and relational contract law. Northwest Univ Law Rev 72(6):854–905

Murto J, Korpisaari P (2024) Employee use of social media: private, public or something else? Eur Labour Law J 16(1):87–108

Noe RA (2020) Employee training and development. McGraw-Hill, New York

Schmid G (2006) Sharing risks: on social risk management and the governance of labour market transitions. WZB Discussion Paper, No. SP I 2006-101, WZB Social Science Center, Berlin

Stone K (2006) Employment protection for boundaryless workers. In: Davidov G, Langille B (eds) Boundaries and frontiers of labour law goals and means in the regulation of work. International Institute for Labour Studies. Hart Publishing, Oxford

Supiot A (2000) The Dogmatic Foundations of the Market (Comments illustrated by some examples from labour law and social security law). Ind Labour Law J 29(4):321–346

Vogenauer S, Weatherill S (2006) The European Community's competence to pursue the harmonisation of contract law—an empirical contribution to the debate. In: Vogenauer S, Weatherill S (eds) Studies of the Oxford Institute of European and Comparative Law. Hart Publishing, Oxford

**Peter Sipka** PhD, defended his doctoral dissertation on employer liability at the University of Debrecen in 2014. The work was later published as a monograph and has since reached its second edition. He teaches labour and social law at the Faculty of Law of the University of Debrecen, and also delivers lectures in several specialised training programmes. His publications mainly focus on employers' liability, the legal risks associated with various forms of employment relationships, and the limits of employers' managerial prerogatives—more broadly, the boundaries of the employer's duty of care in the context of evolving labour law relations. Alongside his academic career, he practises as an attorney, primarily providing labour and corporate law services to international companies. He is actively engaged in the Hungarian labour law professional community, serving as a board member of both the Hungarian Labour Law Society and the Debrecen Bar Association.

# Lifelong Learning and Work in the Future

**Beryl ter Haar**

## 1 Introduction

As elaborated in the introduction to this book and in Chapter 1, lifelong learning is an ambiguous concept. At least for lawyers who like clear definitions to work with. Many chapters in this book therefore explore lifelong learning in relation to different aspects of labour law. One of the things these chapters show is that two main approaches to lifelong learning can be distinguished, namely lifelong learning as a labour market instrument and lifelong learning as a human right to (self-) development.

As a labour market instrument, the aim and purpose of lifelong learning is to keep workers employable. In this context, continuous training and education ensures that the knowledge and skills of workers stay up to date with developments, such as in technology and working methods, approaches, and the overall organisation of work. Therefore, the training and educational activities are focused on what is needed for the worker to stay employable. Often this means that training and educational activities are limited to what is needed for the job the worker is employed or active in.[1] Often, this also means that it is the employer who decides what kind of

[1] An approach that can be found in EU Directive 2019/1152 of the European Parliament and of the Council of 20 June 2019 on transparent and predictable working conditions in the European Union, especially Art. 13 based on which the employer is obliged 'to provide training to a worker to carry out the work for which he or she is employed, such training shall be provided to the worker free of cost, shall count as working time and, where possible, shall take place during working hours.'

B. ter Haar (✉)
Centre for International and European Labour Law Studies (CIELLS), University of Warsaw, Warsaw, Poland

University of Groningen, Groningen, The Netherlands



J. Murto, V. Franca (eds.), *Labour Law and Lifelong Learning*,
https://doi.org/10.1007/978-3-032-11035-0_12

training and educational activities are to be taken. The latter also makes sense, since in this approach, the employer often contributes to the costs and (working) time that are involved with the training and educational activities.[2] This approach largely coincides with the "human capital" perspective which emphasises that education is 'a form of investment in human capital and a key factor for economic growth.'[3] Furthermore, it is argued that investment in human capital may increase the productivity of the individual worker.[4]

As part of a human right, as defined in United Nations Declaration on the Right to Development, lifelong learning could be considered as part of the right of self-development, which would enable a person to continuously develop its talents.[5] In this context, lifelong learning activities are not limited to what is needed for work but are linked to the needs and desires of the individual person. As such, the human rights approach to lifelong learning is broader than that of the labour market approach. The human rights approach aligns with the ideas of Amartya Sen and Marta Nussbaum about capability which centre the development of capabilities of persons to achieve freedom and wellbeing.[6] More particularly, for Sen, capability is about real opportunities for a person in exercising freedoms, such as 'the freedom to be employed, educated, happy, to have shelter and to enjoy a healthy life'.[7] A person's "capability set" depends on a variety of factors, including personal characteristics and social arrangements.[8] This means that different people have different abilities to convert resources and opportunities into real achievements. More specifically, although the idea of choice (freedom) is central in the capability approach, the individual acts 'within specific social and institutional arrangements which could function also as social constraints.'[9] Education is an important factor in con-

---

[2] See especially in this volume Murto J, Lifelong Learning and Labour Law – Mapping the new Phenomenon in the Systematics of Labour Law, sections 4.1 and 4.3.

[3] Boyadjieva and Ilieva-Trichkova (2017), p. 272.

[4] See in general Becker (1993). For a labour law comment on this, see Bueno (2017), p. 477.

[5] Article 1(1) of the United Nations Declaration on the Right to Development, defines the right to development as 'an inalienable human right by virtue of which every human person and all peoples are entitled to participate in, contribute to, and enjoy economic, social, cultural and political development, in which all human rights and fundamental freedoms can be fully realized.' Based on Article 2(1) of the Declaration, 'the human person is the central subject of development and should be the active participant and beneficiary of the right to development.' Furthermore, based on Article 8(1), 'States should undertake, at the national level, all necessary measures for the realization of the right to development and shall ensure, inter alia, equality of opportunity for all in their access to basic resources, education, health services, food, housing, employment and the fair distribution of income.' For academic writing about the right to development in a labour law context, see Novitz and Mangan (2011).

[6] See for a concise summary about labour law, human development and the capability approach: Deakin (2011), pp. 171–173. See in the context of education/lifelong learning: Boyadjieva and Ilieva-Trichkova (2017), p. 269.

[7] Boyadjieva and Ilieva-Trichkova (2017), p. 269.

[8] Boyadjieva and Ilieva-Trichkova (2017), p. 270 with reference to Sen (1999), p. 33.

[9] Boyadjieva and Ilieva-Trichkova (2017), p. 275.

verting resources and opportunities since it 'affects the development and expansion of other capabilities'.[10] In other words, education, including lifelong learning, has a transformative power substantively contributing to identity formation and agency empowerment.[11] This makes lifelong learning an essential aspect of the human right self-development.

The two approaches align when the lifelong learning activities of the individual contribute to a worker's employability for the job that worker is performing for the employer. However, they conflict or at least raise (labour law related) questions when the worker's needs and desires for training and educational activities are not related to the aim of remaining employable for the specific job or work activities the worker is performing for the employer. One of the most prominent questions in this context is whether the employer should contribute to costs and (working) time for lifelong learning activities that are not related to work activities agreed upon in the employment contract or to work activities performed in his business?[12] A further question is whether the answer to the first question changes when the lifelong learning activities not only contribute to the wellbeing of the worker, but when they are also in the interest of society? It might change the answer, because, indirectly, the employer is benefitting from the wellbeing of the society overall, like its infrastructures and institutions. The answer might even be nuanced and, as often is the case, depend on the circumstances, for example to what extend the employer (as a business owner) benefits from those infrastructures and institutions: the more the employer benefits, the more he is expected to contribute to the lifelong learning activities of his workers; the less the employer benefits, the less is expected of the employer.

The list of questions is endless. Many of which have been addressed and explored in other chapters in this book. What makes it difficult to address these questions from a purely labour law, labour market or human rights perspective is that the answers to those questions largely dependent on the dominant socio-economic context of a society.[13] Therefore, the aim of this chapter is to analyse the dominant socio-economic context of the European Union EU). This is interesting, because the EU is one of the driving motivators of lifelong learning policies of its member states. This is followed by a forward look which sketches a new socio-economic paradigm the EU might be heading at, namely a wellbeing paradigm. The wellbeing

---

[10] Boyadjieva and Ilieva-Trichkova (2017), p. 270 with reference to Walker (2012).

[11] Boyadjieva and Ilieva-Trichkova (2017), p. 275.

[12] See in this volume; Sipka, P. Lifelong learning as a contractual issue: is it an employer's obligation or an empty right?

[13] Cf. Adams (2022), Rogowski (2013), Hepple (2011) and Todoli-Signes (2024). Although this view is not supported by all labour lawyers, as some argue that labour law serves its own goals and purposes which are valid and valuable for more than one socioeconomic context. See for example: Weiss (2022), Langille (2024), and Davidov (2016). And more neutral: Davies (2009) and Landau (2023). Indirectly, in this book a more reflexive approach to labour law is taken in the sense that labour law develops in communication with the socioeconomic context it is operating in. See in this volume Murto J, Lifelong Learning and Labour Law – Mapping the new Phenomenon in the Systematics of Labour Law, section 3, who builds, among others, on the ideas of Bruun (2017).

economy paradigm is based on commonalities that are found in academic ideas, theories, approaches that are all dealing with the future of society and work, some of which are already picked up in practice, which makes it not purely fictional or utopian. The chapter concludes with sketching the context of work and lifelong learning in the wellbeing economy.

## 2 EU Socio-economic Context and Labour Market Approach to Lifelong Learning

When reviewing what the dominant socio-economic context is within the European Union (EU), the impression exists that it is that of a social market economy (see Article 3, par. 3 of the Treaty on the European Union (TEU)). However, in the 1990s, the EU made a paradigm shift to a predominantly neoliberal free market economy.[14] In some EU member states, this is more strongly the case (like in Germany, The Netherlands, Ireland, Poland and Hungary) than in other EU member states (like Italy, Spain, France and the Nordic countries). More generally and maybe also most importantly, this shift is visible in EU social policies, including those on lifelong learning, which affect the social policies of all EU member states.[15]

One of the characteristics of the neoliberal free market economy is that it prioritises productivity and (short-term) profit-making for shareholders over the wellbeing of humans and the planet. Consequently, the focus in EU social policymaking lies with those activities of lifelong learning that increase productivity and therewith profits. In other words, the socio-economic context of the neoliberal free market economy favours lifelong learning activities that contribute to the employability of workers and leaves little room for activities that just benefit the needs and desires of the person as a private individual. Within the context of the EU, this is most apparent in programmes like NextGenerationEU and the Just Transition Fund, as well as the titles and tasks of the EU commissioners, especially 'Social Rights and Skills, Quality Jobs and Preparedness', with as main task 'to guide the overall work on strengthening Europe's human capital, from skills and education to culture and sport'.[16] To achieve the main task, the commissioner is responsible for, among others, 'guiding the work on the European Pillar of Social Rights to tackle the **skills and labour gaps**, focusing on **training and education**' and 'embedding a **new culture of preparedness** to help people adapt to change and risks'[17] (emphasis in original).

[14] Cf Ter Haar and Copeland (2010).

[15] Ibid. See more indirectly: Vandenbroucke et al. (2017).

[16] https://commission.europa.eu/about/organisation/college-commissioners/roxana-minzatu_en. Accessed 30 December 2024.

[17] Ibid.

The strongest proof of lifelong learning at EU level being framed in a neoliberal free market socio-economic paradigm, or at least a labour market approach, can be found at Cedefop (European Centre for the Development of Vocational Training).[18] Although it seems that lifelong learning is a social (human) right, since it is part of the first principle of the European Pillar of Social Rights (EPSR),[19] the further description about the importance of this principle, in general, and lifelong learning, in particular, is proof that this perception is wrong. To ensure the implementation of the EPSR, headline targets have been formulated at the Social Summit in Porto (7–8 May 2021). For lifelong learning, this is a target of having at least 60% of all adults participating in training every year by 2030, which means a significant increase from the 2010 target of a 12.5% participation rate.[20] This target is justified by arguments that training for adults is 'paramount to improve employability, boost innovation, ensure social fairness and close the digital skills gap'. All of which are needed in the context of the challenges to recover from the Covid19 pandemic and to face the twin transition (digital and green).

Cedefop, which presents the EU's lifelong learning strategy, emphasises that those (and other) challenges 'can only be addressed through a systematic and integrated approach to adult participation in training'.[21] Because, 'rapid labour market changes, driven by technological advancements and fierce global competition, require continuous skill adaptation to maintain and enhance the EU's economic growth and global competitiveness while ensuring social justice and inclusion'.[22] The EU combines the first principle of the EPSRs with the fourth and fifth principles, which, respectively, deal with 'active support for employment, to uphold everyone's right to timely and tailor-made assistance to improve employment or self-employment prospects' and secure and adaptable employment, which gives workers the right to 'fair and equal treatment regarding working conditions, access

---

[18] Cedefop-lifelong learning programme-the imperative of lifelong learning: https://www.cedefop.europa.eu/en/news/imperative-lifelong-learning. Accessed 12 February 2025. Cedefop is established by: Regulation (EU) 2019/128 of the European Parliament and of the Council of 16 January 2019 establishing a European Centre for the Development of Vocational Training (Cedefop) and repealing Council Regulation (EEC) No 337/75. OJ 2019 L30/90.

[19] The EPSR is available at: https://employment-social-affairs.ec.europa.eu/policies-and-activities/european-pillar-social-rights-building-fairer-and-more-inclusive-european-union_en. Accessed 12 February 2025. The first principle, part of Chapter I: Equal opportunities and access to the labour market, reads as follows:

**1. Education, training and life-long learning**

Everyone has the right to quality and inclusive education, training and life-long learning in order to maintain and acquire skills that enable them to participate fully in society and manage successfully transitions in the labour market.

[20] The European Pillar of Social Rights Action Plan (2021), explanation to the second headline target, available at: https://op.europa.eu/webpub/empl/european-pillar-of-social-rights/en/. Accessed 12 February 2024.

[21] Cedefop-lifelong learning programme-the imperative of lifelong learning.

[22] Ibid.

to social protection and training'.[23] As part of the European Skills Agenda, the Commission explored the use of individual learning accounts as a tool 'to support the upskilling and reskilling of working age adults'[24] to make 'the shift to a modern, resource-efficient and competitive economy'.[25]

The above makes clear that the whole idea of lifelong learning, at least at EU level, which influences the lifelong learning policies and approaches at national levels, is framed in the context of labour market policies only. Except for the very general idea of lifelong learning, nothing in the EU policy documents indicates that lifelong learning could also be approached as a human right, or more particularly the right to (self-)development.

## 3 New Socio-economic Paradigm: Wellbeing Economy

Before elaborating on the new socio-economic paradigm, two caveats. First, the elaboration is brief and on mainlines. As such it may come across as too simple, too naïve, however, it is based on well-developed ideas by in their fields highly respected academics. The brief elaboration here just serves to give a first impression of the difference between the paradigms of the social market economy (which is the main socio-economic context against which background the current European labour law models have been developed)[26] and the current dominant socio-economic paradigm of neoliberal free market economy, on the one hand, and the main contours of the new socio-economic paradigm of the wellbeing economy, on the other hand.

Second, the main contours of the wellbeing economy sketched here cannot be found literally in one theory, idea or approach. Instead, it is based on commonalities that I found in several ideas, theories, approaches, presented in different disciplines, including economics, socio-economics, sociology, political science, business management and labour history.[27] While each of those ideas, theories, approaches, have their own focus and main points, they all seem to have in common the elements that I use to draw the main contours of the wellbeing economy. I think these commonalities are interesting, since it might make it more realistic that a paradigm shift on

[23] Par. 2 preamble of Council Recommendation of 16 June 2022 on individual learning accounts. OJ 2022 C243/26.

[24] Par. 4 preamble of Council Recommendation of 16 June 2022 on individual learning accounts. OJ 2022 C243/26.

[25] Par. 5 preamble of Council Recommendation of 16 June 2022 on individual learning accounts. OJ 2022 C243/26.

[26] Cf. Hepple (2010) and Hepple and Veneziani (2009).

[27] Leading sources of reference for the main contours include: Fioramonti (2017), Raworth (2018), Mazzucato (2021), Hickel (2021), Frey (2018), Collier (2018), Jackson (2021), Schwab and Vanham (2021), Susskind (2020), Srnicek and Williams (2016), Seidl and Zahrnt (2022), Henderson (2021), Banerjee and Duflo (2011), Gorz (1989), Chamberlain (2018), Dermine and Dumont (2022), Graeber 2019, Veltman (2016), Bueno (2017), Méda (2016), Lucassen (2021), Suzman (2021), Andriessen (1990) and Varoufakis (2021).

those common elements might actually take place. Moreover, some of those elements are already being picked up in practice, albeit some more seriously than others.[28]

Of course, it is impossible to look into the future and therefore there is no guarantee that this paradigm shift will take place or to what extent it will take place. Nonetheless, the fact that parts of this paradigm are already being picked up in practice, including that of the EU,[29] makes it interesting to further explore and see what this might mean for work, the meaning of work, and more particularly in the context of this book, for lifelong learning. The description of the common elements that make up for the contours of the wellbeing economy paradigm are based on descriptions that I have written elsewhere,[30] however, the descriptions here have been further developed and adjusted to fit the main topic of this chapter: lifelong learning.

The commonalities that I think that can be distinguished in the main reference sources are:

1. human- and planetary-centred;
2. participation;
3. public-private cooperation;
4. recognition of complexity;
5. value and purpose based; and
6. post-growth and post-productive work approaches.

**Ad 1. Human- and Planetary-Centred**

Within the wellbeing economy paradigm, growth or economic wellbeing is no longer measured by GDP (gross domestic product) and profit-making for shareholders alone. This means that instead of achieving wellbeing indirectly via an increase of (material) welfare, which was the aim of the (liberal) social market paradigm, or through the trickle-down effect of profit-making, which is the goal of the neoliberal free market paradigm, the aim of the wellbeing economy is to achieve wellbeing as a direct goal of human and business activities.

Although it is difficult, if not impossible, to define what wellbeing is, there are determinants, parameters or settings, for society and economic systems that foster or facilitate the creation or achievement of wellbeing.[31] For example, Raworth proposes an economic system that is regenerative and distributive to stay within the planet's ecological ceiling and social foundation respectively.[32] Fioramonti expresses a similar idea in the form of an economy that is 'powered by human relations, which

[28] See for examples at the websites of the Wellbeing Economy Alliance https://weall.org/ and the Doughnut Economics Action Law https://doughnuteconomics.org/. Both accessed 12 February 2025. See for a description of how the EU engages with these ideas: Ter Haar (2024a) and Ter Haar (2024c).

[29] Ibid.

[30] See especially: Ter Haar (2024b) and Ter Haar (2022).

[31] Cf. Frey and Stutzer (2002).

[32] Raworth (2018) Chaps. 5 and 6.

play out in a transformed interaction with natural ecosystems. New businesses create value by connecting people, reducing ecological footprints and achieving the right size rather than pursuing maximisation in scale'.[33] In Fioramonti's view, people would become "prosumers", instead of only consumers, 'capable of making the most of the things they need through local systems of co-production, networks of small businesses and a new form of post-industrial artisanship'.[34] A qualified artisan would fix, upgrade and upcycle products for the duration of a lifetime, which in turn makes professional activities personalised, care-driven and context-specific.[35] This will put families and communities at the centre of value creation and will aspire to the creation of a 'for wellbeing organisation'.[36] Henderson's idea for a collaborative economy built on shared purpose and common missions within businesses that go beyond profit maximisation resonates well with Fioramonti's idea of 'for wellbeing organisations'. More utopian ideas, such as Andriessen's *Eldorica* and Varoufakis' *The Other Now*, present similar economic approaches.

**Ad 2. Participation**

From the first commonality, it follows that participation, in various forms and meanings plays an important role. The idea of stronger participation rights (for workers) is not new,[37] but the scale and form make it interesting. Moreover, part of the idea of a wellbeing economy seems to be forms of direct democracy by all relevant stakeholders. For Frey and Stutzer, for example, (direct) participation is paramount to achieve happiness.[38] Since happiness is subjective and therefore different for every person, having some influence over decisions concerning aspects of life is an important element to achieve happiness. In their ideas, Fioramonti and Varoufakis seek participation, or actually cooperation, in smaller group structures, such as in cooperatives and by regionalising production and services. Henderson reimagines capitalism in the form of a collaborative economy in which companies serve common goals or purposes, often for the common good, which should make companies more attractive for workers since the company directly contributes to (improving) their wellbeing.

Raworth and Schwab also promote a strong participation involvement of stakeholders, including a different balance of power between those stakeholders. For both, it is clear that in the current socio-economic paradigm, the voice of the "economic" stakeholders is too strong. In the wellbeing economy paradigm, this should be more balanced. For Raworth, this means that the wellbeing of people and planet come first and that the economic needs and desires should be at the service of the

[33] Fioramonti (2017), p. 157.

[34] Fioramonti (2017), p. 165.

[35] Fioramonti (2017), p. 168.

[36] Fioramonti (2017), p. 174.

[37] E.g. among many others: Deakin (2004), p. 94, Dukes and Streeck (2023), Mundlak (2020) and Todoli-Signes (2024).

[38] Frey and Stutzer (2002), pp. 133ff. and 174–175.

needs of people and the planet.[39] For Schwab, it means that all stakeholders have to balance their primary objectives and express the need for balance and solidarity: failing to achieve the objectives of one is considered a failure of all.[40]

Building on the ideas of cooperation as being more than mere participation, Raworth promotes a role for the commons. Contrary to the traditional economic idea that the commons will lead to a tragedy, Raworth refers to the groundbreaking works on the commons by Elinor Ostrom who demonstrated that the commons are actually creative when they operate under certain conditions.[41] Within the context of work, the idea of a stronger role of the commons is further explored by Tomasetti. Although Tomasetti underlines several complexities making such a strong role of the commons rather utopian, this might be different when such a role is considered against the background of the wellbeing economy paradigm. In his utopia *Another Now*, Varoufakis sketches a world in which the idea of the commons works well based on the participatory ideas of one-share-one-vote for workers and an evaluation of the performance of business operations by a "socialworthiness-index".[42]

**Ad 3. Public–private Cooperation**

Public–private cooperation differs from public–private partnerships that are known in the current dominant socio-economic paradigm. The World Bank defines public–private partnerships as 'a long-term contract between a private party and a government entity, for providing a public asset or service, in which the private party bears significant risk and management responsibility and remuneration is linked to performance'.[43] Public–private cooperation goes much further. It is underpinned by the idea that both, public and private activities have to contribute to the wellbeing of the people and the planet. This implies that the purpose and objectives of private companies align with government policies, rather than productivity and profit-making for the shareholders.[44]

For Raworth and Collier this means, for example, that the State becomes a facilitating actor that empowers and enables the economic actor.[45] Mazzucato proposes that governments should become a 'goal-oriented stimulator of new ideas from the ground up' to fulfil public purposes.[46] In this role, governments defend public interests through the creation of regulations that are market-shaping in such a way that it

[39] Raworth (2018), pp. 68ff.

[40] Schwab and Vanham (2021), pp. 171ff. (Chap. 8).

[41] Raworth (2018), pp. 82ff; based on Ostrom (1999).

[42] Varoufakis (2021), pp. 41ff.

[43] The World Bank (2020) What is a PPP: Defining "Public-Private Partnership". https://ppp.worldbank.org/public-private-partnership/what-ppp-defining-public-private-partnership. Accessed 13 February 2025.

[44] Henderson (2021), pp. 43ff, Collier (2018), pp. 147–148 and 207ff and Schwab and Vanham (2021), p. 173.

[45] Raworth (2018), pp. 71 and 86, and Collier (2018), pp. 147ff.

[46] Mazzucato (2021), pp. 101–102.

rewards value creation and not value extraction.[47] In turn, this stimulates private entities to employ their business activities for the good of the public interests. The public interests are implied to contribute to the wellbeing of the people and the planet.[48]

**Ad 4. Recognition of Complexity**

In the current dominant socio-economic paradigm, concepts are used that simplify life and society. For example, the *homo economicus* which acts in a rational and predictable manner, and the mechanical equilibrium which will be achieved by markets by balancing supply and demand. In reality, though, humans and markets are complex. Their behaviour and functioning cannot be captured by simplified concepts. Within the wellbeing economy paradigm, this complexity is acknowledged. This is most explicitly done by Raworth in her *Doughnut Economics* which is based on the idea of an embedded economy. This is an economy that nests '*within society and within the living world, while recognising the diverse ways in which it can meet people's needs and wants*' (emphasis in original).[49] Fioramonti also embraces such a view when he translates the economy as a form of development of wellbeing in care (taking) as a core part of the relations underpinning the economic system which works for people and the planet.[50] In Mazzucato, the concept of embedded economy is presented by thinking in terms of circular economy.[51]

Second, instead of the rational *homo economicus*, Raworth sees and treats humans in their diversity as socially adaptable humans who engage in different roles related to the economy, for example as citizens, employees, entrepreneurs, consumers and parents.[52] Within these roles, people engage in a wide range of values 'many times a day as we switch from bargaining to giving to competing to sharing in our constantly changing economic landscape'.[53] Following from this, it is clear that humans are motivated by more than just cost and price, as is presumed with the *homo economicus*, indeed humans are motivated by various social dynamics, underpinned by values, heuristics, norms and networks.

Third, Raworth embraces complexity by a more value and purpose-based approach (see next element), by introducing a code of ethics (like the Hippocratic Oath for medical doctors) for economists as developed by DeMartino.[54] More con-

[47] Mazzucato (2021), pp. 197ff. About the principle of non-extractiveness in the wellbeing economy and labour law, see Ter Haar (2024c, 2025).

[48] This is based on a combined reading of Mazzucato's *Mission Economy* (2021) (with a strong emphasis on the creation of a circular economy) and Mazzucato's *The Value of Everything* (2019).

[49] Raworth (2018), p. 71.

[50] Fioramonti (2017) pp. 167ff and 207ff. More elaborate about the idea of care as a core concept of a socioeconomic paradigm; see The care collective (2020). About the idea of care as a foundational principle of labour law in the wellbeing economy; see Ter Haar (2025).

[51] Mazzucato (2021), p. 198, with reference to Raworth (2018).

[52] Raworth (2018), p. 128.

[53] Raworth (2018), p. 128, with reference to Montgomery (2015). Similar: Collier (2018).

[54] Raworth (2018), pp. 160–162 with reference to DeMartino (2012). Similar: Schwab and Vanham (2021), p. 191 with reference to the "Davos Manifesto 2020".

cretely, Raworth proposes the following four ethical principles, which reflect a lot about her *Doughnut Economics*:

1. *Act in service* to human prosperity in a flourishing web of life, recognising all that it depends upon;
2. *Respect autonomy* in the communities that you serve by ensuring their engagement and consent, while remaining ever aware of the inequalities and differences that may lie within them;
3. *Be prudential* in policymaking, seeking to minimise the risk of harm—especially to the most vulnerable—in the face of uncertainty; and
4. *Work with humility*, by making transparent the assumptions and shortcomings of your models and by recognising alternative economic perspectives and tools.[55]

Similar visions and approaches can be found in the ideas of Henderson, who bases her collaborative economy on the expectation of companies to be committed to 'building an organisation in which every employee is treated with dignity and respect and viewed as a whole human being whose autonomy and worth is to be honoured,'[56] combined with economic and political institutions that are inclusive.[57] The same applies for Frey and Stutzer since happiness (wellbeing) cannot be achieved when humans, in their various roles, are not enabled to pursue their happiness.[58] Collier envisions something similar with his value-based society that 'pragmatically steers capitalism' based on shared senses of belonging and identity.[59]

**Ad 5. Value and Purpose Based**

Any socio-economic system is based on values and purposes, often presented as an ideology. The wellbeing economy paradigm is no different, except that it strives to be pragmatic rather than ideological. The reason is that in many of the ideas underpinning the wellbeing economy paradigm, ideology is considered to be disruptive instead of constructive.[60] The values, purposes and goals underpinning the wellbeing economy paradigm embrace a wider interpretation than those underpinning the current dominant socio-economic paradigm, which are limited to their economic context of productivity and profit-making for shareholders. Henderson, for example, states that a 'genuinely purpose-driven organization is in itself an act that creates shared value since it requires creating the kind of jobs that are needed to begin to address inequality and build a just society'.[61] Schwab and Mazzucato argue something similar based on a stakeholder approach which recognises that value is

[55] Raworth (2018), p. 161.

[56] Henderson (2021), p. 95.

[57] Henderson (2021), pp. 210ff.

[58] Frey and Stutzer (2002), pp. 171ff.

[59] Collier (2018), pp. 206ff.

[60] Ideology is explicitly rejected by Schwab and Vanham (2021), Collier (2018) and Banerjee and Duflo (2011), and implicitly by Frey (2018), Mazzucato (2021) and Raworth (2018).

[61] Henderson (2021), p. 87, and similar Collier (2018), pp. 69ff with the idea of an *ethical firm*. See on this also: Supiot (2021), p. 8.

created collectively, i.e. not only by companies but also 'by educators, scientists, cultural actors, government institutions, [...] society and the natural environment itself'.[62] For Raworth, it means that the success of the economy will not be reflected in 'the metric of money but in the metric that reflects human prosperity in a flourishing web of life'.[63]

Expressing values, purposes and goals is one thing, putting them in practice is another, especially without an ideology that guides directions in decision-making. Therefore, this cannot be seen separately from the other common elements, especially participation and public–private cooperation. These hold structures and include institutions that should lead to achieving and safeguarding the values, purposes and goals. Collier elaborates on how values, without ideology, can be shaped in practice and society. Much of his views are based on the involvement of civil society, community, the commons and how they shape narratives that become a certain standard. Those narratives should be developed from the basic values that can be found in every society, such as feelings of belonging and esteem, and a sense of reciprocity (rights and freedoms come with obligations and responsibilities, etc.). Mazzucato's *Mission Economy* is all about how governments (the State) can regain control over the direction of their policies and facilitate and enable private companies to contribute to achieving those policies/goals. Raworth sets out concrete goals in her *Doughut* with is an indicator for the planetary ceiling that should not be exceeded and social foundation that no one should fall below in an economy that is successful. To achieve those goals, Raworth sets seven ways of thinking as a twenty-first-century Economist: 1. the doughnut; 2. embedded economy; 3. social adaptable humans; 4. dynamic complexity; 5. distributive by design; 6. regenerative by design and 7. growth agnostic.[64] Henderson's empirical evidence-based work *Reimagining Capitalism* provides many examples of how companies operate more value- and purpose-based and what they have gained with it.

**Ad 6. Post-Growth and Post-Productive Work Approaches**

The strong human and planetary-centred approach expressed in the previous five common elements underpinning the wellbeing economy paradigm, almost inevitably leads to a post-growth and post-productive work approach.

The post-growth approach, and for some, like Fioramonti, even a degrowth approach, follows from the move away from a socio-economic paradigm that is driven by productivity and profit-making for shareholders. To a certain extent, this builds on the first commonality which moves away from growth measurement by GDP. Particularly, because GDP fails to include all costs, such as the (over)exploitation of the planet and workers. The ideas underpinning the wellbeing economy

[62] Schwab and Vanham (2021), p. 184, with reference to Mazzucato (2021), p. 194, and more generally Mazzucato (2019).

[63] Raworth (2018), p. 279, and similarly Varoufakis (2021) with his Social worthiness-Index, and Frey and Stutzer (2002), with their recognition that happiness is subjective and can only be achieved when people are enabled to reach for what makes them happy.

[64] Raworth (2018), pp. 24ff.

paradigm embrace a broader interpretation of growth, one that recognises the complexity of people and society (see above element 4), especially the fact that people are motivated by much more than just monetary incentives. Growth, therefore, also includes immaterial aspects like values such as feelings of belonging, (self)esteem and sanctity but also a purpose such as developing and exercising talents as desired.[65] The latter implies that people should be truly free to choose work activities,[66] which could be realised by the introduction of a form of a universal basic income, which frees people from the need to work for income.[67]

Being agnostic to growth, as Raworth calls it, has consequences, among other things, for the meaning of work. Such, because growth, in general, and growth, in personal income, will no longer be the main motivator for people to work. Also, consumerism, as in the gathering of ever more and more material wealth, will no longer be a main motivator, instead the principle of sufficiency will be leading.[68] These fundamental changes raise the question: What will aspire people to work? There is no conclusive answer to this question, especially because this differs per person. However, as presented by Raworth, drawing from a wide array of psychological research, the New Economics Foundation identified five acts that have proven to promote wellbeing: '*connecting* to people around us; *being active* in our bodies; *taking notice* of the world, *learning* new skills, and *giving* to others'.[69] (emphasis in original) Fioramonti (2017), and to a lesser extent Henderson (2021), show in their works how in such a growth agnostic socio-economic paradigm, a post-productive work society can thrive. In such a society, work activities are not performed for economic purposes only or mainly, instead they are performed because they contribute to the wellbeing of society, as well as that of the person performing those activities.[70] This means that work activities that (seem to) have hardly any (direct) economic value in the capitalist, productivity-driven

---

[65] Cf. Raworth (2018), pp. 282–283.

[66] For a comment on the limited freedom to choose work, see Bueno (2017).

[67] Raworth (2018), pp. 199–201, and Andriessen (1990) in his utopia *Eldorica*. Although many pilot projects have proven the benefits of forms of universal basic income, *cf.* Bregman (2018), see in the context of the right to work: Standing (2013). There are also critiques of why a UBI could not work, at least when considered in a capitalist socioeconomic paradigm, for example: Dumont (2022). For others, a UBI alone is not enough, they propose the introduction of a right to laziness, see especially De Becker and Claus (2024).

[68] Raworth (2018), p. 282.

[69] Raworth (2018), p. 283, with reference to Aked et al. (2008). Fioramonti (2017) bases his *Wellbeing Economy* on similar acts. These acts reflect values that Collier (2018) identified as universal in any society.

[70] On the negative effect on the wellbeing of workers of many purely productivity-driven jobs, or jobs with no social purpose; see Graeber (2019).

socio-economic paradigms,[71] such as care, education and art, will be fully recognised for their value in the post-productive work society.[72]

## 4 Work and Lifelong Learning in the Wellbeing Economy

From the above descriptions of common elements that underpin the wellbeing economy paradigm, it follows that compared to the capitalist productivity-driven socio-economic paradigms, lifelong learning is to be viewed from a completely different context.[73] A context in which the person is central. A context in which the person is not considered as part of the production process, either as a commodity or as a capital. A context in which the question is not what the person with its labour, intellect, etc. can mean for the company and the productivity, but what the company and the work activities have to offer to the person. A context in which a person can find and perform work activities that will contribute to feelings of self-esteem, belonging and self-realisation. Particularly, because those work activities contribute to the wellbeing of society and respect planetary boundaries, but most of all, because those work activities match with the talents of the persons and allows the person to continuously further develop and perform those talents.

A context also, in which the person is truly free to choose its work activities,[74] because the person is no longer dependent on work for income. The latter, because wealth, as in the control over land, business activities, technology, knowledge and the power to create money,[75] is distributed by design, including a form of universal basic income,[76] instead of redistribution evened up by economic growth. A context in which governmental policies facilitate lifelong development of talents. A context in which education is not at the service of market-needs rendering it to a purpose of 'the socialization of young people for the successful adoption of pre-defined work

[71] Cf. Mazzucato (2019) and Graeber (2019), pp. 210–212, with references to Lockwood et al. (2017), pp. 1659ff, and Lawlor et al. (2009), and within the context of labour law on the specific topic of care: Encinas de Muñagorri (2024). See also Bueno (2017), p. 480, where he talks about wasted human potential.

[72] Raworth (2018), p. 279 refers to this as "flourishing in the web of life". Fioramonti (2017), pp. 165ff indicates such with the term "prosumers", *i.e.* people who produce and consume just what they need and what is needed in society (which reflects the principle of sufficient). Varoufakis (2021), pp. 61ff expresses the need of societal value of work activities with the "socialworthiness-index" that companies are regularly assessed by.

[73] The sketch here is based on the work narratives that I defined based on the commonalities in Ter Haar (2024b), pp. 39–46.

[74] For an elaborate explanation on why this is not the case in the capitalist productivity-driven socioeconomic paradigms see Bueno (2017).

[75] Cf. Raworth (2018), p. 177.

[76] What form exactly needs to be worked out. Current ideas vary from reforms in taxation to more radical proposals. Cf. Piketty (2015), Raworth (2018), pp. 276–279, Collier (2018), pp. 132, 142–144, and 187. And more radical: Varoufakis (2021), pp. 52–55.

role',[77] but in which education is about developing a person's capabilities to enjoy substantive freedoms and to lead the kind of life a person has reasons for to value.[78] A context, therefore, in which entities that offer work activities, have an obligation to ensure that their work activities contribute to social values while staying within the planetary boundaries, and to encourage people to continuously further develop their talents. A context, therefore, in which governments facilitate structures and institutions that enable people to continuously further develop their talents. Such, because this will contribute to realising public goals, which is the aim of the entities offering the work activities that are performed by people that are able to use their talents to their full potential because they are enabled to keep developing those talents.

To conclude in short, in the wellbeing economy paradigm, lifelong learning is core to the system, because people are aspired to use their talents to their full potential to contribute to the well-being of society which gives them feelings of self-realisation, self-esteem, belonging, etc., which also foster feelings of happiness and wellbeing. Therefore, work in the future will not exist without lifelong learning, because (self-)development is core to the wellbeing economy. More concretely, it means that with the shift from the current dominant socio-economic (neoliberal free market economy) to the wellbeing economy paradigm, lifelong learning will become more of a human right, rather than a labour market instrument. That will also give a more prominent position within labour law, including more expectations and obligations on employers to ensure that workers can enjoy the fundamental right to lifelong learning. At least, that will be the case in the context of the ideal-type wellbeing economy paradigm based on the common elements sketched in this chapter. To what extent that will be the case, only the future can tell.

## References


Adams Z (2022) A structural approach to labour law. Camb J Econ 46:447–463

Aked J et al (2008) Five ways to wellbeing: the evidence. The New Economics Foundation, London

Andriessen J (1990) Eldorica. Met een Reisverslag naar een betere wereld. Het Spectrum, Utrecht

Banerjee AV, Duflo E (2011) Poor economics: a radical rethinking of the way to fight global poverty. Penguin Books, London

Becker GS (1993) Human capital. A theoretical and empirical analysis with specific reference to education. University of Chicago Press, Chicago

Boyadjieva P, Ilieva-Trichkova P (2017) Lifelong learning as an emancipation process: a capability approach. In: Milana M, Webb S, Holford J, Waller R, Jarvis P (eds) The Palgrave international handbook on adult and lifelong education and learning. Palgrave Macmillan, London, pp 267–288

Bregman R (2018) Utopia for realists and how we can get there. Bloomsbury Publishing, London

Bruun N (2017) The old and new foundations of labour law. In: Ahlberg K, Bruun N (eds) The new foundations of labour law. Peter Lang, London, pp 17–35


---

[77] Bueno (2017), p. 477, with reference to Frayne (2015), pp. 78–81.

[78] Sen (1999), p. 14.

Bueno N (2017) From the right to work to freedom from work: introduction to the human economy. Int J Comp Labour Law Ind Relat 33:463–487
Cedefop (2024) The imperative of lifelong learning. https://www.cedefop.europa.eu/en/news/imperative-lifelong-learning. Accessed 12 Feb 2025
Chamberlain J (2018) Undoing work, rethinking community: a critique of the social function of work. Cornell University Press, Ithaca
Collier P (2018) The future of capitalism. Facing the new anxieties. Harper, New York City
Davidov G (2016) A purposive approach to labour law. OUP, Oxford
Davies ACL (2009) Perspectives on labour law. CUP, Cambridge
De Becker A, Claus F (2024) Social security and the right to laziness beyond just basic income. In: Bueno N, ter Haar B, Zekić N (eds) Labour Law Utopias: post-growth and post-productive work approaches. OUP, Oxford, pp 201–220
Deakin S (2004) Workers, finance and democracy. In: Barnard C, Deakin S, Morris GS (eds) The future of labour law: Liber Amicorum for Sir Bob Hepple. Hart Publishing, London, pp 79–100
Deakin S (2011) Labour law and development. In: Langille B, Davidov G (eds) The idea of labour law. OUP, Oxford, pp 156–175
DeMartino GF (2012) Professional economic ethics: why heterodox economists should care. Paper given at World Economic Association Conference on Economics and Society: the Ethical Dimension, February – March 2012
Dermine E, Dumont D (2022) A renewed critical perspective on social law: disentangling its ambivalent relationship with productivism. Int J Comp Labour Law Ind 38:237–268
Doughnut Economics Action Lab (2025). https://doughnuteconomics.org/. Accessed 12 Feb 2025
Dukes R, Streeck W (2023) Democracy at work. Contract, status and post-industrial justice. Polity Press, Cambridge/Oxford
Dumont D (2022) Universal basic income as a source of inspiration for the future of social protection systems? A counter-agenda. Eur J Soc Secur 24:299–318
Encinas de Muñagorri R (2024) Labour law for care and wellbeing. In: Bueno N, ter Haar B, Zekić N (eds) Labour law Utopias: post-growth and post-productive work approaches. OUP, Oxford, pp 155–175
European Commissioner for Social Rights and Skills, Quality Jobs and Preparedness. https://commission.europa.eu/about/organisation/college-commissioners/roxana-minzatu_en. Accessed 30 Dec 2024
European Union (2019a) Regulation (EU) 2019/128 of the European Parliament and of the Council of 16 January 2019 establishing a European Centre for the Development of Vocational Training (Cedefop) and repealing Council Regulation (EEC) No 337/75. OJ 2019 L30/90
European Union (2019b) Directive 2019/1152 of the European Parliament and of the Council of 20 June 2019 on transparent and predictable working conditions in the European Union. OJ 2019 L186/105
European Union (2022) Council Recommendation of 16 June 2022 on individual learning accounts. OJ 2022 C243/26
Fioramonti L (2017) Wellbeing economy. Success in a world without growth. Pan Macmillan South Africa, Johannesburg
Frayne D (2015) The refusal of work: the theory and practice of resistance to work. Zed Books, London
Frey BS (2018) Economics of happiness. Springer International, Cham
Frey BS, Stutzer A (2002) Happiness and economics. How the economy and institutions affect well-being. Princeton University Press, New Jersey
Gorz A (1989) Critique of economic reason. Verso Books, London
Graeber D (2019) Bullshit jobs: the rise of pointless work, and what we can do about it. Penguin Group, London
Henderson R (2021) Reimagining capitalism in a world on fire. How business can save the world. Penguin Business

Hepple B (ed) (2010) The making of labour law in Europe. A comparative study of nine countries up to 1945 – reprint. Hart Publishing, London
Hepple B (2011) Factors influencing the making and transformation of labour law in Europe. In: Langille B, Davidov G (eds) The idea of labour law. OUP, Oxford, pp 30–42
Hepple B, Veneziani B (eds) (2009) The transformation of labour law in Europe. A comparative study of 15 countries 1945–2004. Hart Publishing, London
Hickel J (2021) Less is more: how degrowth will save the world. Penguin Random House, UK
Jackson T (2021) Post growth. Life after capitalism. Wiley, London
Landau I (2023) Human rights due diligence and labour governance. OUP, Oxford
Langille B (2024) The Coast of (Labour Law's) Utopia. In: Bueno N, ter Haar B, Zekić N (eds) Labour Law Utopias: post-growth and post-productive work approaches. OUP, Oxford, pp 17–28
Lawlor E, Kersley H, Steed S (2009) A bit rich: calculating the real value to society of different professions. New Economics Foundation, London
Lockwood BB, Nathanson CG, Weyl EG (2017) Taxation and the allocation of talent. J Polit Econ 125:1635–1682
Lucassen J (2021) The story of work: a new history of mankind. Yale University Press, New Haven
Mazzucato M (2019) The value of everything. making and taking in the global economy. Penguin Books, London
Mazzucato M (2021) Mission economy. A moonshot guide to changing capitalism. Harper Business, New York City
Méda D (2016) The future of work: the meaning and value of work in Europe. ILO Research Paper No .18
Montgomery S (2015) The Soul of an Octopus. Simon & Schuster, New York
Mundlak G (2020) Organizing matters. Two logics of trade union representation. Edward Elgar Publishing, Cheltenham
Novitz T, Mangan D (eds) (2011) The role of labour standards in development. From theory to sustainable practice. OUP, Oxford
Ostrom E (1999) Coping with the tragedies of the Commons. Annu Rev Polit Sci 2:493–535
Piketty T (2015) Capital and wealth taxation in the 21st century. Natl Tax J 68:449–458
Raworth K (2018) Doughnut economics. Seven ways to think like a 21st-century economist. Penguin Random House, UK
Rogowski R (2013) Reflexive labour law in the world society. Edward Elgar Publishing, Cheltenham
Schwab K, Vanham P (2021) Stakeholder capitalism. A global economy that works for progress, people and planet. Wiley, New Jersey
Seidl I, Zahrnt A (eds) (2022) Post growth work. Employment and meaningful activities within planetary boundaries. Routledge, Oxfordshire
Sen A (1999) Development as freedom. OUP, Oxford
Srnicek N, Williams A (2016) Inventing the future: postcapitalism and a world without work. Verso Books, London
Standing G (2013) Why a basic income is necessary for a right to work. Basic Income Stud 7:19–40
Supiot A (2021) Labour is not a commodity: the content and meaning of work in the twenty-first century. Int Labour Rev 160:1–20
Susskind D (2020) World without work: technology, automation, and how we should respond. Macmillan, London
Suzman J (2021) Work. A history of how we spend our time. Bloomsbury Circus, London
ter Haar B (2022) Labour law in a changing world - inaugural lecture on the acceptance of the endowed chair European and Comparative Labour Law at the University of Groningen. University of Groningen Press, Groningen
ter Haar B (2024a) Industry 5.0 key to face Europe's challenge to create a human face. Revue de droit du travail 5:300–304

ter Haar B (2024b) Economic paradigm shifts for labour laws. In: Bueno N, ter Haar B, Zekić N (eds) Labour law Utopias: post-growth and post-productive work approaches. OUP, Oxford, pp 29–50
ter Haar B (2024c) Industry 4.0 + Industry 5.0 = happy marriage between humans and technology. Ital Labour Law e-J 17:189–213. https://doi.org/10.6092/issn.1561-8048/20805
ter Haar B (2025 forthcoming) The freedom to conduct a business, a care paradigm, and Industry 5.0 as pathways for compliance with labour rights in global value chains. In: Newaj K, van Eck BPS, Phiri C, Kalula E (eds) Labour law and employment relations in Africa: a commemoration of the 10th African ILERA Congress. Juta, Lansdowne
ter Haar B, Copeland P (2010) What are the future prospects of the European Social Model? An analysis of EU equal opportunities and employment policy. Eur Law J 16:273–291
The Care Collective (2020) Care Manifesto. The politics of interdependence. Verso Books, London
The European Pillar of Social Rights. https://employment-social-affairs.ec.europa.eu/policies-and-activities/european-pillar-social-rights-building-fairer-and-more-inclusive-european-union_en. Accessed 12 Feb 2025
The European Pillar of Social Rights Action Plan (2021) Explanation to the second headline target. https://op.europa.eu/webpub/empl/european-pillar-of-social-rights/en/. Accessed 12 Feb 2025
The World Bank (2020) What is a PPP: Defining "Public-Private Partnership". https://ppp.worldbank.org/public-private-partnership/what-ppp-defining-public-private-partnership. Accessed 13 Feb 2025
Todoli-Signes A (2024) Labour law and economic policy. How employment rights improve the economy. Hart Publishing, London
United Nations (1986) Declaration on the Right to Development, available at: https://www.ohchr.org/en/instruments-mechanisms/instruments/declaration-right-development. Accessed 20 Feb 2025
Vandenbroucke F, Barnard C, De Baere G (eds) (2017) A European Social Union after the crisis. CUP, Cambridge
Varoufakis Y (2021) Another now: dispatches from an alternative present. Vintage, New York City
Veltman A (2016) Meaningful work. OUP, Oxford
Walker M (2012) Egalitarian policy formulation in lifelong learning: two models of lifelong education and social justice for young people in Europe. In: Aspin DN, Chapman DJ, Evans K, Bagnall R (eds) Second international handbook of lifelong learning. Springer, Dordrecht, pp 181–193
Weiss M (2022) Challenges for labour law. In: von Adamovich E, Zernikow M (eds) Philosophical and sociological reflections on labour law in times of crisis. Cambridge Scholars Publishing, Newcastle, pp 339–353
Wellbeing Economy Alliance (2022). https://weall.org/. Accessed 12 Feb 2025

**Beryl ter Haar** is UW professor and head of the Centre for International and European Labour Law Studies (CIELLS) at the University of Warsaw, Poland, and endowed professor of European and Comparative Labour Law at the University of Groningen, the Netherlands. Her research deals with international and European labour law, especially collective bargaining, social dialogue, new governance, transnational private regulation and the future of labour law. She has published widely on these issues in national and international journals and edited books. She is a member of editorial boards of various (labour) law journals and co-editor of several books, including the book *Labour Law Utopias: Post-Growth and Post-Productive Work Approaches* which was published with an open access by Oxford University Press in 2024. Beryl is co-founder and co-organiser of the Hugo Sinzheimer Moot Court Competition in European and International Labour Law.

# Conclusion

## The Right to Lifelong Learning on the Work Floor: From an Individual Right Over the Collective Dimension Towards a Shift in the Economic Approach

**Alexander De Becker and Beryl ter Haar**

## 1 Introduction

Writing a conclusion with regard to lifelong learning and labour law remains quite a difficult task. The profound analyses of all contributors have closed some gaps within the field of lifelong learning and labour law while, on the other hand, some of them still remain.

This book fills in a gap that has existed for quite some time. The right to lifelong learning on the work floor has already been recognised in the Pillar of Social Rights in 2016. Until today, no real analysis of the legal substance and impact of this right had been granted in legal scholarship.

This book can be summarised in four major clusters: the first cluster deals with the conceptual framework of the right to lifelong working at the work floor, the second cluster deals with the individual right to lifelong learning on the work floor, the third cluster discusses the collective approach of the right to lifelong learning on the work floor while the last one grants insights on the right to lifelong learning at the work floor in relation to the larger context.

The limitations of this research should be acknowledged. The book adopts an EU-centric approach to the topic, which means that the global context is only addressed to a limited extent. As a result, the findings and conclusions are primarily applicable within the framework of EU law. Expanding the analysis to include a broader global perspective could be a valuable direction for future research.

A. De Becker (✉)
Faculty of Law and Criminology, Ghent University, Belgium, Ghent
e-mail: alexander.debecker@ugent.be

B. ter Haar
Centre for International and European Labour Law Studies (CIELLS), University of Warsaw, Warsaw, Poland

University of Groningen, Groningen, The Netherlands



J. Murto, V. Franca (eds.), *Labour Law and Lifelong Learning*,
https://doi.org/10.1007/978-3-032-11035-0_13

## 2 Lifelong Learning on the Work Floor: The Conceptual Framework

First of all, the moment of birth of the concept of lifelong learning is well covered by Flore Claus. She indicates that, legally speaking, the concept of lifelong learning appears in legal documents with regard to labour law in the 1960s. With regard to the legal documents to be researched, it goes without saying that it is the case. The difficulty with the concept of lifelong learning is that it is naturally embedded in labour law and most probably in life as a whole. Murto indicated that labour law itself seems to carry lifelong learning in itself.

These analyses have to lead us to an important new insight. Labour law and lifelong learning are twinned. Not necessarily within the traditional concept of labour law but starting from an opposite angle: lifelong learning has to be understood as an individual element with an individual approach while labour law has two distinct elements (individual and collective labour law) and wants to protect the worker. As Kain finds out, the mere existence of an individual human right to lifelong learning may not yet be fully claimed. It therefore stands to a certain degree at odds with the regulatory framework of labour law which does not start from granting individual rights but rather from protection.

However, the right to education is, at international and at EU-level, recognised as a fundamental right for many decades.

This brings up a new query: as lifelong professional learning is inherent as a part of working, why would the development of the right to lifelong learning not be influenced by the path that the right to strike has followed? It may be needed to clarify this more in depth. Individual fundamental rights do not appear out of heaven. It may take a long evolution.

The right to strike was never explicitly recognised as a fundamental right in the ECHR. Therefore, it remained a hidden treasure with regard to the case law of the ECtHR.[1] While the ECtHR originally was unwilling to grant the right to strike a full recognition as a human right, its case law evolved. Originally, the Court stated that other means were available to the trade unions in order to guarantee the exercise of their freedom of association. Society evolves. The case law in Demir and Baykara linked for the first time clearly that freedom of association implies the right to negotiate collectively for trade unions.[2] This judgement opened the door to going even a step further. In the Enerji Yapi Yol Sen case[3] and even more recently the Humpert case,[4] the Court judged that the right to strike is embedded in the freedom of association and to right to bargain collectively. This last element embeds the right to take collective actions as ultimum remedium. The right to strike may thus be considered as a fundamental right which is a sequel to the freedom of association for trade

[1] ECtHR, Schmidt and Dahlström v. Sweden, 6 February 1976.

[2] ECtHR, Demir and Baykara v. Turkey, 12 November 2008.

[3] ECtHR, Enerji Yapi Yol Sen v. Turkey, 21 April 2009.

[4] ECtHR, Humpert v. Germany, 13 December 2023.

unions. Recently, the ECtHR seems to be more reluctant again to judge in full that the right to strike is a fundamental human right. However, in the Humpert case, the ECtHR still underlines that within freedom of association,[5] the right to strike plays a preponderant role. The limitations to the right to strike which are set out in German law may be considered to be necessary (or at least acceptable) in a democratic society, the Court upholds the right to strike as a fundamental right in the framework of article 11 ECHR. The recent cases Kaya and Almaz seem to indicate that the right to strike belongs to trade unions and may not be considered to real individual rights.[6]

Notwithstanding the recent evolutions, the right to lifelong learning on the work floor could undergo a similar evolution. It constitutes a natural element of the right to work and of the right to education in general seems perfectly fit for such a development. Article 1.4 of the European Social Charter already invokes the effective insurance of the right to work includes providing or promoting appropriate vocational guidance, training and rehabilitation. It thus seems a logical step that the right to lifelong learning on the work floor is considered to be an unavoidable and logical sequel to the right to work.

Queries may arise whether the scope of the right to lifelong learning on the work floor stops at that level. The second cluster namely provides even more new insights.

## 3 The Right to Lifelong Learning on the Work Floor: A Fundamental Individual Right

The right to lifelong learning may then be fundamental and logically linked to the right to work, other queries still remain.

The content of the individual right to lifelong learning on the work floor is another difficult topic to tackle. Matti Urpilainen tries to find an answer to that difficult question. The concept of micro-credentials and an individual learning account further underpins the approach of the existence of such a fundamental right. The approach of the right to lifelong learning (on and even out of the work floor) remains an individual one. It concerns a sort of individual account on lifelong learning which fits well in the larger concept of work and progress in work (and even broader in life). Giorgio Impellizieri perfectly adds to this information that apprenticeships actually are part of the European Charter of Fundamental Rights.

The link between the right to lifelong learning on the work floor and the right to work is obvious. However, it does not stop there. The right to lifelong learning also fits in the larger set of rights of EU citizens. The right to vocational training and personal development in general may not be forgotten. It thus seems that in the future it could be sought to what extent the right to lifelong learning on the work floor could not be linked to article 8 of ECHR. The ECtHR has already judged on

[5] ECtHR, Humpert v. Germany, 13 December 2023, consideration 104.

[6] ECtHR, Kaya v. Turkey, 19 November 2024 and ECtHR, Almaz v. Turkey, 19 November 2024.

numerous occasions that article 8 of ECHR (the right to respect for personal and family life) included a right to personal development and personal identity.[7] This implies the possibility to set up a professional life, according to the ECtHR. The protection of honour and reputation are considered to be part of the scope of article 8 ECHR.[8] Protection against dismissal and the violation thereof can also affect the right to personal development.[9] It seems that the right to lifelong learning as such does not yet fit in this framework. Further developments with regard to not allowing people to participate in vocational training, however, can be useful as it includes the non-possibility of interacting with people of the outside world. It is therefore important to keep an eye on the development of the case law of the ECtHR. Links to the underdevelopment of the possibility to get in contact with the outside world can normally be established in case a person is not allowed to obtain micro-credentials or when a person may not develop his own individual learning account or apprenticeship.

All these contributors (Urpilainen and Impellizieri) deliver a sound foundation for a further step towards the full recognition of an individual right to lifelong learning on the work floor. They set up the basis; it is up to a next set of researchers to further develop the fundamental employment character of the right to lifelong learning.

This group of researchers may also consider examining the broader context of the individual right. In particular, how does the privatisation of educational training affect the substance and implementation of this concept? Moreover, the existence of an individual right does not necessarily imply that each worker must independently identify all possible training opportunities to enhance their skills. This aspect warrants more in-depth investigation in future research.

In short and at the current stance, it can be stated that the fundamental right to lifelong learning is not yet clearly shaped in the current state of the art. That does not mean, though, that the right to lifelong learning on the work floor cannot become an independent fundamental right in the future. It has already been quoted as a right in the Pillar of Social Rights. The conceptual framework needs to be sharpened, and the foundations of this individual right need to be clarified further. The chapters in this book provide an excellent base to start that debate between legal scholars, case law and legal practice.

[7] ECtHR, Volkov v. Ukraine, 9 January 2013; ECtHR, El Masri v. Former Yugoslavian Republic of Macedonia, 13 December 2012.

[8] ECtHR, Pfeifer v. Austria, 15 November 2007; ECtHR, A v. Norway, 9 April 2009.

[9] ECtHR, Ozpinar v. Turkey, 19 October 2010; ECtHR, Volkov v. Ukraine, 9 January 2013.

## 4 The Right to Lifelong Learning at the Work Floor and Collective Bargaining

With the chapter of Johansson starts a new episode in the book: the difficult balance between collective negotiations and the right to lifelong learning on the work floor. It goes without saying that an individual right on lifelong learning on the work floor does in itself not at all exclude the possibility to negotiate collectively about this topic. Collective negotiations leading to binding collective agreements, however, include a certain rigidity which at first glance seems to stand at odds with the individual right to lifelong learning on the work floor. Johanssons statement that trade unions have a stronger and a larger bargaining power which is totally convincible. Trade unions at company level can perfectly assess the needs of the workers in companies.

The outcome of the analysis of De Becker and Franca, however, indicates that in many EU Member States, collective bargaining agreements on lifelong learning are still lacking behind. It seems that the collective aspect of lifelong learning is well embedded in the Nordic countries and in Spain but that most of the other EU Member States are lagging behind. Germany may be a pupil in between, as Ruhwedel and Stein clearly state. The specific German model with Works Councils which really deliver their part to the Mitbestimmung of the company.

At company level, negotiations on lifelong learning and how to fill the individual right seem to be appropriate but the protection of workers in smaller companies may not be lost of view. Therefore, a general framework may be useful at a sectoral level. The right to lifelong learning on the work floor however remains a right which has a partially distinct content depending on the sector. In general, the right to lifelong learning on the work floor has a common socle. For all workers involved, it includes the right to further develop them and to attend vocational training.

As a consequence, national and EU-level have to find out which elements of the development of the social dialogue are desired to fill in. The right to lifelong learning seems to fit perfectly in the scope of the creation of a Matryoshka.

It concerns a multilayered topic where EU Social Dialogue could take care of legal recognition of the fundamental right in order to assure that even in the countries where such a right is still underdeveloped, the right to lifelong learning on the work floor is fully granted and guaranteed. Here seems to lie a necessity for the EU Social Dialogue to play its role. The EU level is the most appropriate level to recognise the right to lifelong learning as a fundamental right in the framework of the existing labour law framework.

At national level, the different social partners can play their own roles. In case national or interprofessional collective bargaining agreements play a preponderant role, it would be useful to create another framework which grants in a Member-State more detailed and substantial content to the right to lifelong learning on the work floor. The regulatory framework of the EU Social Dialogue and the National Social Dialogue can then be filled in with collective agreements at sectoral and at company level. At company level, the employer and trade union can finally decide to apply the most adapted form of the right to lifelong learning on the work floor. This specific outline grants a perfect example of a good and correct application of the principles of subsidiarity and proportionality with regard to the repartition of tasks between the EU Social Dialogue and the national social dialogues.

## 5 The Right to Lifelong Learning and the Larger Context at the Work Floor

Sipka outlines a specific problem which might occur, however, if the outline of the right to lifelong learning at the work floor is fully rendered to the individual employer and the individual worker. It can become an empty box in case one does not take care on a daily basis of the enforcement and respect of the fundamental right to lifelong learning at the workplace. The analysis of Sipka is more than useful as it delivers the knowledge that the fundamental right to lifelong learning is a dynamic right which has to be kept at stake with the ongoing societal evolutions.

Once, the EU Social Dialogue can play its role in full. As a consequence of a full recognition at EU level of such a fundamental right, the case law of the ECJ and the ECtHR will undergo some fluctuations. The basic right which is declared and recognised by the Pillar of Social Rights will be granted more concrete substance. This is primarily a task for social partners at all levels of the EU. In case, the EU takes its fundamental right to collective negotiation, as defined in article 28 of the Charter of Fundamental Rights seriously, major gains can be obtained with regard to the development of this fundamental right. If the EU Social Dialogue, the right to lifelong learning on the work floor may stay a socioeconomic wish which is not translated into a regulatory framework, it becomes than an empty box.

Ter Haar paths to be followed at EU level. The approach has to shift from a pure internal market perspective towards a human-centered perspective. This leads to other perspectives, which she correctly describes as postgrowth and post productive but mainly as a well-being economy.

This is a crucial element for the interplay between the individual right to lifelong learning at the work floor and the role trade union and collectivities have to play in setting up the framework to safeguard this right.

The wellbeing economy does not only concern wellbeing as an individual in general but mainly the development of individual rights in co-existence with a market economy where the focus shifts from pure gain towards humanity. Let us hope that the right to lifelong learning at the workplace can be added to this shift.

**Alexander De Becker** is professor of Labour Law at Ghent University. He has held numerous visiting professorships and the following Chairs: The State as Employer (University of Amsterdam, 2010–2015; University of Leiden, 2015–2017); Excellence Chair University of Turin, 2022; Bologna Chari, University of Bologna, 2025. He has widely published and is recognised as a leading expert in the field of 'The State as Employer'.

**Beryl ter Haar** is UW Professor and Head of the Centre for International and European Labour Law Studies (CIELLS) at the University of Warsaw, Poland and Endowed professor European and Comparative Labour Law at the University of Groningen, the Netherlands. Her research deals with international and European labour law, especially collective bargaining, social dialogue, new governance, transnational private regulation and the future of labour law. She has published widely on these issues in national and international journals and edited books. She is a member of editorial boards of various (labour) law journals and co-editor of several books, including the book *Labour Law Utopias: Post-Growth and Post-Productive Work Approaches* which was published open access by Oxford University Press in 2024. Beryl is co-founder and co-organiser of the Hugo Sinzheimer Moot Court Competition in European and international labour law.

MIX
Papier aus verantwortungsvollen Quellen
Paper from responsible sources
FSC® C105338

If you have any concerns about our products,
you can contact us on
**ProductSafety@springernature.com**

In case Publisher is established outside the EU,
the EU authorized representative is:
**Springer Nature Customer Service Center GmbH**
**Europaplatz 3, 69115 Heidelberg, Germany**

Printed by Libri Plureos GmbH
in Hamburg, Germany